Reverent Irreverence

Integral Church for the 21st Century:
From Cradle to Christ Consciousness

Rev. Tom Thresher, Ph.D.

Published by Integral Publishers
http://www.integralleadershipreview.com
http://www.integralpublishers.com
733 Mermaid Avenue
Pacific Grove, California, USA 93950
831 333-9200

1. Religion 2. Christianity 3. Philosophy 4. Church

For more information about Integral Publishers
russ@integralleadershipreview.com

ISBN: 978-1-61658-445-0

I am grateful for the permission to use material from Robert Kegan and Lisa Laskow Lahey, *How the Way We Talk Can Change the Way We Work*, San Francisco: Jossey-Bass, 2001 and *Immunity to Change: How to Overcome It and Unlock the Potential in Yourself and Your Organization*, Boston: Harvard Business Press, 2009.

Dedication

To
Pamela
Who never takes me seriously,
So made this book possible.

For
My Children

Contents

Foreword by Rev. Bruce Sanguin   ix

Acknowledgments   xiii

Introduction: xv
    Why Integral?   xvi
    A Distinctly Human Project   xvii
    Growing Up with Humanity   xviii
    Personal Story   xx
    Overview   xxiii

PART 1: INTEGRAL THEORY FOR THE INTEGRAL CHURCH

Chapter 1: A Myth for Our Time   3

Chapter 2: Integral Theory   11
    Introduction to Integral Theory   11
       States of Consciousness   12
       Stages of Development   13
       Lines of Development   14
       Types   16
       Quadrants   17
       The Quadrants Become the Big Three   22
    Levels, Lines and the Stories We Tell   23
       Stages, Waves and Levels   26
          Tribal/Magic   28
          Mythic-Literal/Warrior   29
          Traditional/Conformist   30
          Modern/Achiever   31
          Postmodern/Pluralist   33
          First and Second Tier   34
          Integrated/Self-Actualized   35
          Paradoxical/Construct-Aware   37
          Unitive/Trans-Personal   38
    Summary and Room to Roam   40

Chapter 3: Jesus Stories for the Integral Church   **53**

    Talking with Animal Spirits: Tribal/Magic   56

    My God Trounces Your God: Mythic-Literal/Warrior   58

    Follow the Rules and You Will Be Saved: Traditional/ Conformist 62

    We're Just Frisky Dirt: Modern/Achiever   65

    All Perspectives Are True: Postmodern/Pluralist   71

    Dancing Across Systems: Integrated/Self-Actualized   75

    No Belief Is True: Paradoxical/Construct-Aware   81

    Awake: Unitive/Trans-Personal   86

Chapter 4: "Yes ... And" Theology: An Integral View of Scripture   **93**

    John 3:16   95

    The Bible   102

    Sunday Reflections   103

        Temptation   104

        Trinity   108

        Allegory of the Liturgical Year   111

        Belief and Doubt   117

        Man Plans, God Laughs   120

PART II: INTEGRAL CHURCH IN THE WORLD

Chapter 5: Creating a Map for the Integral Church   **129**

    How Can Integral Theory Guide the Integral Church and Help Bob and Susan?   131

    Questions from Integral Theory   136

        The Lines That Matter   136

        States of Consciousness   138

        Stages of Development   139

        Types   140

        Quadrants and the 1-2-3 of God   141

    Creating a Map   144

    How to Fill in This Map   145

    How to Explore Types and Lines   147

    Room to Roam and Integral Church   149

Chapter 6: Permission and Possibilities: The Experience of an Emerging Integral Church   **157**

    The Dynamics of an Integral Community   160

    Mapping Programs   162

       TAGS: Talking About God Stuff   164

       Transformational Inquiry   166

       Faith Formation Study Group   168

       Call to Care   169

       Rummage Sale   169

       Many Stories ... One Community   170

       Earth Stewardship   170

       Medicine Wheel   170

       Women's Book Club   171

       Meditation   171

       Choir   172

       Enlightenment Intensives   173

       Christian Education   173

    Mapping Quadrants, Stages and States   174

    Mapping Lines of Development   175

    Room to Roam   175

Chapter 7: A Revolution of Caring ... One Church at a Time   **183**

Appendix A: Leadership   **191**

Appendix B: Worship   **195**

Appendix C: Faith Formation and Scripture Study   **199**

Appendix D: Talking About God Stuff (TAGS)   **203**

Appendix E: Transformational Inquiry   **211**

Foreword

Rev. Bruce Sanguin

Whether you come from the right, left or center of the church, there seems to be general agreement that the church must change. Some are downright apocalyptic about the potential consequences of maintaining the status quo. A colleague of mine projected current trends into the future, looking at membership, baptisms and adult professions of faith. The numbers gradually, inexorably, work their way to zero by the year 2050. Barring divine intervention of biblical proportions it is clear that mainline denominations, to say the least, are in some trouble. Too often, however, the prescription for change is second and third order—the ecclesiastical equivalent of shifting the deck chairs on the Titanic. What is being called for is a shift of first order proportions. Einstein is reported to have said that it's impossible to get out of a problem with the same mind that got you into it. Tom Thresher aims for change at the level of consciousness: first, seek the heart and mind of Christ consciousness, then see what forms, structures and activities emerge in support.

While there is agreement about the need for change, there is no consensus about how to change or what a new church might look like. Evangelical Christians are increasingly flirting with postmodernist theology and philosophy, attempting to take context and perspective seriously. Many mainline Christians, steeped in the rationalism of modernism and the pluralistic impulse of postmodernism, are getting on board with the "progressive" movement. But I've had some difficulty understanding what exactly is meant by the former so-called "emergent" church and the "progressive" church. In the case of the latter, it is often associated with the shift away from biblical literalism, homophobia, and toward theological and political inclusiveness. Rarely, however, does this inclusiveness encompass our more theologically conservative friends. The emergent church movement is also deeply suspicious that the "progressives" end up denying the Lordship of Jesus Christ. One is left with the feeling that both movements too often are defined by what they are not, namely, those other guys.

This book offers a clear vision of a model for change and what that future church could look like. It doesn't involve trashing those other guys, but rather positively embraces the contribution that each can make to the revitalization of church. Tom's vision of an Integral Church is bold, no less than creating the space for the emergence of Christ consciousness—what St. Paul called the heart and mind of Christ. In doing so, he is tapping into the deep yearning of the growing demographic that identifies itself as "spiritual but not religious".

The bioregion that geographically and culturally defines both my congregation in British Columbia, Canada, as well as the congregation Tom serves in Washington State is known as Cascadia. We enjoy the highest percentage of people in North America (45%) who claim no religious affiliation, yet who regard themselves as spiritual. While these people are certainly interested in talking *about* God, and in living moral and ethical lives, their primary interest revolves around spiritual practices that help them to *experience* the divine. Tom has courageously laid out a vision for the church that is about creating the space, programs and processes to help people connect with God as the deepest expression of Self. Of course, there is precedent for this in our mystical tradition. But where have all the mystics gone? As far as I am aware, Tom is the first to present this goal of helping people realize Christ consciousness as the primary purpose of the church.

This book conveys a sacred wisdom that is born of the wedding between the enlightenment spirituality of the Eastern traditions and the Western world's discovery of the evolutionary trajectory of the cosmos—God as both Formless, Fecund Emptiness beyond time and space, and as Evolving Form immanent within creation. It forges new ground in applying this wisdom to the Judeo-Christian narrative. As a result, new vistas of biblical interpretation and theological reflection open up to the reader.

For many, this book will be an introduction to the Integral map of reality. This is a map that has changed my life and my leadership as a minister by providing me with the equivalent of a new operating system. Once this operating system is "loaded" the universe opens up into a cornucopia of perspectives. We begin to appreciate that the one we call "Christ", and what we mean by the heart and mind of Christ, arises necessarily in, through, and as, the worldviews or big stories that we inhabit. And we grow in hope as we discover that we are able to consciously evolve into bigger, more comprehensive stories that transcend, yet include, our previous stories. This book provides a succinct and clear presentation of the Integral Map. More than this, it offers a series of practices to help those who are ready, willing and able to evolve deeper into Christ consciousness.

I am looking forward to entrusting this book to the people of the congregation I serve. This is saying something. As a minister, I am always on the look out for books that have real depth and yet are not intimidating. This book bears the lightness of simplicity on the other side of complexity. Tom writes with a playfulness characteristic of all mystics who have learned not to take themselves too seriously. The vision of an Integral Church is, I'm persuaded, a gift of Spirit for the 21st century. Nothing less than a vision with this kind of scope will be able to address the complexity of the life conditions we are facing as a species.

In the next decade we will see a profusion of books coming on to the market, written by authors who have been opened up by the power and perspective of Integral thought. This book is a portal that opens into and co-creates the "new thing" God is doing in our world.

Acknowledgements

Basically, I've been sitting all alone in my little hovel grinding out text with no worldly contact. Just kidding! Sometimes I wonder if I am actually the author of this book, for it truly takes a village.

First, I must thank my wonderful wife, Pam Thresher, for the incredible support she has offered. Not only did she provide major editorial help, she never complained as I sniveled and whined about the writing process. Nor did she stop me when I prattled on about the exciting stuff I was learning. She even talked to me about it! My good friend Jim Silva also offered essential support. In weekly conversations Jim shared his extensive understanding of Integral philosophy and Christianity and held my toes to the fire if I tried to gloss over an important point. Ed Frodel offered a spectrum of support. He's been an essential dialog partner, contributed the cover art, wrote a thoughtful piece for the Appendix, and even did an initial edit.

When you are stuck it's great to have stellar intellects to turn to… it's even better when they are good friends. John Forman helped me navigate essential aspects of Integral Theory and nuance important explanations. Salvatore Zambito lent a yogic lens on Yeshua (Jesus) and essential spiritual support when my work took me in unexpected directions. Aiya Maston works with me at the church. I count on her for fresh insight and loving friendship.

Every author needs a goad. Kema Larson played this role and sustained me at every step. She read early versions, gave legal counsel, directed me to publishers, pushed me when I was underperforming, and even nagged me when necessary… all with loving kindness.

This book would not have happened without the inspiration of Karen Sella and Daniel O'Conner in whose living room the idea was born. Nor could it have transpired without the gift of Wilber's *Sex, Ecology and Spirituality* some 15 years ago by Lee LaFollette.

I received indispensable editorial support from Keith Bellamy and Russ Volckmann at Integral Publishers, LLC and from Catherine Exton, who made this book look professional. Many thanks to Kathy Haug who designed the title. My friend, David Korten, with whom I always argue, provided essential inspiration.

Many thanks to my new friend and colleague, Bruce Sanguin, who wrote the splendid Forward to this book. And to Bob Kegan, whose insights undergird so much of my work and whose masterwork, *In Over Our Heads*, set the bar high.

Last, but not least, my profound thanks to the individuals at Suquamish United Church of Christ. Without them there would be no Integral Church.

Introduction

Jesus was not a Christian, he was a spiritual but not religious Jew.

The fastest growing religious demographic[1] in the U.S. is, quite paradoxically, the "spiritual but not religious." I count myself among them and, as my opening sentence suggests, find myself in good company. If you accept the media's portrayal of Christianity then I am the non-Christian pastor of a congregation of non-Christian Christians. My congregation has so little in common with the extremists presented in the media that we sometimes wonder if we are on the same planet. Despite the dominance in the media of (very photogenic) extremist "Christians," I find that what most church goers seek is a mature Christianity that will nurture and support them in the complex and rapidly changing world of the 21st century. This is the job of the Integral Church.

It is crucial to ask whether we are watching the slow and painful death of Christianity in the West. If we are, then we must also ask if there is any reason to save it. Does the church really have anything worthwhile to offer the 21st century? Obviously, I think it does. But still, don't secular humanism, atheism, Buddhism, and various New Age practices offer viable alternatives to Christianity and the church? I believe they do, but they also lack something vital. I will explain the lack with a personal story.

Nearly two decades ago I lived with my (then) wife in the mountains of Northern California, 20 miles from town. We both thought I was having a stroke (I wasn't) and while she was driving me down the mountain I found myself confronting the questions of God, death, heaven and hell. This is interesting because I was not raised a Christian. My parents were not Christians and I had had very little exposure to Christian thought. Yet here I was wondering if I died would I go to hell? I concluded a merciful God would never let anyone go to hell. The fascinating question was: why was a non-Christian wondering about God and hell in Christian terms? Very simply, because I was raised in a Christian culture saturated with the values, perspectives and orientations of Christianity. Even though I had not been raised with these ideas they were *the* categories of thought available to me in this culture.

What secular humanism, atheism, Buddhism and the New Age movement lack (and I am a big fan of these perspectives) is a means of dealing with the cultural roots we all inherit growing up in the West. For all the great insights offered by these other perspectives they inherently exclude the basic cultural dynamics that formed our consciousness. What the church can offer, and that no other institution can, is the means to confront, challenge, transcend and incorporate the foundational mental structures bequeathed to us by our Christian heritage. A mature Christianity need not oppose the legacy of our cultural conditioning. It has the authority to both construct *and* deconstruct the foundational premises that ground our Western culture. Instead of denying the assumptions that formed our consciousness, a mature Christianity challenges and transforms them with an authority unavailable to imported or secular faiths. This, then, is the mission of Integral Church: to provide a "conveyor belt"[2] for the evolution of consciousness from infancy to divinity, that is, from cradle to Christ-consciousness.

Why Integral?

Why integral? Because our destination is Christ and *how we get there matters.* We are children of God, the Divine itself. Awakening into Christ-consciousness is our destiny and cannot be avoided. Perhaps we awaken into our Christ nature at physical death, perhaps through many lifetimes. The good news is that we can awaken (be reborn) long before physical death. We can live, breathe and find our identity in the birthless and deathless eternal now. As the opening of the Gospel of Thomas claims, "Whoever finds the interpretation of these sayings will not experience death."[3] This promise is for everyone. The goal of the Integral Church is to make this promise a reality for all who want it. Again, the purpose of the Integral Church is to carry us from infancy into Christ-consciousness through increasingly expansive understandings of the Christian story and personal transformation.

In this life we can transcend the limits of mind and body. We can be "born of the Spirit."[4] But that is only half the journey. To be fully reborn we must bring that awakening fully into daily life; we must "be born of water."[5] The quality of our rebirth in the world depends upon the *persona* through which it is manifest. As the owners of Western mythology, the church has a unique and powerful role to play in both our awakening and its manifestation. Integral Church is about the full expression of that possibility.

A Distinctly Human Project

We are meaning-making creatures. We do not live life as it is but through the stories we tell about it. Every creature has its habitat, and the habitat of humans is the symbolic realm, especially language. We live, breathe and dance in a realm that transcends (and includes) the physical, and hence has immense power over it. It appears that no other creature lives so fully in the symbolic realm. To the best of our knowledge, no other creature has language of the kind and depth of ours. Cosmologist Brian Swimme claims that the power we derive from the symbolic realm makes us a force of nature, equivalent to land, air, water and fire; the very DNA of plants and animals is shaped by human choice.[6]

You will see me repeat this throughout this book, for it is foundational. We make meaning through the stories we tell each other and the stories we tell ourselves. Our compulsion to make meaning of everything sets us apart from other creatures. Because we possess powerful, self-reflective memories we construct a past and, from it, project a future. We do not remember the past as it is; we reconstruct it in the present every time we remember. We don't remember facts; we reconstruct images into meaningful events that are woven into on-going personal and collective stories in the present. We define ourselves in the stories we tell ourselves and others, moment by moment. As the spiritual teacher Eckhart Tolle explains, our name is a basket in which we collect the bits and pieces from which we will construct our personal story:[7] "I am smart." "I am beautiful." "I am clumsy." "I'm not good enough." We are given these bits and pieces by family, friends and community. With their help we weave together a comprehensive story of "me," which becomes our identity. The development of self, of ego, is the development of a story of "me."

The breadth, scope and possibilities for our individual stories are determined by the stories available to us in our culture and our cultural stories are intimately related to how we obtain a livelihood from our physical environment. One institution plays a pivotal role in the creation of our individual and collective identities: the church. You might look around contemporary Western society and wonder at this statement. Hasn't the church's power and influence been dwindling for centuries? Hasn't there been a precipitous decline in recent decades? There has, but the church nonetheless possesses "a resource as precious as oil and gas."[8] Because religion (and the church as its legitimate institutional form in the West) got its start with the emergence of human awareness, it owns the great stories that provide the possibilities and limitations of our personal identity stories. These stories are precious because, as Ken Wilber argues, "... humanity today, armed with video cameras, will never get a new supply of fresh, believable myths—of Moses parting the Red Sea, or of Jesus born from a biological virgin, of Lao Tzu being 900 years old when he was born, or the Earth resting on a serpent resting on an elephant resting on a turtle, and so on ... " Hence, "the world's great mythic-religious systems are a precious human resource, the only ones speaking to those [early,] unavoidable stages of human growth."[9]

Because religion grew up with humanity it has the power to confer legitimacy on the cultural stories from which we build our identities. In the West, Christianity and the church own the cultural stories, particularly for early personal development. Even if you were not raised Christian, if you grew up in the West, you grew up saturated with the stories and cultural perspective of the church.

Growing Up With Humanity

Religion, and some kind of institutional form we would recognize as "church," grew up with humanity. When the bulk of humanity saw the world as magical, our religion was magical. Spirits lived in the trees and forests; animals embodied the earth's different powers and were thought of as gods themselves; and folks believed that sticking needles in a doll really did hurt the intended victim. When much of humanity outgrew its magical orientation, religion gave birth to the great myths. In Judaism and Christianity the great stories of Creation, the Exodus, the flood, Jesus' birth, death and resurrection provided a mythological context that matched the mythological understandings of the majority of people. During the age of empire, Christianity built great temples and exalted royalty to express the emerging power of collective organization and the rule of law. Down through the ages Christianity, and the other great religious traditions, provided stories, beliefs, practices and explanations that soothed, reassured and generally met the needs of the population as new levels of awareness and understanding emerged.

The Enlightenment changed all that. Modern rationality rejected the magical and mythological stories that were the foundation of the church's authority. Science, art and morality broke away from the church and developed along their own modern and postmodern trajectories, leaving Christianity in its childhood. But in denying the importance of our spiritual nature, modernity left no cultural resources to resist the alienation of scientism and consumerism. Ironically, neither science nor the marketplace can solve the problems they have created. Now, seemingly, only the church has the legitimacy to point beyond itself and invite faith into the modern and postmodern worlds that are starving for its sustenance.

If the church "owns" the cultural stories of the West, it has both the authority and the sacred responsibility to expand these stories to meet contemporary needs. Today, we find a spectrum of churches preaching different stories and claiming them as the One True Story. Even postmodern churches, which celebrate the stories and perspectives of other faiths, claim that diversity is the One True Story. But no church offers a path through all the levels of human development. An objective of the Integral Church is to facilitate human awakening from cradle to Christ-consciousness in one church.

To facilitate the full spectrum of human awakening from in one church is a tall order. In an ideal world shepherding individuals through the various stages of human development might be the responsibility of many churches. Much like our educational system, folks would be supported by a culture and structure appropriate to their faith development. However, unlike our schools, individuals would be free to stay at whatever stage of faith their heart desired. An ideal church system would pass folks along when they had reached the limits of the perspective of the church they attend. In such a system we might find ourselves in a fundamentalist church learning the Bible stories as literally true. If and when we found this perspective inadequate or stifling, we would receive farewell blessings and move to a new church community teaching the Bible in more expansive ways. Obviously, this is not the state of Christianity, hence, the need for individual churches to carry us from cradle to Christ-consciousness.

The stories we tell ourselves and the stories we share about who we are, where we belong and what is important are not trivial. Wars are fought, abortion clinics and Twin Towers are bombed, and families are destroyed over these stories. Contemporary America finds itself in unprecedented "culture wars" that leave us politically, economically and spiritually polarized. Three vast cultural orientations set us in opposition to one another. In the simplest terms they are Traditional, Modern, and Postmodern. Each worldview believes itself to be the one true perspective and, hence, at "war" with the other "false" perspectives. We now live long lives amid rapid change, so we must deal with starkly different worldviews as they come into competition with one another. A new way of seeing is required—one that intrinsically (not just intellectually) recognizes the value of each of these perspectives in the overall development of the individual, culture and society. We call this new perspective "Integral" because it integrates all the previous waves of development into a comprehensive whole. Integral is a profound move beyond the great achievements of Tradition, Modernity and Postmodernity. It truly synthesizes the wisdom from each perspective into a new and compelling story for our times.

Integral is not the end of the story, of course. In fact, it is merely the launching pad for more expansive worldviews and ways of knowing that lead into the full promise of Jesus' life and being. Beginning with Integral, we join the other great faith traditions and Christian mystics like Meister Eckhart, Francis of Assisi, Teresa of Avila and St. John of the Cross in recognizing that our ultimate destiny is oneness with God. The Integral Church is a tentative step in culturally supporting individuals as they seek to develop fully and completely into the promise of the Christ.

Personal Story

I am perhaps the least likely person to write a book about church. My journey has had almost nothing to do with the church or with Jesus. I never came to love Jesus the way many do. The Bible is not pivotal to my understanding of Christianity and my relationship to the church has swung between total disregard and puzzlement. Few things surprise me as much as being a Christian minister. However, after nearly nine years as a practicing pastor, it's clear this is my path and there is nothing I would rather do. I do not worship Jesus nor do I seek to follow Jesus. I am only interested in what Jesus became and in becoming that. The extraordinary experiences that led me to become a minister never included Jesus as lord or savior, only as brother and friend. In the years since those experiences I have had good reason to doubt their veracity or whether they had anything at all to do with Jesus. The paradox is that this questioning, this doubting of the presence of Jesus in my life, has furthered my spiritual awakening more than any other single event.

I was not raised as a Christian. I did not go to church. I have only vague memories of fear associated with my grandmother's Southern Baptist church and being thrown out of Sunday school after a few visits. I was quite perplexed when my high school girl friend took me to her Catholic Church. Why were they standing and kneeling and chanting and singing? Were they crazy? Was it safe? Except for a short sojourn as a "Jesus freak" in the 70's, I felt Christianity was inscrutable and not worth bothering with.

My spiritual orientation emerged most forcefully in my 20's when I spent eight years in a transformative small group process and experimented with psychoactive substances for two of those years. This combination, I discovered later, was fortuitous. The small mentoring group, which met for three hours two evenings a week, provided a supportive structure for my experiments with psychedelics. Psychoactive substances effectively deconstructed my assumptions about reality while the small group held me and helped me to construct a new and more expansive consciousness to respond to what was happening.

Even though I developed a profound interest in personal development and psychology, I didn't study in these fields until much later. Rather, I discovered a knack for, and interest in, economics. I had flunked or dropped out of college some five or six times when I finally returned to school in earnest. I was then in college pretty much non-stop for the next 11 years. I graduated with honors from UCLA in economics and a year later went to Stanford where I completed a Ph.D. in Economic Studies in Education and an M.A. in Economics. Since my advisors in the School of Education were Marxists, and the Economics Department was among the most conservative in the nation, I often joked that I was getting "a communist doctorate and a fascist master's." Interestingly, despite being in the country's most prestigious School of Education, the education I received there paled along side the education I had received in the small mentoring group of my 20's. The most significant part of my formal education was writing a dissertation combining political economy, developmental psychology and the philosophy of metaphor. It was my first sojourn into integral philosophy and theory.

My spiritual understanding was most deeply influenced by Hinduism. While reading Paramahansa Yogananda's **Autobiography of a Yogi**[10] I had an overwhelming experience of something like firecrackers going off in my head. In retrospect, it appears to have rewired my brain. This, added to my experience with the small mentoring group and psychoactives, expanded my awareness in ways I have only recently come to appreciate.

My explorations with psychoactives pretty much ended with college and graduate school. The next leap in consciousness came with divorce in my middle 30's. The existential paradox I had to confront was: "How could I care so deeply for someone and still cause them such pain?" I spent countless hours walking and considering this question. Interestingly, none of these explorations were couched in spiritual or religious language, though they were spiritual to the core. During this time I left my position as a college professor and went fulltime into my avocation as an artist/craftsman. I married a younger woman, moved to the mountains and had two lovely daughters with her.

At this point, I want to share with you some experiences that typically don't make it into a text like this. Some of you will write me off as crazy and immediately give up on the book (thanks for buying it anyway). Others will find me more credible because of it. There has been much discussion of whether to keep this part of the story or not. In the end, I decided to keep it because it illuminates the seemingly erratic journey of the soul as it finds its way into more expansive realms of consciousness. I keep it because some of you may need a "life line" (as I did) on your journey of spiritual awakening and because the journey can never be anticipated.

During the early 90's someone very important to me, let's call her Diana, claimed that she was talking to the deceased mother of a friend. Diana wasn't just getting messages; she was actually listening to the deceased mother speak, as if she were sitting next to her. If Diana hadn't mattered deeply to me, I would have likely written her off as crazy; but I knew Diana well. I was definitely skeptical, but event after event slowly convinced me that something extraordinary was happening. The friend's dead mother was eventually replaced (after delivering, through Diana, convincing messages to nine of her ten children) by other entities and eventually by Jesus. I was incredulous. Yet continuing events, and especially knowledge relayed to me that Diana could never have known, persuaded me that this was real. After more than three years of these experiences, numerous "conversations" with Jesus through Diana, and my own altered awareness, Diana communicated to me that I was supposed to become a minister. I nearly collapsed when she told me. It was utterly obvious in that moment that ministry was what I must do. Equally surprising, I had never entertained the thought prior to that moment. I immediately applied to a seminary in Berkeley. We sold everything, including our fully owned home. Things fell together with uncanny ease: our house sold immediately at full price with no contingencies in an absolutely dead market; I was immediately accepted to seminary; we moved into a beautiful apartment on campus; and by August of that year I was a full-time student.

The story does not end here, however. In fact, the most important part of my journey emerged from questions about the veracity of my experience of Jesus through Diana. Events in recent years lead me to doubt whether Diana was actually hearing Jesus. This was shattering. I had reconstructed myself and built an identity around these conversations. As I came to doubt the truth of my experience with Diana, other explanations presented themselves. Perhaps Diana, who had exhibited a strong psychic capacity, was unconsciously reading my deepest longings and feeding them back to me in the form of conversations with Jesus. Perhaps she was projecting her own Catholic background and, unable to differentiate between an active imagination and reality, believed she was actually speaking to Jesus. Or, perhaps, it was manipulation.

Doubts about the veracity of my experience with Diana shattered the foundation upon which I had built the last decade of my life. What emerged was the direct comprehension that "I don't know." I had no idea if anything Diana communicated was true or not. Unexpectedly, that was just fine. In fact, "I don't know" became the best possible answer. Jesus may or may not have spoken to me, I don't really know. I no longer know if Jesus called me to be a minister and it doesn't matter. It doesn't even matter to me if Jesus existed or not. It's not the point. My journey is not about Jesus; it's about me and my life. Any awakening is not about Jesus, no matter how much I may learn from him. Something powerful moved and I became a minister. My journey continues, seemingly whether I like it or not.

Overview

In the following pages I explore how a church might support individuals on their journey from cradle to Christ-consciousness. In Part I, I present Integral Theory as the orienting framework for Integral Church. I begin with a myth to frame the discussion and keep a note of levity. Italicized passages throughout the book reconnect us with this myth. Chapter 2 summarizes Integral Theory, the comprehensive framework guiding the Integral Church.

Chapter 3 explores "Jesus Stories" for the Integral Church. As keeper of our cultural meaning stories, the church has a unique and essential role to play in Western society. A principal challenge for the Integral Church is to legitimate different stories to support different waves of personal development. It is not enough to say that the stories supporting each wave of development are all equally valid, nor is it sufficient to privilege one story. What is needed is a comprehensive vision that integrates and validates the entire structure of worldviews needed to support individual development.

No exploration of the Integral Church would be complete without a look at scripture. In Chapter 4 I present "Yes... And" theology and explore various scriptures through the integral lens.

In Part II Integral Theory is adapted for use in the church. In Chapter 5 I offer a useful tool to examine how comprehensive a church is in providing support for the spectrum of awakening. In Chapter 6 I apply this analytical tool to the church I pastor west of Seattle. Even though I have led this church from an integral perspective for seven years, I was delighted to discover that important gaps in our programming were uncovered by this tool. The final chapter presents a vision of the Integral Church for our times. Extensive Appendices deal with leadership, worship and a variety of programs you can use in your own Integral Church.

Notes

1 In January 2002, a **USA TODAY**/Gallup poll showed a full third (33%) of Americans described themselves as "spiritual but not religious," an increase of 3% over three years. There is a tendency for those who do describe themselves as "spiritual but not religious" to be among the heaviest Internet users. "Spiritual but not religious" is one of the most rapidly growing religious classifications in the United States. The "spiritual but not religious" classification is one of the most politically liberal demographics (rivaled only by black churchgoers and Jews).

2 Wilber, Ken, *Integral Spirituality: A Startling New Role for Religion in the Modern and Postmodern World* (Boston: Integral Books, 2006) Chapter 9.

3 Gospel of Thomas, Chapter 1.

4 John 3:5, NRSV.

5 Ibid.

6 Swimme, Brian, *The Powers of the Universe*, DVD, 9 hours, (San Francisco, Center for the Story of the Universe, 2004) http://www.brianswimme.org

7 Tolle, Eckhart. *The Power of Now: A Guide to Spiritual Enlightenment*. Novato, CA: New World Library, 1999. Audio version.

8 Wilber, Ken, *Integral Spirituality: A Startling New Role for Religion in the Modern and Postmodern World* (Boston: Integral Books, 2006) 191.

9 Ibid, 192.

10 Yogananda, Paramanhasa. *Autobiography of a Yogi*. Los Angeles: Self-Realization Fellowship. 1946.

Part I

INTEGRAL THEORY
FOR THE
INTEGRAL CHURCH

Chapter 1
A Myth for our Time

Every culture lives within a myth. A myth is not a lie but a Great Story that organizes how we see the world. Like every story, a great myth serves humanity for a while and then loses its elasticity as it becomes burdened with literalisms. We live in a time when the great myths that have served us are wearing out. Unlike other historical epochs, we have a couple of major myths in the process of collapse, another myth just getting traction and yet another myth beginning to emerge. Earlier eras had Great Myths vying for dominance, but there were never so many, and we never had communications that made the death and birth process so visible and frightening.

The great cultural story of the West is Christianity. For centuries, Christianity provided the context in which everything was explained and given meaning. Christianity may have lost credibility in Europe, Canada and the "godless" coasts of the U.S., but it still provides the cultural lynchpin in the heartland of America (and in much of the world). Even if you are not Christian, if you grew up in the U.S., you were saturated with the ontological presumptions of Christianity.

The story that eclipsed Christianity was, of course, Modernity (the Age of Reason). With Modernity's demand for reproducible evidence, doubt seeped into the Christian story, continually chipping away at its revelatory (and subjective) core. But Modernity is no less a mythical orientation than Christianity. (Again, I do not define myth as falsehood, but as an encompassing and compelling cultural story.) In the Modern myth, the individual is no longer bound to serve a higher *authority*, but a higher *principle*. In this myth, the pursuit of self-interest results in the highest good, because both the economic marketplace and the democratic political process ensure that the greatest collective good will be done. The impersonal market and the voting booth replace God as the arbitrator and dispenser of justice.

Like all great myths, Christianity and Modernity both possess great truths and falsehoods. No matter how great, all myths contain the seeds of their own demise. Christianity, over-reliant on subjective revelation, has declined for the past three centuries, most dramatically in the past half century in the West. Modernity with its slavish devotion to rationality is now unraveling with frightening speed. Both Christianity and Modernity have diminished since the 1960's because they are foundationally challenged by Postmodernity. Postmodernity gains its power from the recognition that truth is culturally relative. It can deconstruct any scientific or religious truth by simply pointing to the subjective cultural conditioning of its practitioners.

Of course, Postmodernity is not only destructive, it is tremendously creative and insightful as well. In an alarmingly short time we have seen what might be called the "Green/Pluralist/New Age" mythology gain traction in the U.S. It now stands side by side with Christianity and Modernity as a contender for mythic status, that is, as a Great Story that defines how we see the world and the meaning we give to events.

With such compelling, powerful and insightful mythologies actively available in our culture it is not surprising that we are embedded in culture wars of unprecedented scope. The nature of these worldviews is that each believes its particular orientation to be true and all others false. Leonard Cohen sings, "There is a crack in everything, that's how the light gets in." The culture wars in America have created cracks in all the worldviews. The light that seems to be emerging I call Integral. Of course, Integral has cracks that eventually will let in new light as it reaches its limits. But for now, Integral offers a powerful new lens on the culture wars currently tearing us apart.

To date, Integral Theory is primarily intellectual and theoretical. It has not yet gained the mythological status that carries it into our hearts. Theory tends to be sure of itself; myth is ambiguous. Because myth is ambiguous it can save theory from itself. Theory is based upon reason and rationality; its power and its limits derive from its capacity to narrow and define. But life is neither narrow nor definable. Myth points beyond reason and rationality to that which cannot be said. Myth points to the Mystery that can never be penetrated yet can be known directly.

What, then, is the myth that will save Integral Theory from itself and make Integral Church relevant? This is a perplexing question. As I explore this personally, I discover a wonderful mythology abiding at the heart of my passion for the Integral Church. I know it is mythological because, when I have tired of the intellectual and theoretical explication of Integral Church, something brings me back. Only a great mythological foundation can do that.

Myths are always paradoxical; that's how they create the cracks where the light can get in. Myths bring together the inherent contradictions in life and relentlessly hold them in our face. They won't allow us the respite of resolution. And that is their power. Rather than solving the contradictions, they hold us in the contradictions until the contradictions solve us. Someone said that the opposite of a great truth is not a falsehood but another great truth.[1] The creative job of myth is to hold us in the tension of two great truths until we are changed. Hence, an essential component of an integral mythology is to hold everything as both true and not true. Stated mythically, everything is right and wrong, good and evil. It's all cracked. We will never get it right because that would be the death of Life. It is only when things go wrong that the light gets in and change happens. The Christian myth couldn't be more explicit on this point: the "messiah" Jesus failed to liberate the Jews from Rome when he died on the cross; yet his defeat served as the opening for stunning new ways of knowing and being.

A second component of an integral mythology comes from the remarkable discoveries of science and cosmology regarding the nature of our universe. Something amazing appears to have happened nearly 14 billion years ago. At one moment there was nothing and the next moment there was everything, or at least the beginning of everything. There are (at least) three foundational perspectives on this event. From the objective perspective of science there was a Big Bang. Since this was literally the beginning of time, we can know nothing about what preceded the Big Bang. This was the start of the cosmos and everything that has existed or ever will exist. As cosmologist Brian Swimme[2] argues, we humans are just a recent expression of that Big Bang. The universe took nearly 14 billion years to create us.

Though it has long rejected the scientific story of our origins, the Christian myth is slowly adapting to the scientific evidence for evolution. A dynamic myth, like the Christian myth, can always accommodate new information. From the progressive theistic perspective of Christianity, God was surely the creative spark behind the Big Bang and also the One who set the limiting conditions and patterns for evolutionary development.

There is yet a third component of an Integral myth of our beginnings. Call it the Zen perspective. This perspective sees a radical Emptiness before the Big Bang. As science indicates, the Big Bang did not explode into a preexisting space. The Big Bang created both space and stuff. There was literally no space before the Big Bang. This primordial Emptiness, or Void, pervades the universe in all its aspects. There is nothing that is not simultaneously something and nothing. Emptiness is the ground of being from which all emerges. It is ever present and ever available.

An Integral myth of our origins embraces all three components. I have woven my Integral myth throughout the manuscript because theory easily takes itself too seriously. Much is said in myth that cannot be said otherwise. At its best, myth is playful, disrespectful and irreverent. With this myth I deliberately create a context of irreverence that invites us to step back and laugh at ourselves as we sincerely engage Integral Church. Below, I tell this myth as I would to, say, my twenty-something graduate students or the young adult in all of us who seeks passion, purpose and worthy dreams. Italicized passages will pick up the thread of this myth throughout the remainder of this book.

You will likely notice a bias in this story. I do not come from a Christian, theistic orientation, but from a more Eastern perspective; this myth expresses that orientation. I invite you to modify and adapt it so that it resonates with your soul.

• • •

Before the beginning there wasn't something and there wasn't nothing; there was only an incomprehensible Emptiness. Our sight only reaches to the beginning of Something, what scientists call the Big Bang. First there wasn't; then there was.

In that first instant, three things were born: Christians call them Father, Son and Holy Spirit. Linguists identify them as I, We and It. Cosmologists call them subjectivity, communion and differentiation. Length, width and height; then, now and future; whatever you want to call them, they are the building blocks of what is. Their source and essence is Emptiness, for that is where they come from.

There is something truly amazing about Emptiness; it's very intelligent. Not in the way we think of intelligence, but in very quiet way. Since it is nothing, it has nothing to lose. It can play with everything. Since it is beyond time, it can't possibly waste time; it has forever to do just as it pleases.

Of course, it is not an "it" but that's the only way I can talk about it. And since it isn't an "it," it has no itness or selfness to lose so it can play and play and play.

Perhaps it's frightening that the Emptiness, I sometimes call it the Great Mystery, can afford to be so reckless with all that is. But I will tell you a secret. We are that Emptiness! The Great Mystery that created everything didn't make us… it is us. We made ourselves in this form, and every other form. Why? Well, why not?

Another way of saying this is that when God created the universe He or She had us in mind. In that moment nearly 14 billion years ago He was creating us! Could She ever abandon us? Never! We know Him directly as Emptiness; we receive Her as Love.

All the animals and plants and rocks know that they are this Great Mystery; they just don't think about it. We think about it and we get confused. We can't find Emptiness when we look, but when we don't try, we can feel it. We have felt it since we were born. It is the most common element in our lives, so simple we ignore it.

I assumed it couldn't be important because it wasn't rare or cool or exciting. It was just something that was always there and so it was invisible. Then one day, when I was in crisis, a wise teacher told me that I was looking in all the wrong places. He told me I already had what I was looking for. (Actually, he and others told me this for a long time). When I finally stopped looking everywhere else, I noticed an incredible spaciousness inside of me. I was walking around with the whole universe inside. It was pretty weird…and wonderful. This wasn't some delusion; everything about it said that it was true. This was Emptiness, the Void, Great Mystery (and I swear it was laughing).

Sometimes we call this Emptiness God. I don't particularly like the word God because I get mental images of this guy with gorgeous white hair and six pack abs touching Adam's finger. But other people really like to call Emptiness God. They want to be in relationship with someone. I can't blame them; I'm just not wired that way. When I step back into the Void, it is loving, but not like pop songs. I just think of it as another way that Emptiness plays.

When I say Emptiness plays, I mean it plays with such abandon that I sometimes tremble in fear. Remember, the Void can't die because it was never born; it can't waste time because it doesn't exist in time; it can't get lost because it has no place to go. But all those things can happen to me! (Or so it seems). That's the dilemma of being human. We think we were born, so we believe we can die. Being human is like this crazy rollercoaster and Emptiness loves it all. It loves the joy and it loves the sorrow. It loves the ecstasy and the pain. It loves birth and death just the same. And it's running the show!

We could try to avoid our pain, our sorrow and our suffering by escaping into the Void, but we might miss out on whatever Emptiness has in store for us. In the language of Christianity, we might miss God's purpose for us. But since we are Emptiness, how could we ever do anything but what Emptiness has us do? This really confuses us. It seems that we have free will, yet how could we? How could we not? This is where our big stories, our myths, help. Our brains can't figure this out, and if they did, they'd get it wrong. So we create stories, great big stories, to point to what we can't figure out…go figure!

Emptiness (God or Great Mystery or Spirit or whatever) is on a great adventure called awakening. Of course, Great Mystery is always already awake, but what fun is that? The real fun is not in being awake, but in awakening. So Spirit creates this giant game of hide and seek; it forgets so it can wake up all over again.

In a great flash Emptiness flared forth. In that great flash it created itself in some very simple particles, and then some elements, mostly hydrogen. We think of hydrogen as so much stupid gas, but it knew something; it knew to fall together. In its bones it knew that someday it would sing rock and roll, even if it took billions years. After all, what's a few billion years to hydrogen? So it fell together and it fell together. And as it fell together, it got hotter and hotter and became a sun, and then many suns, and then galaxies full of suns. Some suns got really big and exploded and created new stuff, stuff we smart humans can't create, like gold and uranium and iron. Some of this stuff clumped together around suns and formed planets.

Here's something amazing about planets humans just recently figured out (of course both Mystery and hydrogen knew it from the beginning). If planets are just the right size, amazing things can happen. If they are small, they turn into big rocks, like Mercury; if they are real big, they stay gaseous, like Jupiter. But if they are just about the size of Earth, they stay liquid, solid and gas. Our earth has a solid iron core that is so hot it melts all the rock around it for miles. Then it has a solid crust, like giant islands floating around on the mantle of melted rock. In these crazy conditions life happens. That's what happened here. The earth, which is really made up of the uni-

verse, which is really Emptiness, created life. Just as the stars created galaxies and planets, so Life created more complex life and more complex life.

At some point, Great Mystery needed a good laugh... so it made humans. The Bible says God formed us out of a clump of mud. Still, we think we are very special because we believe we are separate from everything else. That's crazy, of course. How could we be separate? But we believe we are and because of this we take ourselves very, very seriously. We think we're old, but we're really brand new. We're like a fun new toy for Spirit. Our minds are the reason. They change! Animals, trees and rocks can't change their minds; they have to die and pass on DNA. Most animals grow up quickly and stay there; we humans are like children most of our lives. That's why we're such a delight to Spirit.

Just when Emptiness thought it couldn't possibly find a better creature in which to play hide and seek, humans started talking. Talking changed everything, because when we talk, we think differently. Before long we stopped thinking just in images and feelings; we started thinking in symbols. This doesn't sound like much, but it has both confused us terribly and given us power over the whole world. The ancient writers of the Bible recognized this. They spoke of how we were created in God's image and how we lost touch with Spirit when we started thinking and judging (ate of the Tree of Knowledge of Good and Evil). They spoke of God giving us dominion over the Earth. That wasn't true back then, but those writers recognized the possibilities of symbolic thought and language. Today we humans truly have dominion over the Earth. The beliefs we form with our language and thought have made us a force of nature; animals must adapt to us or die. Of course, if they die, we die too. This has been true now for some time, but we're just seeing it.

How will this story play out? What does the Void have in store for us? Will we destroy the Earth and ourselves? Can Emptiness let that happen? There's no way to know. What we can do is listen to how God or Emptiness or Allah or Spirit wants to play this out. In listening, we grow and we remember who we really are.

Are you still awake?

Notes

1 I believe the original quote was from Niels Bohr: "The opposite of a trivial truth is false; the opposite of a great truth is also true."

2 Swimme, Brian and Thomas Berry. *The Universe Story: From the Primordial Flaring Forth to the Ecozoic Era*. San Francisco: HarperSanFrancisco, 1992.

Chapter 2
Integral Theory

Spirit delights in theory. In theory, Emptiness can get most lost and revel in the game of hide and seek we call awakening. Fortunately for Spirit or Emptiness, humans nearly always confuse the map with the territory. That is, they mistake their theories for reality…then they fight to the death to preserve them. All the while Reality, Wholeness, Beauty and Love (all names for Spirit) are hiding in plain sight. So, my friends don't take what I say here too seriously lest you get lost as well.

Introduction to Integral Theory

This chapter explores Integral Theory and Chapter 5 applies the theory to the Integral Church. This is not intended as a comprehensive description of Integral Theory as there are many excellent synopses and original works as well.[1] My purpose here is to offer the basics and extract those dimensions that are most relevant to the ongoing practice of Integral Church. Rigor is not the goal as the day-to-day practices of Integral Church exhibit dynamic qualities and idiosyncrasies that are never adequately accounted for in theory, even one as far reaching as Integral Theory. Instead, I use Integral Theory as a roadmap that both instructs and demands questions of any community striving to be more inclusive in its approach to Christian faith, practice and awakening.

Integral Theory claims to integrate "Life, God, the Universe and Everything"[2] in one comprehensive framework. Integral Theory is foundational to the Integral Church as it seeks to integrate all the fields of science, all the disciplines of the social sciences, all of our meaning-making systems and worldviews, as well as our psychological and spiritual understanding, both East and West, into one comprehensible model. It promises to do this using five broad categories: States of Consciousness, Stages of Development, Lines of Development, Types and Quadrants. I will briefly introduce you to these components of Integral Theory, and then in subsequent sections, go into greater depth.

States of Consciousness

States of Consciousness refer to transient experiences that are part of everyday life. The great wisdom traditions refer to three natural States: waking, dreaming, and deep formless sleep. My model is slightly more differentiated. States of Consciousness become more expansive as we move from Gross to Subtle to Causal to Witnessing to Non-Dual. I develop this spectrum below.

We generally think of ourselves as bodies (the Gross realm), which contain a mind (the Subtle realm) that has thoughts. Our thoughts sometimes give way to intuitions from deep within (the Causal realm). This common perception is the opposite of the holarchy[3] of States of Consciousness. Rather, Gross awareness is contained within Subtle awareness, which is contained within Causal awareness, etc. The full spectrum of States is available to us at all times but we don't notice them. This will become clear as I describe each State.

Gross States of Consciousness refer to bodily sensations received through our five senses. A feeling in my stomach tells me I am hungry. A pinprick causes pain. Wonderful tastes give me pleasure. Loud noises drive me away. All of these are States arising at the Gross level.

Subtle consciousness takes us into the mental realm. If I *think* about what I want to eat to relieve my hunger, or how I want to hit the guy that stuck the pin in my arm, or how what I am tasting reminds me of my mother's cooking, I am in Subtle consciousness. When we dream we enter the purest form of Subtle consciousness as the body drops completely from our awareness and we live in a world created entirely by our mind.

Causal consciousness moves beyond thought. Most of us are so engaged with the chatter of our minds and our bodily sensations that we seldom notice the realm of silence beyond thinking. Please join me for a moment in a simple exercise in Causal consciousness: Close your eyes and ask yourself "I wonder what my next thought will be?" Then wait for your next thought to appear. Most folks will find that there is a gap, a pause of silence, before the next thought appears. That gap is the realm of Causal consciousness. Knowing is not a product of thinking in Causal awareness, knowing comes as intuition or sensation. It comes as a whole picture, not a string of thoughts.

If you hang out in the silence between thoughts (Causal consciousness), you might *notice* that you are hanging out in silence. This is not a thought about the silence, it is a very simple awareness that you are not thinking. If you have a thought about the silence, it can take you back into Subtle consciousness or you can simply notice the thought. The simple noticing of the silence between thoughts, as well as noticing thoughts and bodily sensations, without getting absorbed in them is Witness consciousness. You simply notice that you are silent, or thinking or feeling, without any judgment or opinion. It is as if a totally impartial observer were simply watching all that went on with you.

Gross, Subtle, Causal, and Witness consciousness all exist within the world of duality; there is an observer and something observed. In Non-Dual consciousness all distinction between observer and observed disappears. You are one with all that surrounds you. There is no distinction.

The salient feature of States is that they are *temporary*. States of bliss, anxiety, clarity or various altered states come and then depart; they aren't permanent. On a daily basis, we may experience moments of great insight and clarity (Causal consciousness), or narrowed perceptions induced by fear or anxiety (Gross consciousness), or a semi-dream state when we are tired or day dreaming (Subtle consciousness). All of these provide "lenses" through which we engage the world for awhile… and then they change. Such are the many States of Consciousness.

• • •

States of Consciousness get short shrift here because they are best expressed mythically. Paul speaks of being lifted up to the third heaven. Do we think he was lifted off the ground and up into the air? Some might, but most agree that this is a metaphorical way of describing an altered state of consciousness that profoundly affected how he saw the world. Altered States of Consciousness are the royal road to God consciousness; they are the tastes we get along the way. Just when you think nothing's happening in your life, you suddenly perceive the patterns shaping your destiny and you are amazed. Mystics talk about them; rock bands and evangelical churches produce them. They're like cookie batter or icing on the cake. They can't last long, but while they do they are totally yummy!

Stages of Development

While States of Consciousness are temporary, Stages of Development are permanent. Stages represent the milestones of growth and development of human consciousness; they are enduring acquisitions. Language, for example, is a permanent acquisition associated with a stable Stage of Development. Once achieved, language is always available (baring some physical impairment), and each stage provides the foundation for the next Stage of Development. Each Stage of Development is like a rung of a ladder. Stepping up a rung demands that we leave the previous rung. Yet we cannot abandon or destroy the previous rung as it provides the structure for the current rung. In the language of Integral Theory each stage is said to "transcend and include" the previous stage if there is to be healthy development. "Stages," "levels" and "waves" are roughly synonymous and are used to describe different aspects of development. "Stages" indicate the stability and universality of development. "Levels" highlight development's sequential and hierarchical nature. And "waves" emphasize the fluid and overlapping process of development. The flow of development of human consciousness I call Stages can be divided in any number of ways depending upon how you want to differentiate one Stage from another. Eight levels appear to offer enough differentiation to guide the Integral Church without undo complexity. These eight stages are described in some detail below and expanded in the following chapter.

Lines of Development

We all experience being better at certain things than we are at others. Some of us excel at mental activities while others are caring and kind; still others dazzle us with their physical prowess. These varying capabilities or Lines of Development are explored by Harvard psychologist Howard Gardner as "multiple intelligences."[5] Every individual has a variety of intelligences such as mental, emotional, musical, moral, aesthetic, interpersonal and more (somewhere between one to two dozen lines have been identified). These intelligences are not equally developed in everyone or in the same combination. Some who astound us with their compassion may not be able to "find their way out of a paper bag"; or we may know a mathematical genius who hasn't a clue socially. The differing combination of intelligences helps to explain the immense diversity we observe in human personalities. We all have the full spectrum of intelligences, but some are just more developed than others.

Just as Stages develop through a sequence that transcends and includes the previous Stage, so too, Lines of Development progress through different levels that transcend and include the previous levels. Moral development provides a good example. Research indicates that we progress through at least three levels of moral development from childhood to adulthood.[4] The first is called pre-conventional or egocentric and is typical of early childhood. Morality, at this stage, is "all about me," what I want and what is right for me. As children begin to learn their culture's rules and norms, they grow into conventional or ethnocentric morality; moral considerations are determined by the children's group, clan, tribe or nation and their moral consideration is confined to those groups. Everyone outside their group is "other," or "alien." If an individual's moral intelligence continues to develop, he or she may enter the post-conventional or worldcentric level, which includes care and concern for all peoples regardless of race, color, sex or creed.

The developmental lines of greatest relevance to the Integral Church are found in the subjective experience of the individual. Researchers have identified some two dozen relatively autonomous Lines of Development. Some of the more important developmental lines are listed below with the life question posed by that intelligence:

- Cognitive: What am I aware of?
- Self: Who am I?

- Values: What is significant to me?
- Moral: What should I do?
- Interpersonal: How should we interact?
- Intrapersonal: What do I see when I look inside myself?
- Spiritual: What is of ultimate concern?
- Needs: What do I need?
- Emotional: How do I feel about this?
- Kinesthetic: How should I physically do this?
- Aesthetic: What is attractive to me?
- Psycho-sexual: What is the nature of my sexual identity?
- Nature: What is my relationship to the natural world?
- Worldview: How do I see the world around me?[6]

While all of our multiple intelligences help to create the *persona* that we live through, two are particularly important to personal and spiritual development: the cognitive and self Lines of Development. Cognition asks "What am I aware of?" The self line refers to the sense of "I am."

Cognition leads the way in development. As we become cognizant of new ways of seeing and knowing, we can be drawn into them. But our thinking can only take us so far. To enter fully into a new Stage of Development we must bring other Lines of Development into this new Stage (though not necessarily all). We will likely want our morals, our interpersonal relationships, our emotions and other Lines of Development to reflect the new Stage of Development. Since the self (the ego or *persona*) has the job of integrating the Lines into a coherent whole ("who I am"), it is responsible for bringing "the rest of me" into that new sense of identity. We might look at cognition as "the talk," perceiving a new wave of consciousness. The self is "the walk" that brings all of "who we are" into a different order of consciousness. Cognition is often one, two or more stages ahead of the self in the evolution of individual consciousness.

The self-sense, or the ego, is the place of action. As mentioned, the self has the job of pulling all the various intelligences together into a coherent self. It then has its own developmental process, which is described in some detail below. Self is particularly important to the Integral Church because development of the self is more or less synonymous with both human and spiritual development.

• • •

OK, Lines of Development sound really boring when you talk about them theoretically. But this is where the action is. This is where you find the differences between people that make them really interesting. Remember the girl everyone liked even though she wasn't the prettiest girl in the school? Remember the really smart guy that just didn't have any friends? What about the jock? The princess? The shy one? The obnoxious one? How bored do you think God would get if She only played one role?

With all these Lines of Development happening at once in different ways, in different people, we get drama, and more drama and even endless drama. It really mixes things up for humans. We've discovered we are a force of nature that is shaping all life on this planet…and all we can think about are our personal dramas. The great challenge of our time is to get past our drama before we destroy ourselves. Now isn't that dramatic?

Types

Wilber call the fourth component of Integral Theory "Types." Types refer to "horizontal" differences that occur at each Level of Development. A popular typology is the Myers-Briggs Type Indicator, which categorizes personality types according to feelings, thinking, sensing and intuition. Another popular typology, The Enneagram, offers a similar exposition across nine types of personalities. Your personality type will manifest differently at a different Stage of Development. Other Types include race, gender, social class, sexual orientation and ethnicity.

Gender offers an example for the importance of Type. Research by Carol Gilligan[7] indicates how men and women go through the same levels of development, but "facing in different directions," or in a "different voice." Focusing on moral development, Gilligan found that both males and females develop through the egocentric, ethnocentric and worldcentric levels of moral development; but women do so with an orientation toward relationship, care and responsibility while men develop with an orientation toward autonomy, justice and rights.

• • •

Types are like lines: sterile, boring categories until you look closely. We look around and we see people of different shapes, sizes and colors and we immediately think, "Wow, these people are really different from me!" But it's really just part of the game. What if you were playing hide and seek with your friends but you couldn't hide behind anything? Wouldn't that be a silly game? Types are the same. Spirit hides behind different skin colors, in masculine and feminine bodies, or behind different personalities just for the fun of finding itself again. You've played this game. Remember the person who looked weird or scary to you because they looked so different? Then you got to know them and they became your best friend. That's Emptiness discovering itself behind the masks of different Types.

The Quadrants

States, Stages, Lines and Types come together in the Quadrants. Quadrants provide the really big picture and are best introduced by returning to our myth.

Before there was time, and before there was space, Emptiness had a problem, how to make something from nothing. The Hindus say that Vishnu dreamed the world into existence while sleeping on a snake of infinite coils. Christians say that God created the world out of chaos in six days. Science says it just happened with a Big Bang. Let's say you are the Creator. How would you design a universe, especially a universe you wanted to grow and change and stay interesting? You would want rules that everything would follow right from the beginning. You would want these rules to be really simple, so even hydrogen could understand them. And you'd want them to be dynamic and versatile so things would keep going and changing. Well there's this really smart guy with a bald head and geek glasses[8] who said you might be able to get everything going (and keep it going) with just two rules. First rule: everything has an inside and an outside. This seems obvious because we can't imagine anything without an inside and an outside. Second rule: there are individuals and there are groups. Well "Duh," you say, "Of course there are individuals and groups. How else could it be?" But that's just the point. It's obvious to us because that's how our universe is made. Perhaps it could have been different, but it isn't and it seems to work.

Anyway, if we want to avoid creating any more problems for ourselves, or for the other creatures, it helps to know how the universe works. We've created lots of messes because we didn't look at the whole picture, or even at a big piece of the picture. We're usually concerned with our little corner of the world and how to make things easier for ourselves. But now we have this problem: we've discovered we have all this power and don't really know what to do with it. So we need the biggest map we can find to guide us. We need to listen carefully to the Silence (Emptiness, God) within us so we know what to do.

• • •

States, Stages, Lines and Types come together in Wilber's famous Quadrants. Ken Wilber is not the only important integral theorist, but he must be credited with bringing Integral Theory into a coherent whole. The integral perspective is summarized by his Four Quadrant model (see Figure 2-1).

We begin with four basic ways of looking at anything: from the *inside* and the *outside* of the *individual* and the *collective* (remember, these are the building blocks of our universe). Four basic questions arise from this starting point:

- What do I see when I look through my eyes, hear with my ears, perceive with my mind? (That's the perspective from the *inside* of the *individual*, the "I" or "me.")
- When I look at you, what do I see? (When I look at you or anything from an objective perspective, what kind of "it" do I see? That's the *outside* of the *individual*.)
- What do I experience when I hang out with my friends and we feel like we really understand each other? (That's the *inside* of the *collective*, the "we.")
- How do all the things I see or understand fit together? (That's the *outside* of the *collective*, the "its.")

These perspectives are summarized in Figure 2-1.

For simplicity, the interior of the individual (I or me) is referred to as the "Upper Left" Quadrant, the exterior of the individual (it) as the "Upper Right," and so on. The Upper Left Quadrant is investigated by the fields of psychology, spirituality, and phenomenology and asks "Who am I?" The Upper Right is investigated by the empirical sciences like physics, biology, and chemistry and asks "What is it?" The Lower Left is investigated by cultural anthropology, hermeneutics, and ethics and asks "Who are we?" The Lower Right is studied by sociology, economics, political science and systems theory and asks "How do the 'its' fit?" (See Figure 2-2)

Before moving on, I'll share an example I use with students. I ask for a volunteer to walk across the room. When they have returned to their seat I ask the class a series of questions: What did you observe? What were they wearing? How fast did they walk? These are questions from the Upper Right Quadrant, the exterior of the individual.

The next set of questions comes from the Lower Right Quadrant, the exterior of the collective. This Quadrant takes the perspective of an objective witness observing how the parts fit together: What are they walking on? How was the floor made? Where was the lumber milled? Were the workers paid a living wage? Where did their clothes come from? How were they paid for?

Observation is no longer sufficient when we move to the Upper Left Quadrant, the interior of the individual. To get information we must ask the individual: How did it feel? What were you thinking? What did you expect? Finally, we probe from the Lower Left, the interior of the collective. Was the person stylish? Did their stride or posture suggest how they were feeling? What do we imagine this person is like?

Figure 2-1: The Quadrants

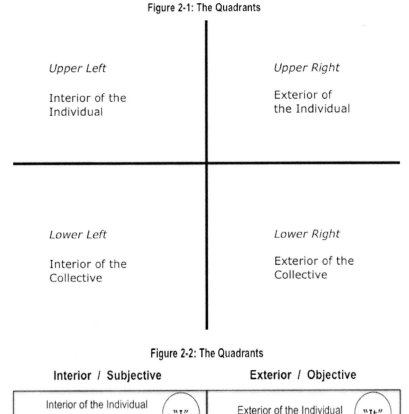

Figure 2-2: The Quadrants

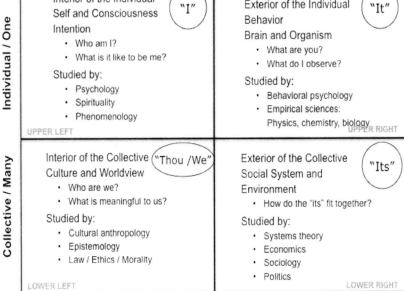

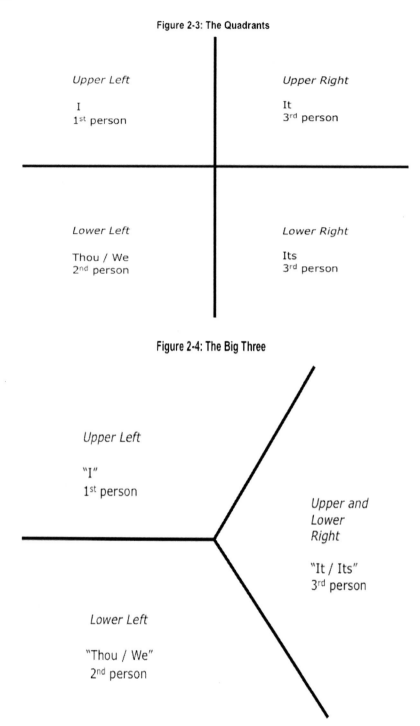

Figure 2-3: The Quadrants

Upper Left

I
1st person

Upper Right

It
3rd person

Lower Left

Thou / We
2nd person

Lower Right

Its
3rd person

Figure 2-4: The Big Three

Upper Left

"I"
1st person

Upper and Lower Right

"It / Its"
3rd person

Lower Left

"Thou / We"
2nd person

It is not as if these are concepts just floating around in space. The Quadrants, when considered as the Big Three of I, We and It, are so fundamental to how we think and how we know that they are embedded in language itself. Language is built upon the relationship among 1st, 2nd, and 3rd person perspectives: I, We and It.

The Big Three are also referred to as Self, Culture and Nature; The Beautiful, the Good, and the True; Father, Son, and Holy Spirit; and as Subjectivity, Communion and Differentiation. "Self" refers to the 1st person perspective, "Culture" refers to the 2nd person, and "Nature" the 3rd person perspective. "The Beautiful" is 1st person since "beauty is in the 'I' of the beholder," and entirely subjective; "The Good" refers to how we are together (2nd person, Thou/We); "the True" points to what is objectively verifiable (3rd person, It/Its).

The Quadrants Become the Big Three

Let's take another look at the Quadrants as developed by Wilber. Notice in Figure 2-3 that the Upper Left Quadrant, (the interior of the individual), is referred to as "I" and "1st person." This is the perspective from "inside the individual." It is the subjective, 1st person perspective. The Lower Left, the "inside of the collective," refers to the collective sense of us together. When I engage with you as a person, you are more than just an object, you are a "thou" with whom I engage "subject to subject" and together we form meaning; we become "We." This is the 2nd person perspective: the subjective sense of being connected ("We" or "Thou/We").

Both the Upper Right and the Lower Right Quadrants are "objective" in the sense that they take a stance separate from "me," or separate from "us." It is as if I am a third person standing apart from you (or myself) and considering you as an object (Upper Right), or a third person standing apart from some interaction and considering how they relate (Lower Right). By combining the two right hand Quadrants, we have the objective realm of "it" and "its." (See Figure 2-4).

Levels, Lines and the Stories We Tell

We need more story to make sense out of Stages of Development. This part of Integral Theory can really upset people because they think it implies some people are better than others. They aren't, of course, but these are the games the mind likes to play. Waves of development are simply Spirit, Emptiness or Great Mystery ramping up the game. With animals, waking up isn't hard because they can't fool themselves the way humans can. Animals are always directly in touch with Emptiness, but they don't know it. They don't have minds like ours that tell them they aren't directly connected to Reality, so they're always connected. Now with humans, Spirit devised a wonderfully wicked game of hide and seek. With humans, Spirit can become delightfully confused and lost. In hide and seek, the best game is the one in which everyone is really hard to find. So this vastly intelligent and creative Universe (that created everything in silence) developed noisy humans to really mix it up. Noisy humans, who think in language and symbols, can change a lot in one lifetime. So Spirit gave us a bunch of changes to make and lots of places to hide in the process of becoming aware of who we truly are. Boring old theory calls these changes levels or waves of development. Myth calls them the life you are living!

Integral theorists are not the first to think about waves of development. Paul, Jesus' great publicist, talked about thinking as a child and then putting away childish things as we grow. The Zen guys laid it out in a story of a boy finding and taming a bull. Christianity even explains how we go through each wave of development, but people don't recognize it because it's too close to them. It's called the Liturgical Year. Funny name, huh? For traditional Christians, the Liturgical Year is like a whole different calendar. Instead of being based on the sun, it's based on the life of Jesus, the Son. Instead of January, February, and so on, it begins with Advent, then Christmas, Epiphany, Lent, the Passion, Easter, and Pentecost. Pretty cool! People who worship Jesus find this a very important way to see the world. But I think there's another way to see the Liturgical Year, as how Spirit takes us through each wave of development on this crazy roller coaster of life. I'll tell you the story.

It begins with this young girl, Mary, getting pregnant by the Holy Spirit. (Try explaining that to your parents!) Her husband, Joe, is mad as hell, but has a dream where an angel tells him it's true and that Mary will have a special baby they should name Jesus. Joe believes it, so, Mary is off the hook. I don't know if this is how it really happened or not, but it's a great story! If you look at it with mythical eyes, it tells us a lot about how we become aware. We don't become aware of something all of a sudden; it generally dawns on us over time, just like growing to a baby.

So the first part of moving into and through a new wave of development is getting a clue. My name for Advent is "Wuz' Happenin'?" The cool thing is that if you hang out in "Wuz' Happenin'?" long enough, you actually do get a clue. Suddenly you get it; that's Christmas. The baby Jesus is born. I get it! My word for Christmas is "Wow!" You've had these experiences, and they are wonderful. You suddenly begin to see the world in whole new ways; you understand things you didn't understand before; a lot of your old problems get solved; and life opens up for you. The Bible writers called this opening Epiphany, and they tell about it with three wise men bringing Jesus very valuable gifts. Most of us think we would be really happy if we could stay in Christmas and Epiphany all the time, but Great Mystery knows that even epiphany stuff gets boring after awhile. Anyway, we're only half way through our journey through a wave a development. The next step can really stink.

Have you noticed that wherever there is light there is also dark? That there's also a shadow? Christmas and Epiphany are like this great burst of light and it takes us awhile to see the shadow, but it's always there. In the Bible story, Lent begins right at the pinnacle of Epiphany. In the Bible story, Jesus has just been baptized in the river by John. A dove descends from heaven and a voice says, "This is my son in whom I am well pleased" (only it was in Aramaic, not English). Well, it doesn't get better than that as far as epiphanies go. What does Jesus do? Does he party? Does he tell everyone how it is? No, he goes out into the desert to be alone for a really long time.

Here's the great wisdom in this story: right in the middle of the best-ever epiphany, Jesus realizes there's a downside, a shadow. There's a bunch of stuff inside him that he's ignored because all the epiphanies have been so exciting. The church calls it Lent, I think Jesus would have called it "Oh Shit!" (I know that's not nice language, but it's the best way to describe it). Suddenly, he is aware that the wonderful insights of Epiphany have their limits, and he has to descend into the dark side of himself. That's just how the world is. If he wants to see all of Truth, he's got to look into the darkness as well.

As Jesus explores the shadow, he discovers that the darkness is deeper than he imagined and will demand more courage than he thought possible. In the Bible story, Jesus has to go to Jerusalem. In Jerusalem people want to kill him, and he has to go right to them! Church folks call this Passion Week; he might have called it "Oh God!" as in "Oh God do I really have to do this?" During Passion Week, Jesus is betrayed by his friends, deserted, arrested, stripped naked, beaten, made fun of, forced to drag a cross through the city and then nailed to it until he dies. It's not a pretty story, but it points to something really important: everything you think is true must collapse before you can get to the next level. Jesus has to let go of everything, even his belief in God.

Now here's the surprise. Just when he thought all was lost, he gets resurrected. He dies and comes back to life. Yeah, I know that's pretty hard to believe. But the Bible says that's what happened. I don't say it's true or not true. What's important to me is what it tells us about our own lives. It says that when you think all is lost, you must surrender, give in and let go. That doesn't sound like a good Marine, but it's what the story's telling us; give in, because when you give in, miracles happen. When you stop trying to run your life and let the intelligence of the Universe run it, amazing things happen. You're reborn! Christians call this Easter, I call it "Ahhhhh," because of the peace of letting go.

You might think at this point that you're done, but you're not. What you've done is gone all the way through a wave of development. Now you've got to pick up the pieces. In the Bible it happens after Jesus has been resurrected, hung out for awhile, then been lifted up into heaven (that's a whole other story). One day, as Jesus' closest followers are hanging out together, tongues of flame come out of the sky and touch them and they speak in different languages. This is pretty weird, but it points to finishing the process. When Jesus was around, the apostles didn't really have to figure stuff out for themselves because they could just ask him. But once he was gone, really gone, they had to figure it out for themselves. The tongues of fire are a symbolic way of saying they got it. What it means for us is, when we've made it all the way through a level of development, we can't just leave it behind; we've got to clean up the mess we made with all this dying and resurrecting. We have to find out what was really good about what we just came through to move ahead. Christians call this time Pentecost. I call it "Who's gonna clean up this mess?"

Whew! Fortunately, our transitions through different waves of development are not always this dramatic, but the drama makes a good story, don't you think? We're lucky many people have gone through most of this before us and can help us, because we have something like eight waves of development to go through on our journey from cradle to Christ-consciousness. What I've described here is the journey through one Stage of Development. Once we've cleaned up the mess enough, we're likely to begin a new Advent, a new "Wuz' Happenin'?"

Why do we do this? Because this is the game, this is hide and seek on a cosmic scale. Spirit is running the show. It will let us stop for as long as we want at any part of the journey. But it promises that if you hang in there, it will be the best ride of your life.

• • •

Even though the full breadth of the integral perspective is relevant to the Integral Church, some aspects are more pertinent than others. In particular, the interior dimensions of the individual (both States of Consciousness and Stages of Development; the Upper Left Quadrant) and the way in which we construct meaning together (Lower Left) are particularly relevant. While the socio-economic context (Lower Right) and the health and well-being of congregants and their families (Upper Right) are important, I contend that church, in general, and the Integral Church, in particular, serve best when they focus on the interior dimensions and thereby promote the meaning-making of individuals and communities. As individuals evolve through more expansive waves of development, their action in the world becomes more resonant with the movement of Spirit. Action then emerges as timelier and more relevant. In this section I will take a closer look at some of the important interior dimensions individuals move through on their journey from cradle to Christ-consciousness.

Stages, Waves and Levels

There are numerous ways to slice up the progression through ascending Stages of Development. Integral Theory generally uses eight basic levels and I will follow that convention. Using some of the different descriptive names for each, they are:

- Tribal/Magic/Impulsive/Symbiotic
- Mythic-Literal/Warrior/Power/Opportunistic/Egocentric
- Traditional/Conformist/Mythic/Rule-Role Mind
- Modern/Achiever/Rational
- Postmodern/Pluralist/Individualist
- Integrated/Self-Actualized/Integral/Strategist/Autonomous/
  Systemic
- Paradoxical/Construct-Aware/Magician/Alchemist/Jester/Holy Fool
- Unitive/Trans-personal/Ironist

At first glance, this may appear to be far too much detail for practical application in an Integral Church. It is true these categories overlap and intermix in practice (they are "waves" after all), but they are sufficiently distinct as categories that they will be instantly recognizable in your congregation. Furthermore, they provide essential elements of a roadmap for the Integral Church.

An important caveat is in order at this point: the levels of development do not refer to *people*, they refer to *perspectives*. Any individual incorporates many of these levels and likely inhabits different ones throughout the day. In fact, each of us contains all of the levels up to (and slightly beyond) our center of gravity. Our center of gravity refers to the orientation or perspective we favor when we view the world around us (more about this below). From moment to moment we may shift into higher or lower levels of awareness, but we tend to settle back to our center. As I discuss below, one job of the Integral Church is to create programs and settings where individuals experiment with higher orders of consciousness with safety and support.

The question inevitably arises: "What is my level?" This, of course, states the question inaccurately. The same query can be stated more precisely as: "What perspective do I gravitate to?" Or "Where do I find my center of gravity?" The obvious value of reframing this question is it then emphasizes the important caveat above: the levels point to perspectives we can inhabit at different times. And, yes, we will have a preferred perspective. A simple way you can explore the question, "Where is my center of gravity?" is to pay attention as you read the descriptions below. The earlier perspectives (those you have already transcended and included) will seem quite familiar. This does not mean your center of gravity is in these earlier levels; rather, these are perspectives you have long since mastered and readily enter at will.

Notice, as you read the descriptions, when they become a bit confusing, or when they don't resonate with you, or when your attention begins to drift, then you are moving into unfamiliar territory. More complex and encompassing perspectives beyond our comfort zone does not imply we are lacking in any way. Every one of us will find a level of consciousness or a perspective beyond our comprehension in this moment. There may be times when a previously baffling perspective becomes obvious to us, and then it slips away. This is all perfectly natural as we move into and out of a perspective.

On our journey of personal and spiritual development, there is no demand to move into more expansive perspectives. Each level of development has its own blessings and curses. A more expanded level of awareness may alleviate the suffering of the previous stage, but it brings its own unique form of suffering, a form of suffering particular to that stage. Many wonderful lives are lived at one Stage of Development, for all are equally wonderful manifestations of Spirit.

Let's examine these categories more deeply. You will notice that I use two names and a color for each wave of development. The second Descriptor (e.g., Magic) describes the perspective of the individual whose center of gravity is at that level. The first label (e.g., Tribal) refers to the worldview that supports it. I will say more about worldviews in Chapter 3. Color (e.g., purple) is a neutral designation used by Wilber.[9] The following descriptions are a blend of the work of James Fowler, Suzanne Cook-Greuter, Bill Harris, Steve McIntosh, Ken Wilber and Robert Kegan.[10]

Tribal/Magic (Purple)

The Tribal/Magical wave of development (which is also described as "impulsive," "symbiotic" or "naïve") is generally observed in the West in young children from about ages two to six and is foundational to all higher orders of consciousness. As mature adults we may find the most meaningful and beautiful times in our lives are imbedded in our Magical awareness.

For the individual inhabiting the Magical wave of development, the world is literally seen as magical. Everything is alive; spirits inhabit trees, animals and wind, and they all talk to us. Word magic dominates: "If I say it is so, it is so." God is literally a fantastical, magical being. The Bible stories are literally true. Moses really did part the Red Sea, Jesus really did walk on water and the earth was truly made in six days.

Among primitive tribal cultures (not modern Native American tribes) the world is perceived as mysterious and threatening; it is fear driven and a spectrum of rituals are practiced to placate the spirits. Priests, shamans or chiefs are quasi-divine beings who make ritualistic requests of a magical God to elicit safety and security for the tribe. Individuals are expected to sacrifice self for kin and tribe and to obey chiefs, customs and taboos without question. Purple (Tribal/Magic) cultures generally survive by foraging, herding and engaging in primitive horticulture. "Truth" from the Magic perspective consists of the tribe's myths and stories as presented by chiefs and shamans. "Beauty" is found in family, children, symbols and fetishes, drumming and dance. "Goodness" is for the good of the gods and the good of the tribe.

Every wave of development makes its important contribution to the process of evolution (both individually and culturally); every wave also has its distinct pathology. The Purple wave of development imbues us with family and kinship loyalty, providing a sense of enchantment with the world and intimacy with nature. An expansive imagination and profound innocence permeate this perspective. On the down side, Magic is superstitious, often violent, enslaves the individual to the group and promotes docility.

Suppressed individuality and an emerging ego identity often initiate the transition out of Magic awareness. Fear of death and ongoing attacks from outsiders, as well the allure of freedom and power associated with the warrior culture, provoke the emergence out of Purple.

Mythic-Literal/Warrior (Red)

The Mythic-Literal/Warrior perspective (also known as the "opportunistic," "egocentric," "mythic-literal" or the "power" Stage of Development) emerges in middle childhood, around ages 7 through 12 in contemporary Western culture.

For Warrior consciousness, life is a zero-sum game. For Red, there are only winners and losers; the goal is to gain power over others. God is mighty, powerful and entirely anthropomorphic. He must be respected, feared, bargained with and prayed to. The Warrior expresses him- or herself forcefully and "to hell with anyone else." You may recognize Warrior consciousness in yourself as road rage. Red's motivation is to gratify oneself now and only trust oneself. For the Warrior, the world is full of threats and predators; the quest for personal honor and avoidance of shame are consuming drives.

Mythic-Literal/Warrior cultures may engage in primitive agriculture, trading and, of course, raiding. "Truth" is manifest in the existing distribution of power. "Beauty" arises from the spoils of conquest and the symbols of power. Contemporary Warrior consciousness is expressed in gangs, rap music and punk rock, which are often used by our militaries to imbue frontline soldiers with the Warrior perspective for their own survival. "Goodness" derives from personal power, pleasure, prestige and respect.

The pathologies of the Warrior Stage of Development are obvious. It tends to be violent, ruthless, continuously at war and self-serving in all its actions. Yet this wave of development contributes essential aspects to the evolutionary spiral as the source of initiative and individual empowerment. Individuals may be driven beyond Red consciousness by parenthood, spiritual experiences or vulnerability brought on by illness or injury, as well as by the desire for security and belonging.

Traditional/Conformist (Amber)

This perspective is also known as the "mythic," "conformist," "mythic-membership" or "concrete operational" Stage of Development. Traditional/Conformist ways of knowing generally emerge in early adolescence when teens realize that not only are they looking at others, but that others are looking at them. As Erik Erikson said, early adolescents are always performing on an invisible stage.[11]

Self identity, at this developmental stage, is defined by one's relationship to the group. This may include peers, family, race or ethnicity, nation or sexual orientation. For this reason, Conformist consciousness is intensely ethnocentric, as in "my group, right or wrong." Amber relies upon legitimate, external authority. This may include a priest or minister, a teacher, a book, a rock-star or fashion model. There is one, and only one, truth that is spoken through divinely recognized earthly authorities who deliver this truth through a recognized chain of command. The apostolic succession of Catholicism comes to mind as does TV's endless airing of celebrity opinions.

Amber's spiritual orientation, particularly in the West, tends to be theistic. God is other and we are essentially different from God. The Traditional/Conformist faith story is seen as "everybody's belief" and is generally comprised of a consistent, but unexamined clustering of values and beliefs. The symbols of the faith are multi-dimensional and evocative. Power is inherent in the symbol itself.

The Conformist perspective sees the world as "black or white," good or evil; ours is a world badly in need of law and order that can only be saved by obedience to God's supreme law. Individuals willingly sacrifice themselves and their desires to the group's transcendent purpose (which will save humankind). This "black and white" understanding provides a clear and unequivocal moral code that demands obedience. Both individual and collective salvation comes through adherence to the "rule of law" as set forth by God (in the *Bible*, the *Torah*, the *Qu-r'an* or Mao's *Little Red Book*).

Not surprisingly, pathological expressions of Conformist consciousness take the form of rigid intolerance, prejudice, dogmatic fanaticism, inflexible fundamentalism and chauvinism. On the other hand, the contributions of Amber to overall human development are huge. Conformist consciousness, with its nascent ability to take the perspective of another, provides the fundamental building blocks of civil society. This includes our sense of civic duty, law and order, respect for authority, moral clarity, as well as a deep sense of loyalty, hope and purpose.

Typical of trading, agrarian and maritime economies, Conformist consciousness finds "Truth" in the scriptures of the mythic order (the *Bible*, the *Qu-r'an*, the *Tao Te Ching*). "Beauty" resides in children and family, wholesome art that represents the "One True Way," and in country and gospel   music. "Goodness" is equivalent to God's will as interpreted by the legitimate representatives of the Divine.

Amber conformity is often challenged by higher education and the cognitive dissonance caused by scriptural contradictions. Higher education typically challenges fundamental assumptions of scripture while critical analysis of scripture reveals many contradictions. Both can initiate the deconstruction of Traditional/Conformist ways of knowing and point the way into the Modern/Achiever Stage of Development. The obvious power of science and the inherent challenge it poses for traditional ways of knowing can also inspire movement to the next order of consciousness.

Modern/Achiever (Orange)

The Modern/Achiever typically shows up in late adolescence and is generally considered the destination for "adulthood" in Western culture. Orange is also known as "formal operational" or the "rational" wave of development. The individual inhabiting the Achiever Stage of Development strives to better him or herself, to live well and improve society. Whereas Conformist consciousness sees one's self primarily in relationship to others, Achiever consciousness can stand outside the relationship and reflect upon it. This capacity to objectively stand outside the system is the foundation of science. Hypothetical-deductive reasoning allows evaluation of different perspectives and the possibility of choosing the "one best answer."

The individual inhabiting Orange consciousness tends to be self-directed (rather than relying on some external authority), goal oriented, empirical and materialistic. Doubt, particularly well-reasoned doubt, plays an important role in this wave of development. Previous roles and beliefs can be questioned, faith stories are demythologized and the power of external authority is diminished as personal authority strengthens. The Achiever brings critical reflection and the logic of science to stories received from traditional faith. A well reasoned atheism and agnosticism are consistent expressions of a "spiritual" orientation from this perspective.

Orange sees life as an assortment of opportunities for improving living standards and social position. There is a drive to escape oppressive, dogmatic systems and to demystify the material world. The achievement of wealth, status, social progress (through science and technology) and individual excellence motivate the individual inhabiting Achiever awareness. Individual autonomy and competition are also hallmarks of this order of consciousness.

The dignity of modern western culture is found in Achiever consciousness. This dignity includes meritocracy, that is, rewards based on individual initiative and effort. Upward mobility, the creation of a healthy middle class and individual excellence are also products of this perspective. The wonders of science and technology that have increased human life spans, health and wellbeing also derive from Achiever consciousness. The pathological downsides are, of course, equally pernicious: extreme materialism, nihilism, exploitation, selfishness, greed and unscrupulousness.

Achiever consciousness is intimately connected with the industrial economy and capitalist market systems. "Truth" is found by objective means and proved materially (scientifically). In other words, truth is that which is disclosed by reason. "Beauty" is found in fashionable, even glamorous, symbols of power and prestige. Both classical music and jazz are associated with modern consciousness. The "good" is that which brings progress, liberty, material wealth, status and opportunity, in other words, "the good life."

The desire to move beyond Achiever consciousness may be triggered by spiritual experiences, disappointment and disillusionment with the ability of possessions to bring genuine happiness. Feelings of emptiness, guilt and the allures of the "counter culture" may also motivate one to look to the next wave of development, Postmodern/Pluralist.

Postmodern/Pluralist (Green)

Postmodern/Pluralist awareness (also referred to as "affiliative consciousness," and "holistic thinking,") reached a critical mass in the U.S. during the 1960's as the limitations of modernity, science and capitalism entered the public awareness. Popular confidence in technology dwindled as people noticed that science could not solve all our problems or make us happy. The Green perspective strengthened as questions of justice increased and we realized that capitalism could not unravel the problems of global poverty and inequality. We became acutely aware of exploitation, the corruption of existing hierarchies, environmental degradation, the shallowness of materialism and the suffering of others. Marginalized groups, especially people of color and women, were recognized and given a greater voice.

Individuals inhabiting Green shift from the individualistic orientation of Orange to a more socio-centric orientation. Such individuals exhibit sensitivity to the feelings and perspectives of others (especially those previously unheard), and the relativity of experience and belief. Consensus becomes the preferred mode of decision-making; hearing every voice and finding common ground the ideal.

The Pluralistic perspective is just that, pluralistic. Green believes that more perspectives reveal more of reality, that there is validity to every perspective, and that life is more dialectical than linear. Individuals inhabiting the Pluralistic stage become increasingly self-reflective, opening to the many "selves" within. Ego boundaries become more porous, which enables greater acceptance of paradox and uncertainty. An emerging 4th person perspective allows one to stand back and evaluate an entire system (as opposed to a 3rd person perspective which looks at particular relationships). This showed up in the U.S. in the growing awareness of personal and cultural conditioning. Awareness of our propensity for defensive self-deception led to deep questioning of the "establishment" culture and economic system. The information economy emerges with and supports Pluralistic consciousness just as the industrial economy emerged with modern Achiever consciousness.

"Truth," from the Pluralist perspective, is necessarily subjective because everyone's truth is a reflection of their social location: the nexus of their race, class, gender, age and sexual orientation. "Beauty" is found in nature, modern art, tribal/folk art, New Age music, 60's music and psychedelia. Sustainability defines the "Good" that is best for all people and the planet.

The pathologies of the Green wave of development are now a vocal part of the American culture wars. A critical view sees Pluralism as value relative: terrorists flying planes into the Twin Towers merely reflect their values which, according to Green, are as true as anyone else's. Pluralism easily becomes narcissistic. Extreme relativism morphs into "my truth is my truth so I'll do whatever I damn well please." Anything that smacks of hierarchy is bad, despite the hierarchical judgment in that position. There is often remarkable contempt for both Achiever and Conformist ways of knowing.

Despite the downside of the Pluralist wave, its contributions to evolution are vast. Green brings a worldcentric morality, increased recognition of human potential combined with heightened responsibility for *all* people and for the earth itself. Compassion and inclusion come to center stage; the feminine is raised up and celebrated along with renewed spiritual freedom and creativity.

The drive to move beyond the Pluralist orientation may be triggered by dissatisfaction and the weariness with constant seeking. The failure of the counter culture to deliver the cures it promised fosters a deep desire for results. Leaving one wave of development and entering the next always entails the loss of familiar ground and the unknown possibilities and dangers of the next. The individual reaching the limits of Green must either look back to Orange for answers or forge ahead into the unknown territory of expanding awareness.

First and Second Tier

An important developmental transition occurs at this point which is particularly relevant to the Integral Church. This transition is the shift from "first tier" to "second tier." The salient aspect of this shift concerns how other developmental waves are perceived. In first tier, all the stages we have discussed so far (Magic, Warrior, Conformist Achiever, and Pluralist) see their own perspective as "The Truth." In contrast, second tier awareness becomes deeply cognizant that all perspectives are partially true and that each makes its own essential contribution to the spiral of development. American culture wars reflect this first tier orientation and the absolutism of each perspective. Steve McIntosh elaborates on the conflict among traditional, modern, and postmodern orientations:

> *Each of these stages [tends] to see the other existing worldviews primarily for their pathologies, discounting the progress and stability these other worldviews are continuing to bring to the world...For instance, modernists tend to view the postmodern worldview as some kind of politically correct fashion [statement]. Postmodern sensibilities are often dismissed as "airy fairy." Likewise, traditionalists often see those who fail to ascribe to their worldview as misguided sinners or worse. And postmodernists also tend to vilify modernists and traditionalists as the real cause of the world's problems. In fact, postmodernism can be intensely antimodern, despite the fact that modernism represents the next crucial step for the majority of the world's population.*[12]

Because appreciation of the contributions of each previous level emerges and deepens in second tier, it is the realm and goal of the Integral Church. Second tier awareness sees across systems of belief and integrates them in ways no previous level can. This integration is not just intellectual; it permeates to the level of the self such that the personal sense of self is no longer threatened by competing perspectives. Integral Church aspires to this wave of development as it holds the fabulous spectrum of human complexity in the loving embrace of Spirit. The following two waves of development (Self-Actualized and Construct-Aware) I call Integral.

Integrated/Self-Actualized (Teal)

What I call the Integrated/Self-Actualized wave of development also goes by the names "Integral," "Autonomous" and "Strategist." When I speak of the Integral Church, I am pointing, in a general way, to the waves of development beginning with second tier and moving beyond. "Integral" emphasizes the critical shift from first to second tier, especially the emerging capacity to value and support all the previous waves of development. If, as Wilber argues, the church has a unique role (because it owns the great cultural myths) to become a conveyor belt for individuals into more inclusive levels of awareness, then appreciation for all the stages is paramount. This appreciation really begins with the Self-Actualized wave of development.

In moving past the Pluralist way of knowing, Self-Actualized awareness not only deals with paradox and ambiguity, but actually finds them to be sources of inspiration. Teal consciousness is actively reflective in the face of complexity, change and multiple time horizons (such as past, near future, distant future). This reflective action involves self-guided education across   different modes of learning (mental, emotional, and kinesthetic, for example), feedback from different sources and deep attention to inner workings.

An emerging understanding of the role that our personal meaning-making stories play in what we perceive and how we respond is foundational to the Self-Actualized consciousness. Increasingly, an individual inhabiting Teal makes use of previously disowned parts of the self to consciously construct new stories of self. These new stories can then function more coherently with personal goals. The plasticity of personal boundaries (founded in the security of a deeply settled sense of self), permits awareness across systems of relationships and processes (an expanded 4th person perspective).

Self-Actualized awareness recognizes Pluralism's failure to offer realistic solutions for global problems while simultaneously celebrating the great contributions of Pluralist, Achiever, Conformist, Warrior and Magical waves of development. Self-Actualized consciousness awakens to new understanding of a vast universe interior to the individual. At this stage, individuals have an autonomous, tolerant, insightful presence combined with high self-esteem. Teal is the highest Stage of Development achievable by the separate sense of self.

The awakening of second tier consciousness corresponds with a global systems economy. Truth is found in the harmonization of science and spirituality. Unlike the Pluralist wave, which perceives truth as relative and unattainable, the Self-Actualized perspective finds that "Truth" can be approximated, especially with the development of higher forms of consciousness. "Beauty" is found in nature, in the arts of each level in their emergent phase and in the unification of opposites. "Goodness" resides in the evolutionary process itself and in the health of the entire spiral of development.

Folks inhabiting Teal can come across as elitist, insensitive, aloof and impatient. They are often preoccupied with their own development and self-fulfillment. Despite this, the contribution of this wave is immense. In addition to the appreciation of the previous waves of development, the Self-Actualized perspective brings a renewed insistence on achieving results. This insistence is focused by a practical, worldcentric morality and a passion for resolving the culture wars that cause so much suffering.

An individual may be inspired to reach beyond the Self-Actualized level by powerful spiritual experiences or by glimpses of Construct-Awareness. Such experiences can trigger realization that a separate self-sense, no matter how beautifully developed, is both a blessing and a limitation. Such glimpses can motivate profound questioning into the very structure of ego and its active deconstruction.

Paradoxical/Construct-Aware (Turquoise)

The Paradoxical/Construct-Aware level of development also goes by the names "Magician," "Alchemist," "Jester," and "Holy Fool." The transition to Construct-Awareness is often instigated, as with all transitions, by reaching the limits of the previous wave of development, in this case Teal. The difference between this transition and other transitions is in the capacity to observe the transition as it occurs (a 5th person perspective). Prior levels tend to be so thoroughly held by their perspectives that the transition is perceived as "fatal:" a blind leap from the known to the unknown. The transition from Self-Actualized to Construct-Aware also has a certain "fatality" about it since the individual is entering an unknown realm. But this transition has a transparency not available to other levels. The transition from Teal to Turquoise in the individual can now be observed from a witnessing presence. On the one hand, witnessing offers a perspective that makes the transition less frightening; on the other hand, witnessing permits much deep questioning of foundational beliefs.

The individual at the Construct-Aware wave of development comes to realize (to physically, mentally, and emotionally "grok") that all objects are human-made constructs. The ego, space and even time are all based upon layers and layers of symbolic abstraction that become evident to Construct-Awareness. The quest, then, is to uncover the limits of the rational mind and to *unlearn* the automatic, conditioned responses that are based on memory, everyday cultural reinforcement, even language.

Profoundly interested in the deep processes of "being," the Construct-Aware individual becomes ruthlessly compassionate. Construct-Awareness understands that spiritual awakening is not about reinforcing some comforting story—it is about the hardnosed destruction of self in the service of freedom. Compassion, from this perspective, is about freedom, not comfort. The concerns of the Turquoise are planetary: beyond one's own culture, beyond one's lifetime. Whereas Self-Actualized awareness sees clearly across systems, Construct-Aware awareness sees across systems of systems, or across paradigms.

The individual at the Turquoise wave fully accepts the tension of paradox as part of human existence and can commit deeply to service, both of self and others, with humility. It is understood that no level of abstraction or cognitive insight can reveal the fullness of truth, but, paradoxically, truth can be known directly.

Turquoise, by its paradoxical nature, is difficult to express in prose. Poetry is better. My favorite expression comes from the Santana/Everlast song, "Put Your Lights On:"

Hey now, all you sinners
Put your lights on, put your lights on
Hey now, all you lovers
Put your lights on, put your lights on

Hey now, all you killers
Put your lights on, put your lights on
Hey now, all you children
Leave your lights on, you better leave your lights on

Cause there's a monster living under my bed
Whispering in my ear
There's an angel, with a hand on my head
She say I've got nothing to fear

There's a darkness living deep in my soul
I still got a purpose to serve
So let your light shine, deep into my home
God, don't let me lose my nerve
Lose my nerve[15]

The Construct-Aware wave of development initiates the active deconstruction of the self-sense or ego. Turquoise can manifest as remarkably productive action in the world or (since it is fairly rare and often misunderstood) as despair or apathy. Glimpses of non-dual reality draw the Construct-Aware individual toward the Trans-Personal level of Development.

Unitive/Trans-Personal (Indigo)

The Unitive/Trans-Personal wave of development[14] is something of a catchall phrase for several Stages of Development beyond Construct-Awareness. The successful deconstruction of the separate self-sense in Turquoise opens the door to several levels of trans-personal awareness. That is, awareness beyond identification with ego. While these Stages of Development are very important (the home of sages, saints, Buddha's and Christs) they are so rare, we are unlikely to encounter them in our lives nor in an Integral Church.

This wave of development produces a paradox for the Integral Church. While Indigo points to the desired end of development, awakening into Christ-consciousness, the church can do little to promote this awakening. The path of personal and spiritual development is, at least partially, intentional up through Self-Actualized (Teal) awareness and into Construct-Awareness (Turquoise). Somewhere in Turquoise the self can no longer push the agenda because the self cannot willingly destroy itself. To explain, I turn to Wilber.

There are two important dynamics of Spirit. Wilber calls them Eros and Agape.[15] Eros is the lower reaching up to the higher, seeking greater unity; Agape is the higher reaching down to the lower, drawing it into greater unity. The spiritual seeker questing after more expansive ways of being is Eros in the broadest sense. Agape is what we Christians call Grace. Eros, the pursuit of unity, characterizes the earlier waves of development. But the ego cannot willingly destroy that which it is wholly dedicated to preserving: the ego. At some point Grace (Agape) takes charge and we are drawn forward. (Grace, of course, is active from the very beginning, but is less recognizable in earlier Stages of Development). While we cannot lead the way into our own egoic destruction, we can make ourselves (spiritually) accident prone, that is, available to Grace. Contemplative practices, such as prayer and meditation, facilitate this opening. But we are no longer in charge, nor can we maintain the illusion of control. So, while the Integral Church can proactively support development into the Integral waves, the best it can offer is clear and compelling stories to contextualize the movements of Grace in the Trans-Personal realms. Without a cadre of fully awakened teachers, the Integral Church can carry us through the Integral Stages (Teal and Turquoise). Hence, I will offer only a brief overview of Indigo.

In Indigo (and beyond) Truth is known directly by a fully emptied presence and boundless radiance. Knowing proceeds from a still center, a post-conceptual unity awareness. Trans-Personal awareness finds the universe as its territory and eternity its timeframe (not endless time, but the timeless present). Truth is immanent and self-revealing in all moments; interconnectedness and non-separateness are experienced directly (not conceptually). Existence consists of changing states of awareness within timeless Spirit. This is the Christ-consciousness, the profound recognition that human will is an illusion. "Not my will but thine" is not a prayer, but a simple statement of fact. Individuals inhabiting Trans-Personal awareness are unequivocally accepting of whatever is, with no need to interfere. Yet there is action, the action of an unassuming presence (*wu wei* in the Taoist tradition).

Second tier consciousness is the goal of the Integral Church. Teal and Turquoise are not better than first tier waves of development, but they can include first tier Stages of Development in a more expansive embrace. There is no drive or desire for all or even most of the individuals in an Integral Church to inhabit these Integral Stages of Development. The intent is that the *institution* becomes integrally informed. That is, the institution holds the space for individuals to evolve through successive waves of development.[16] Each Stage has its blessings and its curses. Each Stage offers gifts and essential building blocks to the full spectrum of awareness. And every individual will find a center of gravity that suits their life's needs (until it doesn't). It is the role of the Integral Church to provide support and possibilities for this evolution.

Summary and Room to Roam

As a summary, I bring Integral Theory together with some graphics (see graphics at end of chapter). I begin by changing Wilber's Quadrants into the Big Three (I, We and It) and adding the Stages of Development. Notice that the Stages are represented by concentric circles to indicate that each Stage transcends and includes the previous Stage. This is the foundational diagram to which I add Lines of Development, States of Consciousness and Types. I add each of these separately to preserve clarity. Finally, I bring Quadrants, Stages, Lines, States and Types into one graphic.

Let's begin with Wilber's four Quadrants:

- The Upper Left: the interior of the individual, "I," 1st person perspective.
- The Lower Left: the interior of the collective, "Thou/We," 2nd person perspective.
- The Upper Right: the exterior of the individual, "It," 3rd person perspective.
- The Lower Right: the exterior of the collective, "Its," 3rd person perspective.

These are summarized in Figure 2-5.

The Quadrants are simplified into the Big Three by combining the two right hand Quadrants, since both bring a 3rd person perspective. See Figure 2-6.

Let's add the Stages of Development to the Big Three (Figure 2-7). In this chapter I have emphasized the development of self so these stages are indicated in the Upper Left "Quadrant." When I discuss the different worldviews that support the levels of personal development (Chapter 3: Jesus Stories for the Integral Church) they will be indicated in the Lower Left Quadrant.

Another way of depicting levels of development is as waves (see Figure 2-8). I add this graphic only to emphasize that Stages of Development are not rigid, like floors of a building. They flow together in ways that are not captured by the concentric circle model.

Lines of Development refer to aspects of our overall *persona*. As indicated in Figure 2-9, individual lines can be at different waves of development. These are the multiple intelligences that comprise the richness of who we are as individuals. They are interior to the individual and are represented in the Upper Left Quadrant. (Of course, there are different Lines of Development in the other Quadrants, which I have excluded for simplicity.)

States of Consciousness are also represented in the Upper Left Quadrant because they are part of the interior of the individual (see Figure 2-10).

Finally, Types cross cut all dimensions and levels as indicated in Figure 2-11.

Figure 2-12 integrates Quadrants, Levels, Lines, States and Types into one visual. The worldviews that support each Stage of Development are elaborated in Chapter 3: Jesus Stories for the Integral Church. These are the meaning-making stories we create collectively and are therefore indicated in the Lower Left "Quadrant."

Room to Roam

As previously indicated, the goal of the Integral Church is to facilitate individual development through the Stages of Development (as far as folks want to go). In Chapter 5, I use Integral Theory to create a map churches
can use to become more integrally informed. In addition to evaluating program offerings, it is important to discover what tools the church possesses to facilitate this development. The notion of "Room to Roam" is a particularly useful tool in this regard.

Terri O'Fallon brings together Stages of Development and States of Consciousness. [17] She and her colleagues call it "Room to Roam" to indicate the room consciousness can have to roam about between States and Stages. I introduce it here in its original form. I will modify the idea in Chapter 5 to reflect possibilities for nurturing personal development in the Integral Church.

In the section entitled States of Consciousness, I mentioned the three great States as waking, dreaming, and deep formless sleep. Another way to speak of these is as Gross (waking), Subtle (dreaming) and Causal (deep formless sleep). I added to these Witness and Non-Dual. All States of Consciousness are transient and all are available to us no matter our level of development. Let's review these States of Consciousness so you can get a clearer picture of how powerful the Room to Roam idea is.

Gross consciousness refers to our normal, everyday awareness; our awareness of concrete sensations: the things we encounter with touch, taste, smell, sight and hearing.

Subtle consciousness refers to the mental realm. The Subtle realms of consciousness are vast. They include "dreaming, imagination, thinking, emotions, shamanic experiences, psychic experiences, experiences of non-embodied beings, experiences of light, archetypes, etc.,"[18] the entire mental realm.

Causal consciousness is one of vast openness, emptiness and formlessness. Above, I referred to it as the silent realm between thoughts. Causal awareness has no images, sounds or content of any kind.

Witness consciousness impartially observes all States of Consciousness. According to Dr. O'Fallon, "This is the ever-present transcendental state…simply because it can witness all the changes of state."[19]

Finally, the Non-Dual state emerges when the Witness becomes one with all that it is witnessing.

These different States of Consciousness are combined with the Stages of Development in Figure 2-13. Please note that there is no correlation between States and Stages in the graphic. Gross consciousness, for example, is not necessarily associated with the Warrior or Magic Stage of Development.

If an individual has a center of gravity, say, at the Achiever perspective, but can also access the Witness state of consciousness then his or her awareness would have the Room to Roam depicted in Figure 2-14.

An individual who inhabits the Self-Actualized Wave of Development but has access primarily to the Gross realm (they don't experience a world beyond their five senses) will have Room to Roam depicted in Figure 2-15. These two individuals would have a common ground, or "We" space depicted by the cross hatched area in Figure 2-16.

These two individuals will have relatively equal territories to roam with their consciousness and have a good deal to share, but they are also likely to perceive different realms. The Self-Actualized individual will have a cross-systems view that won't quite be comprehensible to the Achiever, while the Achiever will be able to step back into the Witness in a manner foreign to the Self-Actualized person.

• • •

Well, there's Integral Theory in a nutshell. Don't worry if you don't grasp it all at this point. The theory is vast and comprehensive. Thankfully, we now have nearly enough theory to map an Integral Church.

One remaining piece is essential for creating a map for the integrally informed church. I playfully refer to this piece as "Jesus Stories for the Integral Church." As mentioned, the church "owns" the great myths that form consciousness in the West. The church has both the legitimacy and the responsibility to expand its foundational stories to meet the needs of individuals as they progress along their journeys from cradle to Christ-consciousness. The next chapter lays out the cultural stories that support each wave of development.

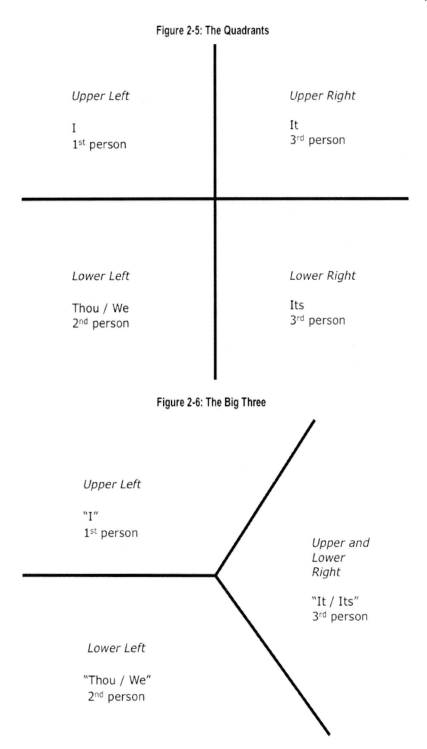

Figure 2-5: The Quadrants

Upper Left

I
1st person

Upper Right

It
3rd person

Lower Left

Thou / We
2nd person

Lower Right

Its
3rd person

Figure 2-6: The Big Three

Upper Left

"I"
1st person

Upper and Lower Right

"It / Its"
3rd person

Lower Left

"Thou / We"
2nd person

42

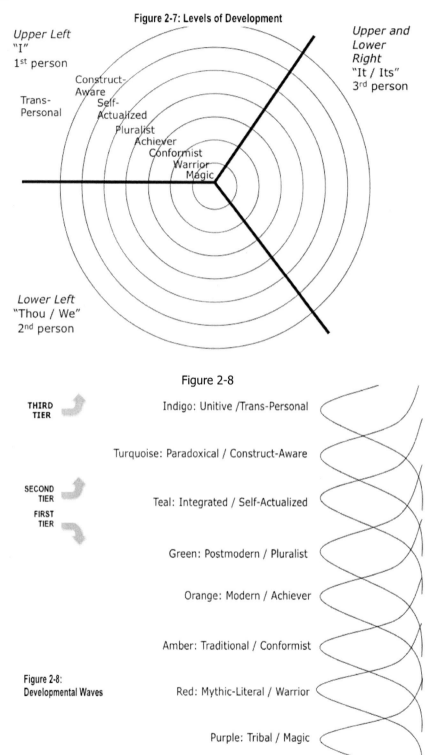

Figure 2-7: Levels of Development

Upper Left
"I"
1st person

Upper and Lower Right
"It / Its"
3rd person

Trans-Personal

Construct-Aware
Self-Actualized
Pluralist
Achiever
Conformist
Warrior
Magic

Lower Left
"Thou / We"
2nd person

Figure 2-8

THIRD TIER

Indigo: Unitive /Trans-Personal

Turquoise: Paradoxical / Construct-Aware

SECOND TIER

FIRST TIER

Teal: Integrated / Self-Actualized

Green: Postmodern / Pluralist

Orange: Modern / Achiever

Amber: Traditional / Conformist

Figure 2-8:
Developmental Waves

Red: Mythic-Literal / Warrior

Purple: Tribal / Magic

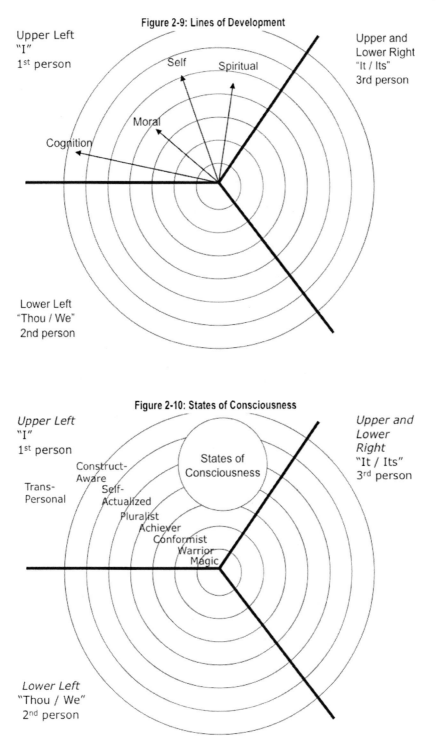

Figure 2-9: Lines of Development

Upper Left
"I"
1st person

Upper and
Lower Right
"It / Its"
3rd person

Self

Spiritual

Moral

Cognition

Lower Left
"Thou / We"
2nd person

Figure 2-10: States of Consciousness

Upper Left
"I"
1st person

Upper and
Lower
Right
"It / Its"
3rd person

Trans-
Personal

Construct-
Aware

Self-
Actualized

Pluralist

Achiever

Conformist

Warrior

Magic

States of
Consciousness

Lower Left
"Thou / We"
2nd person

44

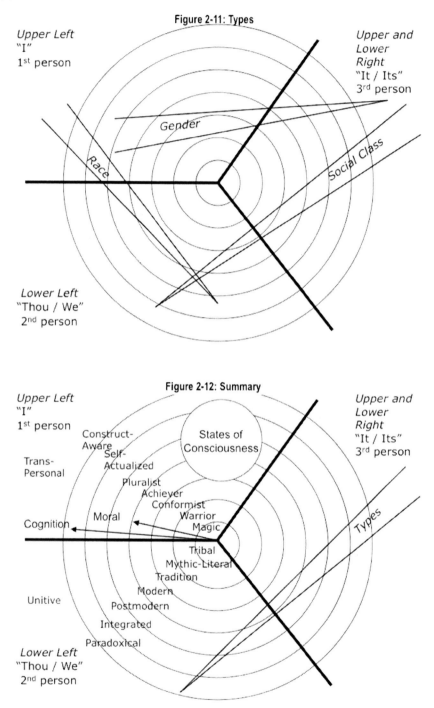

Figure 2-11: Types

Upper Left
"I"
1st person

Upper and
Lower
Right
"It / Its"
3rd person

Gender

Race

Social Class

Lower Left
"Thou / We"
2nd person

Figure 2-12: Summary

Upper Left
"I"
1st person

Upper and
Lower
Right
"It / Its"
3rd person

Construct-
Aware
Self-
Actualized
Pluralist
Achiever
Conformist
Moral
Warrior
Magic

States of
Consciousness

Trans-
Personal

Cognition

Types

Tribal
Mythic-Literal
Tradition
Modern
Postmodern
Integrated
Paradoxical

Unitive

Lower Left
"Thou / We"
2nd person

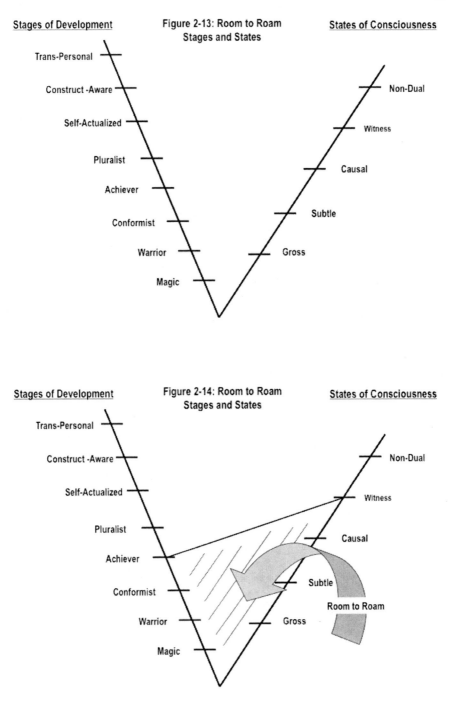

Stages of Development — Figure 2-13: Room to Roam Stages and States — States of Consciousness

Stages of Development — Figure 2-14: Room to Roam Stages and States — States of Consciousness

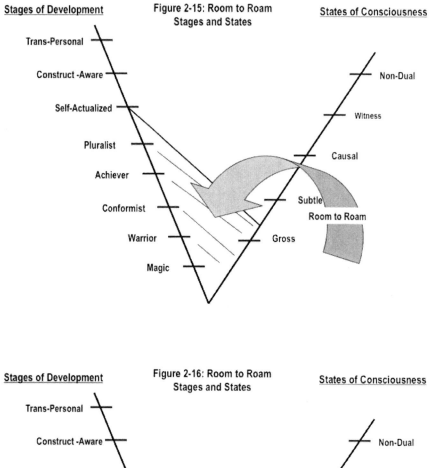

Figure 2-15: Room to Roam Stages and States

Stages of Development

States of Consciousness

Trans-Personal
Construct-Aware
Self-Actualized
Pluralist
Achiever
Conformist
Warrior
Magic

Non-Dual
Witness
Causal
Subtle
Room to Roam
Gross

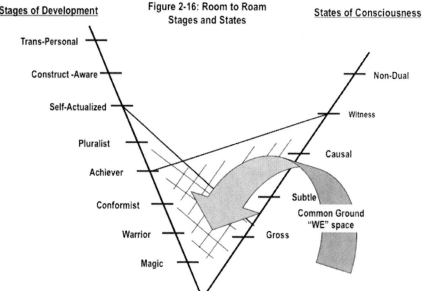

Figure 2-16: Room to Roam Stages and States

Stages of Development

States of Consciousness

Trans-Personal
Construct-Aware
Self-Actualized
Pluralist
Achiever
Conformist
Warrior
Magic

Non-Dual
Witness
Causal
Subtle
Common Ground
"WE" space
Gross

Notes

1 This exposition of Integral Theory is a synopsis of a variety of sources. I am grateful for the incredible work that has been done to develop this elaborate and comprehensive understanding.

Wilber, Ken. *The Integral Vision: A Very Short Introduction to the Revolutionary Integral Approach to Life, God, the Universe, and Everything*. Boston: Shambhala, 2007.

Wilber, Ken. *Integral Spirituality: A Startling New Role for Religion in the Modern and Postmodern World*. Boston: Integral Books, 2006.

McIntosh, Steve. *Integral Consciousness and the Future of Evolution: How the Integral Worldview is Transforming Politics, Culture and Spirituality*. St. Paul, MN: Paragon House, 2007.

Wilber, Ken. *Sex, Ecology, Spirituality: The Spirit of Evolution*. Boston: Shambhala, 1995.

Kegan, Robert. *In Over Our Heads: The Mental Demands of Modern Life*. Cambridge, MA: Harvard University Press, 1994.

Beck, Don Edward and Christopher C. Cowan. *Spiral Dynamics: Mastering Values, Leadership, and Change*. Malden, MA: Blackwell, 1996.

Kegan, Robert. *The Evolving Self: Problem and Process I Human Development*. Cambridge, MA: Harvard University Press, 1982.

Gilligan, Carol. *In a Different Voice: Psychological Theory and Women's Development*. Cambridge, MA: Harvard University Press, 1982.

Wade, Jenny. *Changes of Mind: A Holonomic Theory of the Evolution of Consciousness*. Albany, NY: State University of New York Press, 1996.

Fowler, James W. *Stages of Faith: The Psychology of Human Development and the Quest for Meaning*. San Francisco: HarperSanFrancisco, 1976.

Schumacher, E. F. *A Guide for the Perplexed*. New York, Harper and Row, 1977.

Smith, Huston. *Beyond the Post-Modern Mind*. Wheaton, IL: Quest Books, 1982.

Cook-Greuter, Suzanne. "A Detailed Description of the Development of Nine Action Logics in the Leadership Development Framework: Adapted From Ego Development Theory." Cook-Greuter and Assoicates, LLC, 2002. http://www.cook-greuter.com.

The Blog That Ate Mind Chatter. Bill Harris. Feb-April 2008. http://www.centerpointe. com/.

2 Wilber, Ken, *The Integral Vision: A Very Short Introduction to the Revolutionary Integral Approach to Life, God, the Universe, and Everything*. Boston: Shambhala, 2007, Cover page.

3 A holarchy is, in Arthur Koestler's definition, a hierarchy of holons, where a holon is both a whole and a part. Think of a bicycle gear. The gear has coherence, is identifiable, has a "wholeness" about it. Yet it is also part of the bicycle, which dictates its function. The gear is a holon, a whole/part, and the bicycle is a holarchy, a system which uses subservient parts that have their own characteristics and wholeness. We say the gear is "nested." In the case of States of Consciousness, each State is nested within the next higher State. Each State has it's own wholeness yet is part of a larger whole. Hence, States of Consciousness are a holarchy of increasingly expansive States.

4 Munsey, Brenda. *Moral Development Moral Education and Kohlberg*. Birmingham, AL: Religious Education Press. 1980

Gilligan, Carol. *In a Different Voice: Psychological Theory and Women's Development*. Cambridge, MA: Harvard University Press, 1982.

5 Gardner, Howard. *Frames of Mind: The Theory of Multiple Intelligences*. New York: Basic Books. Tenth edition, 1993.

6 Wilber, Ken, *Integral Spirituality: A Startling New Role for Religion in the Modern and Postmodern World*. Boston: Integral Books, 2006, 60.

7 Gilligan, Carol. *In a Different Voice: Psychological Theory and Women's Development*. Cambridge, MA: Harvard University Press, 1982.

8 Ken Wilber

9 Wilber, Ken, *Integral Spirituality: A Startling New Role for Religion in the Modern and Postmodern World*. Boston: Integral Books, 2006, 68. The use of color to differentiate waves of development was first popularized by Don Beck and Christopher Cowen. Beck, Don Edward and Christopher Cowen, *Spiral Dynamics: Mastering Values, Leadership and Change*. Hoboken, NJ: Wiley-Blackwell, 2005.

10 See Note 13 for references.

11 Erikson, Erik H. *Childhood and Society*. New York: Norton, 1950.

12 McIntosh, Steve, *Integral Consciousness and the Future of Evolution: How the Integral Worldview is Transforming Politics, Culture and Spirituality*. St. Paul, MN: Paragon House, 2007, 75.

13 Santana, *Supernatural*. (Nashville, TN: Artista, 2003) track 3.

14 The Unitive/Transpersonal wave of development is actually the beginning of a third tier path of development. The third tier points to evolution of the individual beyond their identification with ego.

15 Wilber, Ken. *Sex, Ecology, Spirituality: The Spirit of Evolution*. Boston: Shambhala, 1995.

16 It is most likely that one or more individuals in leadership roles will identify with the Integral waves of development or this model would not have much traction within a church.

17 O'Fallon, Terri, "Leadership and the Interpenetration of Structure and State Stages: A Subjective Exposé," *Integral Leadership Review*, Volume VII, No. 5, November 2007.

18 Ibid.

19 Ibid.

50

Chapter 3
Jesus Stories for the Integral Church

Believe it or not, your life is just a story. All the stuff you tell yourself about your life, well, that's your life. So pay attention!

When Emptiness made the Universe, it knew something we generally forget; it had nothing to work with. It was empty, no-thing, void, zilch. This wasn't a problem for the Creator; it knew it was all a giant dream. And it knew that forgetting it was all a dream would just make it more exciting. So Emptiness created from nothing. When physicists look inside atoms, they find all kinds of particles that don't really seem to be there…and lots of emptiness. Perhaps they've found the real stuff of the universe.

We humans live in a reality created by our minds. Not one we created, but a reality given to us, by parents, friends, neighbors, rock stars, movie heroes and, of course, TV. Our reality is being created even before our birth. This doesn't mean that there isn't real stuff all around us; it means that how we understand, the meaning we give to stuff, and even what we see, is constructed in our brain. We view the world through the lenses our mind uses to filter reality. If we wore pink-colored goggles all the time, our world would look pink. We wouldn't think it was wrong, in fact, we would think it was reality. If someone lifted the goggles from our eyes, we would scream and beg to return to "reality."

God loves living through us because we change. We don't wear the same colored goggles throughout our lives. We discard old goggles at different times, like when we become teenagers, when we become adults and when we grow old. We change our goggles whenever we see through a different story. And if we can't find a new story or a new set of goggles, we don't take the old ones off, because no one can live without goggles!

All of this reality-bending, goggle-switching can be kind of scary if we're really attached to a particular set of goggles. So we create great big stories to catch us when it's time for a change. When we were really young, we believed in Santa. We counted on him to bring us cool stuff at Christmas. But it wasn't too scary when we found out that Santa wasn't real because we discovered our parents were Santa all along. Other transitions aren't so easy because our culture doesn't offer the same assurances. Like when we find we can no longer believe in the Big Sky God of traditional Christianity. If we can't believe in "Our Father who art in Heaven" in a literal way, we don't have a lot of good alternatives. We can become an agnostic, an atheist, a New Ager, or a Progressive. But a lot of people will try to talk us out of these alternatives, while no one keeps trying to convince us that Santa is real. Still we can trust that the story we need will be there somewhere.

● ● ●

Personal development is dangerous. When we move from one wave of development to another, our very identity appears to be at risk. Whenever we inhabit a developmental perspective, we invest deeply in it. We believe the thoughts we think, the values we hold and the emotions we feel are *who we are*. We believe the way we see the world is the way the world is. Changing all or any part of this complex we call identity feels like a threat to our very existence.

The Integral Church supports and encourages personal development, which makes development feel risky. A guiding premise of Integral Church is "do not seek to emulate the wise, seek what they sought."[1] The Christian equivalent is "seek ye first the kingdom of God." Since changing the foundational supports of our identity can feel a lot like death (and it is in a way), it is essential that the Integral Church provide appropriate supports for the changes folks may be willing to make. This chapter will explore how the Integral Church offers cultural support in the form of variations on the Christian story that resonate with each developmental stage. These are the worldviews (Lower Left Quadrant) that contextualize, challenge, nurture and support us on our journey of spiritual awakening. I call them "Jesus stories for the journey."

The Integral Church supports personal development by creating a cultural context in which it is safe to open oneself to spiritual change. This context is created, in large measure, by a spectrum of legitimated understandings of the Christian story. These stories must answer important questions: Who am I? What is the purpose of life? Where are we going? And why are we important? The following "Christian" stories provide just that: ways of understanding the cosmos and our place in it for each of the personal perspectives (Stages of Development) discussed in the previous chapter. In this way, when someone feels pulled into a more expansive way of being there is a legitimate cosmology ready to receive them.

I will explore each story using the foundational categories of traditional Christianity: God, prayer, sin, salvation, heaven, hell, evil, death and resurrection and, of course, Jesus. I will then ask how each developmental perspective answers the ontological questions: Who am I? What is the purpose of life? Where are we going?

A theoretical distinction may be helpful here. In the discussion of levels of development, I included all four Quadrants in the description. The description of each wave includes how it feels to inhabit that perspective (Upper Left), the cultural stories and worldviews that support the perspective (Lower Left) and the behaviors and institutions associated with that perspective (Upper and Lower Right). Since the church has such an important role as the owner and legitimator of our cultural-meaning stories (Lower Left Quadrant), this chapter is dedicated to those stories. It is the job and challenge of the Integral Church to welcome, present and legitimate these stories for the congregation so that they are genuinely available for folks on their personal spiritual journeys.[2]

• • •

Spirit (or Emptiness or God) has a favorite game: hide and see. God hides from herself and has the great fun of discovering herself over and over again. Hide and seek is tough to play in animal form. Animals don't really know how to hide, so seeking isn't much fun. Animals and plants and rocks know directly that they are Spirit. Since they don't have thoughts, it never occurs to them that they aren't Emptiness… nor does it occur to them that they are. Whatever is, just is. So how would Spirit hide? With humans it's very different. We think. Better yet, we think in symbols. We think "latte," and a steaming milk and coffee drink comes to mind. This ability to think in symbols brings us great power and extraordinary confusion. We keep thinking our symbols are the real world.

Spirit couldn't be happier! There is no better place on earth to play hide and seek than in humans. Not only do we confuse ourselves with our thoughts, we do it in layers and levels that keep Spirit's game of hide and seek going throughout our lives. Maybe this is what the Bible means when it says we are made in God's image. Anyway, the Universe (or Spirit or God or Emptiness) leaps into the world with us at birth. Spirit completely forgets itself and enters an amazing, wonderful and totally magical world. It begins the game of seeking almost immediately, using the limited tools of its young body. Of course, it seeks clues and direction in the obvious place, the stories of the culture. The first story it finds that makes any sense at all is Magic, the Tribe's essential story.

Talking with Animal Spirits:
Tribal/Magic (Purple)

Christianity has generally opposed the Tribal worldview. The church has long considered all things "pagan" as evil and sought to eliminate them from human existence. As such, there isn't really a positive Christian story from the Tribal perspective until, interestingly, we get to the Postmodern/Pluralist worldview. The Pluralist perspective, with its inclusive and relativistic stance, loves magic and gladly claims a highly romanticized view of tribal spirituality.

Tribal spirituality, termed animism, attributes souls or spirits to animals, plants and other entities, as well as humans. Animism may also attribute souls to natural phenomena, geographic features, everyday objects and manufactured articles.

The idea of *a God* is foreign to the Tribal worldview. Rather there are many gods and spirits that inhabit this world, all of whom must be appeased. Jesus is a quasi-deity, a magical character with special powers to appease and influence the spirits. Sin is failure to perform the appropriate rituals to appease the spirits and hence bring danger to the tribe. The help and intervention of beneficent spirits or ancestors is sought through prayer and ritual sacrifices; the instructions and guidance received through divination are obeyed. The spirit survives the death of the body and goes to live in a really wonderful place called heaven. Prayers for the deceased help guide them through the dangers of the nether world of evil spirits (purgatory) to the promised land of abundance and glory, which is salvation. Hell is to become lost and wander the earth as a ghost, for souls may resurrect from the land of the dead as humans or animals to influence life on earth. Saints, in particular, are called upon to intervene and may be seen in ink blots, tree bark and other phenomena. Literal resurrections, consistent with the Purple perspective, even show up in our Bible. Jesus was visited by Moses and Elijah.[3] After Jesus' death, "The tombs broke open and the bodies of many holy people who had died were raised to life. They came out of the tombs, and after Jesus' resurrection they went into the holy city and appeared to many people."[4]

In the Tribal worldview, "who I am" is not separate from my tribe, clan or kin. One's purpose is to do what is needed by the tribe to promote survival. There is no question of "where are we going?" for all is cyclical and stable.

The Tribal worldview, as mentioned, has been consistently attacked by Christianity. The church has aggressively sought to destroy all vestiges of paganism. What it could not destroy it usurped, Christmas and Easter being the most flagrant. Nonetheless, the Tribal worldview and Magical consciousness have seen an enormous resurgence in recent decades. One reason is that the Pluralist wave of development has a deep affinity for Magic as it rebels against rationality and searches for alternative voices of wisdom. Computer technologies enhance this resurgence by creating fantastic images with deep credibility. Since Purple consciousness is foundational to all higher levels of consciousness, we find great comfort and satisfaction in its landscape.

For these reasons, observing the Tribal story in a contemporary mode is useful, particularly in movies. Many successful movies such as The *Lord of the Rings* and *The Golden Compass* express this worldview. *The Lion, the Witch and the Wardrobe*, from the *Chronicles of Narnia,* is a wonderful example. The author, C.S. Lewis, (a Christian theologian) frames these stories to teach the basics of Christian theology in a magical context. Many contemporary movies use this magical, animistic context to recount great mythic tales of the battle between good and evil (part of the next wave of development supported by the Mythic-Literal worldview). Of interest here is how the traditional Christian story of Jesus is framed in a flagrantly animistic, pagan setting.

In *The Lion, the Witch and the Wardrobe* Christ is not a person, but a lion named Aslan, and Satan is Jadis, the witch. While humans are the principal players, they are inadvertent heroes in a magical world of exotic non-human and semi-human creatures with souls and minds of their own. Towards the end of *The Lion, the Witch and the Wardrobe*[5] the Passion of Christ is played out in this utterly pagan setting. Two girls (Mary and Mary Magdalene?) watch as Aslan voluntarily submits to humiliation (beating and shaving) by semi-human abominations. Aslan, like the Jesus of tradition, willingly accepts death as a sacrifice for one who is undeserving (a sinner) and is resurrected, bodily.

Clearly, the Tribal worldview, which supports magical consciousness, is alive and well in American pop culture. If we avoid assigning as much value to the Purple as to higher waves of development, it is a rich and wonderful foundation for more expansive ways of knowing and offers richly textured cultural stories.

The Tribal story frames Magical awareness and infuses our lives with awe, wonder, imagination and innocence. Intimacy, vulnerability and family loyalty are grounded in the innocence of Magical consciousness as it is supported and sustained by a Tribal worldview.

• • •

Emptiness loves magic! It loves magic so much it never forsakes it entirely. No matter how sophisticated we become, we always have a core of magic... some part of us is always Tribal. For all its awe and wonder, magic consciousness has its downside. It gets knocked around by just about every outside force. The young human rebels and says, "Alright, enough! No more getting pushed around, I'm taking control. I'll lie down here in the middle of the grocery store and scream until I get my way!" And it works. Spirit has found another clue to its own awakening. It can make demands through this little body and mind and get what it wants. It doesn't just have to beg and look cute; it can demand action. So, a new search begins, the search for a story that can support this new opportunity.

My God Trounces Your God: Mythic-Literal/Warrior (Red)

If there is a "bad boy" of spiritual development, it is Warrior consciousness as supported by Mythic-Literal cultural stories. From this perspective, God is an avenging, but just, warrior who is capable of compassion, at least occasionally. He, and it is always a "He," is to be feared, for He is out to get you. In fact, for Red, fearing God is the beginning of wisdom. Jesus is the one and only son of God, sent to bring both justice and reconciliation. The magical, Mythic-Literal Jesus walks on water, raises the dead, multiplies loaves and fishes, heals the blind and crippled and will ultimately judge the worthy and unworthy.[6]

Consistent with the egocentric nature of this wave of development, Warrior prayer can have the flavor of a conversation with a Mythic-Literal God about warrior stuff. Prayer can be a request to convert or destroy others, or entreat favors for oneself.

Red cultures have stringent rules for purity and conduct as in The Ten Commandments or Jewish purity rules. To sin is to go against the rules. If we break these rules, we go to hell where Satan punishes deserving sinners. Salvation is being saved from the wrath of God. The saved go to heaven, victorious in the battle against evil, and receive their just reward. Satan is the source of evil; he is in an ongoing battle with God. The battle between God and Satan began in heaven but continued on earth when Satan and his followers were cast out of heaven. Physical death opens a passageway to either inglorious disgrace in hell or glorious victory in heaven. When Jesus returns in his flaming chariot, the just and faithful will be bodily resurrected and lifted up to live in heaven forever.

The Mythic-Literal story answers our basic ontological questions in a very straightforward manner. Who am I? I am a creation of God, made in His image. What is my purpose? My purpose is to obey God in everything I do. Where are we going? Our destination is heaven on earth where God's chosen people will live in peace and prosperity for a thousand years, i.e., forever.

To get the feeling of the Mythic-Literal Christian story, experience this scolding by David Crowe in his article "Katrina: God's Judgment on America."

> All America watched with concern--wondering what the outcome would be--as Hurricane Katrina swept through the waters of the Caribbean and slammed into the Gulf Coast states of Alabama, Mississippi and Louisiana. And now we know...or do we?
>
> ...Americans are asking, "Why did this happen?"
>
> The answer is found in understanding that man is not in control. God is! Everything in the sky, the sea and on earth is subject to His control.
>
> Psalm 107:25-33 says, "He raiseth the stormy wind which lifted up the waves of the sea...He turns rivers into a desert, and springs of water into a thirsty ground; a fruitful land into a salt waste, because of the wickedness of those who dwell in it."
>
> Was there wickedness in New Orleans, Alabama and Mississippi?
>
> Well, let's see. There was the burgeoning Gulf Coast gambling industry, with a new casino that was to open on Labor Day weekend...
>
> And then there was the 34th Annual gay, lesbian and transgender "Southern Decadence" Labor Day gala...But what is a little sodomy and immorality if it brings in money to the temple and gives everyone a little fun?
>
> Further, there is the well-known corruption, drugs and immoral playground of the French Quarter, Bourbon Street and New Orleans itself, one of America's wink-and-a smile getaways for fun and pagan pleasure...and more money for business and government.
>
> ...What Americans observed on their television sets was a stunning, even prophetic snapshot of precisely what the Psalmist--over 2000 years ago--depicted for a people who are under ungodly leadership...a window into the future of all Americans under the anti-God, morally challenged, secular princes in state, local and federal government. Far too many

of our elected officials erroneously believe we can profitably
engage in government-approved sin, without consequence for
both the righteous and the unrighteous!⁷

Typical of the Red story, Crowe cites scripture narrowly and literally. The basic message is: God said he would devastate sinners and that's what he did with Katrina. You had better behave!

The popular book and movie series *Left Behind* picks up a similar theme. In the first movie, airplane passengers slowly realize that friends, spouses and children are missing. They simply vanished, leaving clothes, possessions, and even their eyeglasses behind. On the highways, drivers are whisked away causing massive accidents. The rapture has begun. God has claimed His chosen, leaving all others behind to face Armageddon. In a taped message from a pastor, who also disappeared but made the tape three years earlier, it is explained that:

You are watching this tape because millions of people have
disappeared, babies and children, still innocent in God's eyes,
have vanished. There is much to fear, but not for those who
are missing because they have placed their faith in Christ
alone for salvation. They have been taken to heaven by Jesus
himself.⁸

God has pronounced his judgment and the righteous have been rewarded while the unrepentant must suffer.

Modern sensibilities rail against or mock the Mythic-Literal story, while fundamentalists and others literally await Jesus' coming. It is a story with tremendous power in our culture today. The progressive church, in particular, finds it hard to stomach. One of the stumbling blocks for progressive churches occurs when its commitment to radical inclusivity confronts the Red worldview. Pluralistic values insist that we accept all ways of understanding as equal so as to not marginalize any group; hierarchy is the great boogeyman of Pluralism. But the Mythic-Literal worldview is strictly hierarchical and staunchly exclusive. So the challenge for the Integral Church, which includes and emerges from the Pluralist developmental wave, is the inclusion of Mythic-Literal stories and Warrior consciousness. Successful integration recognizes both the beauty and limitations of the Mythic-Literal frame.

The limitations of Red are legendary: egocentricity, win/lose morality, violence and intolerance. At the same time, Warrior consciousness and the Mythic-Literal worldview inspire initiative, personal empowerment, action orientation and an emerging individuality not present in the Tribal/Magic perspective. In the West,

Warrior consciousness is developmentally appropriate among youth in the seven to twelve age bracket. It can be celebrated and managed in the appropriate educational setting. In the broader church, Warrior consciousness and the Mythic-Literal worldview are celebrated in dance, drumming and ritual. The Mythic-Literal/Warrior Story has an important place in the Integral Church yet must be watched, for it holds tremendous sway with our psyches; it is invigorating, lively, fun and powerful. When held wisely it is a great source of energy.

• • •

As fun as it is to prove that we are right and trounce those who disagree with us, it does get tiring. Not only do you trounce others, you also get trounced, and that hurts. Mind you, Emptiness doesn't mind. It could trounce and be trounced for a lifetime and get a kick out of it each time. Remember, Spirit is both the trouncer and the trouncee, so it lives both sides of the story…always. It's the human that gets tired. We begin to think, maybe we could have some rules for this game. Wouldn't it be more fun if we had a ref? Maybe each and every struggle isn't a life and death struggle after all. Maybe we could put some limits on our battles; maybe we wouldn't get so worn out. Maybe there's more to life than fighting and struggling. These insights lead us on a search for a new story. If there is a story out there that supports my new insights, they just might be true. And Spirit is off on a new quest.

Follow the Rules and You Will Be Saved: Traditional/Conformist (Amber)

The Traditional worldview, which supports the Conformist Stage of Development, might also be termed conventional or mythic. The Traditional worldview derives its power from the great Christian myths that have formed the cultural perspective of the West for centuries.

While the Traditional is built upon the foundational myths of the Christian tradition, these myths are not taken as literally as in the previous stage. Instead, the great mythological stories must be justified and explained with reasons, while the Mythic-Literal worldview is taken at face value (or at least as presented by accepted authority). Amber sees a world of laws and rules created by a God "out there" who communicates his desires to select individuals: the prophets, Moses, Abraham, Jesus, the pope. These laws exist because God gave them to us. Traditional faith stories are also "conventional" in that "my faith is everyone's faith." It is assumed that this is "how it is." Tevye, in the classic *Fiddler on the Roof,* expresses it wonderfully.

Here in Annatevka we have traditions for everything, how to eat, how to sleep, how to work, how to wear clothes. For instance, we always keep our heads covered and always wear little prayer shawls. This shows our constant devotion to God. You may ask, how did this tradition get started? I'll tell you...I don't know. But it's a tradition. And because of our traditions everyone of us knows who he is and what God expects him to do.[9]

In the Amber world, God is "up there," but He (again, always "He") is much more caring than the Red God. This is a God who judges us severely, but fairly, for our own good. This is a God who loves and forgives our sins by taking human form and coming to us as Jesus. "Jesus, the son of God, comes as the eternal lawgiver, the bringer of complete salvation if one believes the myths and dogmas and follows the codes, commandments, and covenants given to the chosen people and found in the one and only true Book (the *Bible*)."[10]

Sin, in this worldview is *not* conforming to God's laws, *not* pleasing God, and doing harm. Sin is the source of all evil. Salvation, then, is being saved from evil and from God's justice. To be saved is to be forgiven for the sins we all commit and the evil we create and for which we should be punished. Jesus' willing sacrifice for us, undeserving sinners all, is proof of God's love. When we die, we leave this world and go to the next. Those who are saved go to heaven, a place of bliss where God dwells with the Saints forever. Hell, and its eternal damnation, is reserved for those who refuse God's forgiveness and rebel against Him. Resurrection is solely for Jesus until the end times when he will return and retrieve his faithful, if not physically, at least spiritually. Since God is distant but personal, we can seek God's help through prayer. We can ask God to intervene in human affairs and do things for us.

The Traditional/Conformist answer to "Who am I?" is that I am a child of God, created in His image. This does not mean that we look like God, as in the mythic-literal worldview, but that we have the attributes of God: reason, creativity, compassion and love. Our purpose is to live our lives as one who is saved and to share this good news with everyone we can. In so doing, we help bring forth the Kingdom of Heaven on earth.

For Amber, scripture is the source of direct knowledge of God's plan for humanity. Hence, all authority resides in scripture and the interpretation of that word by God's appointed (called) clergy. The following excerpt offers the formulaic flavor of this worldview.

God's Plan of Salvation

The Bible says there is only one way to Heaven
> *Jesus said: "I am the way, the truth, and the life: no man cometh unto the Father but by me." (John 14:6)*

Good works cannot save you.
> *"For by grace are ye saved through faith; and that not of yourselves: it is the gift of God: Not of works, lest any man should boast." (Ephesians 2:8-9)*

Trust Jesus Christ today! Here's what you must do [to be saved]:

Admit you are a sinner.
> *"For all have sinned, and come short of the glory of God;" (Romans 3:23)*

Be willing to turn from sin (repent).
> *Jesus said: "I tell you, Nay: but, except ye repent, ye shall all likewise perish." (Luke 13:5)*

Believe that Jesus Christ died for you, was buried, and rose from the dead.
> *"For God so loved the world, that he gave his only begotten Son, that whosoever believeth in him should not perish, but have everlasting life." (John 3:16)*

Through prayer, invite Jesus into your life to become your personal Saviour.
> *"For whosoever shall call upon the name of the Lord shall be saved." (Romans 10:13)*

What to pray:

Dear God, I am a sinner and need forgiveness. I believe that Jesus Christ shed His precious blood and died for my sin. I am willing to turn from sin. I now invite Christ to come into my heart and life as my personal Saviour.[11]

A less extreme view is articulated by Rev. Tex Sample in the classic expression of the Conventional worldview, the sermon. This excerpt exemplifies another aspect of the Traditional worldview: God is a person with whom we can be in relationship. In Amber faith, God is always "other." There may be some opening to a third person scientific understanding of God, but never a first person ("I am God") orientation.

> *...God takes on the sin and evil of the world, takes it into God's own reality and suffers that sin and that evil on behalf of the world. That, indeed, is one of the basic actions of God in relationship to the world, to suffer sin and evil and death*

for the world. When you go through the worst time of your life I would urge you to know that the only person who suffers more than you, and those hurt and victimized by that event, the only person that suffers more is God.[12]

If you grew up in this tradition, if you were hurt by this tradition or if you consider the tradition to be ludicrous, it is worthwhile to remember how many of our basic expectations of civil society emerge from this worldview. The Traditional/Conformist orientation brings us law and order, civic duty, respect for authority, moral clarity, loyalty, hope and purpose. One of the great challenges of the Integral Church is to fully embrace the contributions of the Traditional orientation without having to fully believe it.

• • •

"Damn! Duped again! Just when they convinced me if I followed the rules I'd be OK. Now I find out they lied! Damn! They said that God always answers our prayers, but my son still died. That's not what I prayed for! I'm taking matters into my own hands.

"It's getting so much more complicated! I can't trust the people I thought had all the answers. I can't trust the priest. I can't trust the government. I can't even trust business people. They all want something from me. Can I trust myself?"

Emptiness is getting closer! It's having a harder time hiding from itself. The game of hiding is getting close to finding, or so it seems. The direction of the seeking has now changed. No longer are we looking outside for clues to the game; we're starting to look inside, at our own thinking. This is a revelation. And, of course, revelation needs validation in yet another new story.

We're Just Frisky Dirt:
Modern/Achiever (Orange)

Rationality is the great destroyer of Christian mythology. Reason, with its achievements in science and technology, has fundamentally trashed the believability of Christian mythology for a huge portion of Western culture. The popular movie *Dogma* reflects the modern caustic attitude of many toward both Traditional and Mythic-Literal Christianity. In the opening scene, the fallen angel Loki is talking with a Catholic nun.

Nun: *"You don't believe in God because of Alice in Wonderland?"*

Loki: *"Through the Looking Glass, "...that poem, The Walrus and the Carpenter, that's an indictment of organized religion. The walrus with his girth and good nature, he obviously represents either Buddha or, with his tusks, the Hindu god Ganesha. That takes care of your Eastern religions. Now, the carpenter, which is an obvious reference to Jesus Christ who was raised a carpenter's son, he represents the Western religions. Now, in the poem what do they do? What do they do!? They dupe all these oysters into following them and then proceed to shuck and devour the helpless creatures en masse. Now, I don't know what that says to you, but to me it says that following these faiths, based on mythological figures, insures the destruction of one's inner being. Organized religion destroys who we are by inhibiting our actions, by inhibiting our decisions, out of fear of some intangible parent figure who shakes a finger at us from thousands of years ago and says 'do it and I'll f---ing spank you.'"[13]*

The Modern worldview usually takes a third person orientation to God. If God is addressed at all, it is in non-personal terms like Creator, Parent, or Mystery. Secular Humanism[14] is the dominant, though by no means only, Modern faith story. The Modern worldview, particularly in the guise of Secular Humanism, finds the universe comprised of inert, fundamental particles brought together by random chance and shaped by evolutionary pressures. A distinct, supernatural God is not needed for the laws of the universe to operate. Jesus, to the degree that he is considered at all, is seen as a universal humanist teaching worldcentric love and morality. Prayer, of course, makes no sense to the Modern rational mind; who would you pray to? Heaven and Hell are empty categories except as they point to conditions on earth. They may be appropriate metaphors of human existence, but they point at nothing beyond the physical. If there is salvation, it is to be saved from Traditional/Conformist thinking as the once popular bumper sticker pleads "Dear God, please save me from your followers." Evil comes from irrational, unhealed thinking and the systems it supports. When the body dies, we simply cease to exist. Resurrection is delusional dreaming.

The ontological question "Who am I?" is answered simply: I am nothing more than "frisky dirt."[15] In other words, I am nothing more than molecules colliding and interacting in remarkably complex patterns, driven by powerful, but impersonal forces. This is not a dance with a dancer, but a set of adaptive responses to the pushes and pulls of a hostile world. The only purpose I could have is to help this world be a better place for me, my children and loved ones. And that is where we are going: we are creating a better world through scientific reason and its technologies.

This bare-bones summary sounds harsh and antithetical to the foundations of Christianity. But a well-reasoned agnosticism or atheism is, I believe, fully consistent with the path of awakening and spiritual development fostered by the Integral Church. A much more generous and nuanced take on Secular Humanism comes from an anonymous writer to the blog *Andrew Sullivan: the Daily Dish*, below.

This passage is characteristic of the Modern/Achiever orientation that brings authority into itself. Individuals at Orange become the authors of their own lives and can feel empowered to construct their own theologies. This individual constructs his own theology as a mixture of Secular Humanism and Christianity. This is a well-reasoned, heart-felt, and compassionate statement that likely serves this person well on his or her spiritual journey.

> *I am an atheist (who was once a Christian)...I would describe my own embrace of science and secular humanism as being motivated by a form of faith that is deeper than Christian faith. I believe that if Jesus lived today, he would be a secular humanist and would reject Christianity, just as he "rejected" Judaism and inspired Christianity. Christianity was once the vehicle for the boldest and most honest thinking about reality, the brotherhood of man, and the human condition. I think in light of the advances in science and our exposure to other religious traditions, it is time again to humanize further our understanding of "God" (or the source of all truth, goodness, and beauty) and come to a more universal understanding of religion....*

> *Heaven is not some place where we will go when our body dies. It is the world that we all yearn for and that each man of faith and good helps to realize in his small way through the march of human history. Hell is not some burning pit for the doomed and unsaved. Rather, it's a metaphor for the eternal separation from this community of the saints that the wicked are doomed never to realize by their rejection of what is good and beautiful. What are miracles? They are not supernatural gifts from an all-knowing God. Rather, they are what men of faith and good appreciate in this universe, despite all that is broken, evil and ugly.*

> *I find that I am better able to love and appreciate Jesus as a humanist imagining him as a man than when I was a Christian and imagined him as a God or a spiritual presence. Jesus was a man, therefore he is one of us and we can truly become like him....*

Humanism then does not reject Christianity, it completes it...I continue to be transformed by Jesus's love and he continues to inspire my humanist faith, faith that there is yet some good in this earth, that we can all be redeemed by love, and that we should all choose life and should try to live it fully in a spirit of peace and brotherhood with all mankind. It makes no difference to me whether Jesus was born of a virgin or rose bodily from his grave after three days. These are signs that the wicked demand because they do not have the heart to see the divine in Jesus and in all of us without such signs. Blessed are those who follow Jesus not having seen and without any need for signs and wonders.[16]

For the past 300 years and more, Christian mythology has been attacked by Western rationality. Stories that support some attitude of faith have taken several forms. One is Secular Humanism, reflected somewhat savagely in *Dogma* and articulated sensitively in the article above. Liberal Christianity has also engaged the modern mindset, and in some wonderfully elegant ways. Theologians like Marcus Borg, John Dominic Crossin, Bishop John Shelby Spong, among others, bring a sensitive and insightful second person perspective to the Christian faith. Bishop Spong articulates this more "Christian friendly" modern story:

My newest book, Jesus for the Non-Religious, ... is written for those people who are committed to the Jesus experience, but because they are citizens of the 21st Century cannot twist their minds into First Century pretzels in order to say "I believe" to the traditional explanations offered by the biblical writers. Rather I seek the reality of the Jesus experience that made these explanations seem appropriate.

I do not believe, for example, that Jesus was born of a virgin in any biological sense, but I do believe that people found in Jesus a God presence that caused them to assert that human life could never have produced what they believed they met in him.

I do not believe that Jesus expanded the food supply, so that with a finite number of loaves he could feed more than 5,000 people in the wilderness, but I do believe that people found in him that which satisfied their deepest hunger and so they referred to him as the "Bread of Life" that is never exhausted.

*I do not believe that the deceased body of Jesus was re-
suscitated physically on the third day and was restored to the
life of this world as, at least, the later gospels assert, but I do
believe that in him and through him people found a way into
that which is eternal and so they portrayed him as breaking
through and transcending the limits of death.*

*I do not believe that Jesus defied gravity to ascend into
the heavens of a three-tiered universe to be reunited with
the God who lives above the sky, but I do believe that Jesus
opened the door to that realm in which life can become so
whole and so fully human that we enter God's divinity and
God's presence in a new way.*

*I do not believe that 50 days after the Easter experience
the Holy Spirit fell on the disciples as a mighty rushing wind,
accompanied by tongues of fire, as the Pentecost story in the
Book of Acts relates, but I do believe that when we are open
to God's eternal presence we are also open to see another so
deeply that tribal identities fall and we can communicate with
one another in the universal language of love and discover
that in Christ there is neither Jew nor Gentile, male nor female, but a new humanity.*[17]

As with Spong, Modern Christian theologians often respond to the challenge
of modernity by stating what they are *not* or what they *don't* believe and offering an
alternative view. A coherent, modern, and popular Christian story is still developing.
I believe the best claimant for the status of a viable, modern and popular Christian
story to support Achiever consciousness is *The Da Vinci Code*.[18] In a 12 minute seg-
ment it lays out a modern Christian story:

- The true story of Jesus has been hidden by the church to perpetuate its
  power.
- Jesus was a great man, not God or the Son of God.
- He did very human things, like marry Mary Magdalene and impregnate
  her just before his death.
- Mary Magdalene was the true Holy Grail, and the succession of heirs to
  Jesus' crown is the true power and gift of the Grail.

So, here we have a spectrum of stories vying for the soul of the Modern spiritual
seeker. They range from the sarcastic (*Dogma*) to the passionate (the anonymous
atheist), from the reasoned (Spong) to the provocative (*Da Vinci Code*). This is just
what one would expect as modern Orange deconstructs traditional Amber, a variety
of stories vying to be the definitive myth of our culture.

Not surprisingly, both Mythic-Literal and Traditional Christianity find themselves at war with the Modern worldview. From the Integral perspective this is a pointless battle, first, because the battle has already been lost and, second, because the Modern/Achiever perspective offers benefits and orientations that are essential for the ongoing evolution of the faith. On the physical level, our improved health and longer life spans (both products of the Modern/Achiever wave of development) allow us more time than any previous generation to explore who we are and express our souls' desires. We have greater wealth, science and technology facilitating a blossoming of wider and more expansive perspectives. Finally, the ethic of individual initiative and excellence motivate challenging explorations into the foundations of the Christian story.

• • •

"Oh, we have achieved so much! But something's missing. What could it be? We've achieved longer lives and greater health. We're wealthier than ever. We even explore space. What could be missing?"

OK, this is where the story gets really interesting. For most of the journey up to this point, our individual psyches could change and count on finding a cultural story to support it. But now we are at the edge of our culture's well-defined stories. We are in the midst of figuring out what's beyond Modern; we call it Post-modern for lack of a better name. It gets even better because the Magical and Warrior parts of our selves get a chance to come roaring back after being suppressed for so long. We thought we had all the answers and now we discover we don't. We thought we were approaching the end of knowledge only to discover we are still at the beginning. All that soft, mushy stuff that artists and poets and mystics have been telling us has some truth to it. Yikes!

As always, Spirit loves this. After all, it's empty. It has nothing to lose, nowhere to go, nothing to do but enjoy the ride. So it goes looking for a new story to hang out in, one that's mushy, slippery and not very sure of itself.

Every Perspective Is True:
Postmodern/Pluralistic (Green)

The most eloquent statement of the Postmodern worldview supporting Pluralistic personal development, comes from author and entrepreneur Paul

Hawkins. Though not stated in spiritual, much less Christian terms, the quote below carries a prophetic quality which qualifies it as a "religious," or more precisely, a "spiritual but not religious" faith story. The quote also captures many of the salient features of the Postmodern story: there is something greater than the individual (community), it is diverse, no one is in charge, there's no dogma, and it is classless. It encapsulates the primary social concerns of the Green wave of development: indigenous people, the environment and social justice. Finally, it is dynamic and self-renewing. Speaking at the Bioneers conference in 2006, Hawkins summarizes the findings of his recent book *Blessed Unrest: How The Largest Movement In The World Came Into Being and Why No One Saw It Coming.*[19]

> *It is my belief that we are part of a movement that is greater and deeper and broader than we ourselves know or can know. It flies under the radar of the media, by and large. It is non-violent, it is grass roots, it has no cluster bombs, no armies and no helicopters. It has no central ideology. A male vertebrate is not in charge...The unnamed movement is the most diverse movement the world has ever seen. The very word movement, I think, is too small to describe it. No one started this worldview; no one is in charge of it; there is no orthodoxy; it is global, classless, unquenchable, and tireless. The shared understanding is arising spontaneously from different economic sectors, cultures, regions, and cohorts. It is growing and spreading worldwide with no exception. It has many roots, but primarily the origins are indigenous cultures, the environment and social justice movements. Those three sectors, and their subsectors, are intertwining, morphing, enlarging. This is no longer simply about resources, or infractions or about injustice. This is fundamentally a civil rights movement, a human rights movement; this is a democracy movement. It is the coming world.*[20]

In sharp contrast to Modernity, the divine reenters the scene with Green. The Postmodern god is a god of radical inclusivity where no one is left out and every faith offers an equally valid window into the divine. The Postmodern God is also politically correct: the feminine is included or preferred, or gender is avoided, when referring to a deity. Jesus is seen as one of many, equally valid, spiritual teachers. Sin has nothing to do with whether I am good or bad. Sin is hurting others; it is oppressing others; it is not living up to our potential. Without sin as "badness," evil drops out as an important category. We are all correct within the worldview we inhabit. We don't need personal salvation in the Pluralist worldview; rather *we* need to save the world…from us. Since all paths ultimately lead to God, all faiths have responsibility for helping the world.

Most fundamental categories of Christianity are renamed and reinterpreted. Heaven becomes Enlightenment or Nirvana. Heaven is an inner experience that brings peace to oneself and the world. Hell is to be alienated from this inner world and the community. Death is a great mystery. It is not to be feared because there is resurrection of sorts: our essence, our eternal Authentic Self, is reincarnated so we can continue to emerge from ego constraints in new and more wonderful forms. Prayer returns as a meaningful practice in the Postmodern world. How you pray is up to you as long as its not petitionary prayer.

Who am I? Postmodernity answers: "I am a child of the Universe in all its wonder and magnificence; in that sense I am a child of God." Our purpose is to make the world better for *all* of God's creatures. We are heading toward a world where we will live in harmony with all creatures great and small.

As part of his attack on the New Age Jesus, S. E. Ray (Pontifical Council for Culture, Pontifical Council for Interreligious Dialogue) does a fine job of summarizing the components of the Postmodern "Jesus Story" outlined above.

> In the last quarter-century, the New Age Jesus has rapidly become known as one who taught mystical teachings related to those of various clandestine orders and traditions, and that early Christian doctrine involved Buddhist teachings like reincarnation and meditation. Moreover, these works present Jesus as a Gnostic revealer of mysteries whose deeds have a symbolic rather than historical importance….
>
> The Jesus of today's movement is seen as someone who could equally speak for Buddhism or Hinduism as for any form of Christianity….
>
> What is known as the "New Age" is now being presented as "new gospel" within and without the church universal. … They all teach we are all divine and fully connected to God without need of any mythical redemptive works of Christ. Each esoteric framework including Theosophical-Occult,

Pseudoscientific, and Metaphysical declares that Jesus is not the unique son of God of orthodox Christianity, nor is his role as a spiritual teacher, though acknowledged as important, in any way exclusive. They will agree that Jesus is divine, but not more so than any other person.

The New Age presents Jesus Christ as the enlightened master or world teacher of the Piscean astrological dispensation. That Jesus is a man who, through a series of occult initiations, that is considered to have taken place over multiple reincarnations, completes a process of spiritual evolution (or occult initiation). Through this he achieves the office of "the Christ" and joins a fellowship of other ascended masters...According to A Course in Miracles, Jesus was merely a man, but the first to remove the veil of unreality created by the ego and to fully understand the illusory nature of sin and evil. In doing this he was able to practice true forgiveness that the Course defines as denying the reality of one's own sin and that of others. Jesus is thus the preeminent example of right thinking as promoted by the New Age. [21]

An eloquent, and very positive, variation of the Green "Jesus Story" comes from the movie *1 Giant Leap*. Postmodernity's expansive worldview is exemplified as much in the style of this movie as in the dialog. Weaving through the comments are musicians all over the world, creating a collective song from their homes, listening through headphones and adding their part to the music of the world. The commentary in the section entitled "God" begins:

Monk: *God by any name, Buddha, from whatever tradition, Jesus, if you are calling them you are calling God.*

Rabbi: *In Judaism we don't believe that Judaism is the only way to God. For a Jew, that's the way to God. For someone who is not Jewish there's no need whatsoever for him to convert to Judaism. He can reach God by his own emotions, by his own intellect, in his own style. So you can have millions of styles all aiming at the same direction.*

Baha'i': *Look at these flowers here in our garden. There are very many flowers in various colors. And that's how you find it in the world. We have whites, we have Indians, and so on, Blacks. Bahaullah says that's good; in that way God beautifies this world. But we are flowers in one garden.*

American woman: He loves everybody. He doesn't care if you're black, white or purple.

Hindu priest: No African, no European, no Hindu, no Ishmael, we are all … One.

Hindu priest: No religion, no caste, no color, One!

Buddhist monk: I think from a Buddhist point of view it is never said that there is only one path…almost any path which is based on compassion.

Minister: I am the God, you are the God, God is within us. You have to sink deep into yourself, to know yourself, maybe then you will realize the God within. And at the same time you will realize the same God exists in other persons.

Polynesian man: We on earth create the body and then, when the time is right, God gives the spirit. We believe we are an echo of God. We were given the same powers as God.[22]

This style of this presentation captures an important aspect of the Postmodern worldview: all views are held as equally valid and generally presented without comment or evaluation. Additionally, all religions point to the same God, but with different voices and different vocabularies. The essential message: All is One!

The Postmodern worldview and Pluralistic perspective are remarkable achievements for spirituality in the Western world. They also represent a fundamental stumbling block for the emergence of the Integral Church. Since the Postmodern/Pluralist wave of development is the last step before the emergence of Integral, second-tier awareness, it marks an important transition for the church. One of the great contributions of Postmodernity to Integral Church is a reawakening of the sacred and the spiritual with new creativity and freedom. Caring and inclusion, responsibility for the earth, a worldcentric morality, and celebration of the feminine all emerge with the Pluralist wave of development as supported by Postmodern stories. It is from this platform an Integral Church emerges.

• • •

"Whew, what a ride! Every step I take the world slips out from under me. It's all so, so relative! Is there anything solid here? I'm tired of agreeing

with everybody, maybe some people are wrong! Is that blasphemy? Will my friends reject me if I say someone might be wrong? Can I say that someone is better? Do we have to listen to how everyone feels about everything? Can't we just get something done? Will anybody know what I'm talking about?"

Dancing Across Systems:
Integrated/Self-Actualized (Teal)

In personal development, the shift of identity from the Pluralist perspective to the Self-Actualized orientation is a momentous change. This shift to second-tier consciousness is distinguished by the integration of all the previous waves of development. It is vital that the Integral Church offer Christian stories commensurate with this developmental milestone.

This move into second-tier consciousness, supported by the Integrated worldview, is the beginning of Integral and the goal of the Integral Church, even though development continues beyond this stage. Since Integrated/Self-Actualized awareness is quite new on the Western scene, the cultural stories that support it are scarce. Accordingly, Chapter 4 explores scripture from an integral orientation.

We begin our Integral Christian story with Wilber's take on the Integral God.

> Put bluntly, there is an archaic God, a magic God, a mythic God, a mental God, and an integral God....
>
> An archaic God sees divinity in any strong instinctual force. A magic God locates divine power in the human ego and its magical capacity to change the animistic world with rituals and spells. A mythic God is located not on this earth but in a heavenly paradise not of this world, entrance to which is gained by living according to the covenants and rules given by this God to his peoples. A mental God is a rational God, a demythologized Ground of Being that underlies all forms of existence. And an integral God is one that embraces all of the above.

*Which of those Gods is the most important? Accord-
ing to an integral view, all of them, because each "higher" stage actually builds upon and includes the lower, so
the lower stages are more fundamental and the higher
stages are more significant, but leave out any one of
them and you're in trouble. You are, that is, less than
integral, less than comprehensive, less than inclusive in
your understanding of God.*[23]

In other words, from the Integral perspective, no one understanding of God is paramount. The God of each developmental wave is included, but not with equal status. The "god" of Green awareness is more complex, expansive and inclusive than the Amber "god." We say that the Postmodern/Pluralist God is more *significant* (or "higher") because it includes more waves of development. But the Traditional/Conformist God is more *fundamental* because it is a foundation from which the Green god emerges (after working through the Orange stage). The Integrated/Self-Actualized orientation includes all of these "gods" as essential. What emerges is a rich array of "gods" we turn to as we inhabit different waves of development throughout our day.

Correspondingly, prayer is commensurate with our sense of God, and praying, according to our need in the moment, is most appropriate. As previously discussed, having a center of gravity at a particular wave of development means we prefer a particular way of seeing, or set of lenses. During a day we likely inhabit several different waves of development. When I am in pain or frightened, I may inhabit the Mythic-Literal perspective of winner/loser, perceiving the world as a threatening place. So praying to a protector God to intervene and save me is most fitting. At another time, I may need the comfort of a loving, personal God, and I may pray to God, the Father. And, at yet another time, submersion in the emptiness of ultimate Mystery is what is needed, and silence is the appropriate prayer.

This developmental sense of God and prayer is enriched through the lens of the four Quadrants, condensed to the Big Three. Wilber calls this the 1-2-3 of God. There is the God within: our direct experience of the Divine. There is God the Other, the Beloved with whom we can be in relationship. And there is God the Universe, Nature, the Ground of Being. Hence, we have God as Self (1st person), God as Other (2nd person), God as Nature (3rd person): the 1-2-3 of God. This, of course, does not define God; rather it is the

Integral insight into the many ways we perceive that which is intrinsically unknowable. From a Quadrant perspective we can reverse the 1-2-3 of God to get the 3-2-1 of prayer, a process of personal investigation. First, recognize a problem (3rd person perspective); second imagine having a conversation with it (2nd person perspective); and third, bring it into yourself and recognize it "as you" (1st person perspective).

• • •

Even though I distinguish between the personal stages of Self-Actualized and Construct-Aware (the next wave of development), the cultural worldviews are not well differentiated, in part, because Integral understanding is very new to our culture. I distinguish Integrated/Self-Actualized from Paradoxical/Construct-Aware according to the experience of *self* in both waves of development. The individual inhabiting Integrated/Self-Actualized awareness has reached the highest level of development the self, or ego, can attain, what Abraham Maslow[24] called self-actualized. It is a highly integrated, and integrating, wave of development. A principle quest for this Stage of Development is the integration of science and religion, as reflected in the stories below. In contrast, the Paradoxical/Construct-Aware wave begins the process of deconstructing the self as it moves toward trans-personal waves of development. The stories under that heading tend to be much more disruptive.

I consider *The Universe Story,*[25] as told by Brian Swimme and Thomas Berry, *Evolutionary Christianity*[26] as developed by Michael Dowd, and *Darwin, Divinity and the Dance of the Cosmos*[27] by Bruce Sanguin the best representatives of an emerging Integral story for our time. These stories exemplify and support the integrative nature of consciousness emerging at the Integrated/Self-Actualized wave of development.

In *The Universe Story,* great discoveries of physics and biology are presented in an evolutionary context beginning with the Big Bang. As Swimme says, that creative moment is still bringing forth unimaginable beauty. Swimme does not present the universe story in any religious context. Rev. Michael Dowd, however, connects it to the Christian narrative in his reflection on the United Church of Christ's statement of faith:

> Here is the Sacred Story of Life, in a nutshell:
>
> God planted the Universe as a seed, smaller than a mustard seed, at the center of God's own heart 14 billion years ago,

and it's been expanding there and growing more interdependent and aware ever since. First, there was a stupendous explosion of light and energy that some call the Big Bang and others call The Great Radiance. Immediately Creation began cooling into elementary particles and then into the first elements: hydrogen and helium. As the Universe continued to expand and become increasingly complex, its inner, spiritual potential became increasingly able to realize itself. With God as the inner life-force of the process, Creation self-organized into galaxies, stars, and planets. Our solar system formed four and a half billion years ago from great clouds of metal-rich stardust—which had themselves formed from previously exploded supernovas. In and through Earth, Creation continued to complexify and deepen its spiritual awareness—through bacteria and multi-celled organisms, through plants and animals, until finally, just a moment ago (geologically speaking), Earth became so complex and highly organized that it became capable of thinking about itself—and that's us.

The human is a being in whom Creation, after some 14 billion years of development, has reached such a degree of cooperation and complexity that Creation can now, consciously, reflect on itself, its meaning, who it is, where it came from, what it's made of, and where it's going. We are nature discovering its own nature and learning about the divine presence within and beyond everything...We are not separate beings in the Universe, who live on Earth; we are a mode of being of the Universe, an expression of Earth. We are the natural fruit of evolution. We did not come into this world, we grew out from it in the same way that an apple grows out from an apple tree!

Through this Sacred Story of Life we are coming to a deeper and broader understanding of what must be included as "the image of God." From this perspective, we can now understand how the entire Universe is being created in the image of God! Humanity is that dimension of the Universe that enables Creation as a whole to honor and celebrate the Creator's loving presence. Our own special role is to enable the body of life to reflect on and to celebrate itself and its deepest mystery in a special mode of conscious self-awareness. The revelation of God in Jesus Christ reveals the Way for humanity to fulfill this destiny.[28]

In this story, the fundamental categories of Christianity take on new meaning once again. To the best of my knowledge, Dowd is one of very few telling a cultural meaning story from a Christian perspective appropriate to the Teal wave of development. According to this story, God is an intimate name for reality or the whole. God not only looks down from above, but looks through the eyes of every creature. Jesus is not the unique son of God to be worshiped but someone to emulate…to find out what he knew. To worship Jesus is to become like Jesus.

To speak of sin and salvation we must speak of the Universe as a whole. Ours is a universe of nested wholes, or what have been called *holons*. Holons are "whole/parts." Everything is a holon because everything has a wholeness to it and is simultaneously part of a larger whole. If reality is constructed of nested holons, then sin is what separates us; that is, any action or thought that separates us from ourselves, from each other, or from God. As Dowd asserts, "If reality is comprised of wholes [holons], then sin is doing anything to serve myself at the expenses of the smaller wholes that make me up or the larger hole that I am part of."[29] Again according to Dowd, Original Sin is "whatever it is that came into existence with language that removed us from the immediate intimacy with God that all the other creatures enjoy."[30] We are born into sin because language separates us from the direct perception of the divine. Salvation, then, is to reconcile with the whole. If God is the Whole, composed of nested wholes or holons, then to the degree that I am reconciled to any cell in the whole of God, I am saved.

Death is natural and generative, for things to be born other things must die. Correspondingly, resurrection is much bigger than what happened to one guy 2000 years ago. Resurrection points to a truth about the whole human race and the history of life. As Dowd expresses it, "Good Fridays always catalyze Resurrection Sundays."[31] Just as first generation stars must explode for second generation stars and planets to form and create life, so too breakdowns and chaos consistently cause creativity and new forms of life to emerge.

In the Integrated story from Evolutionary Christianity, heaven is not some place in the sky. The Kingdom of God is here and now. Dowd: "When the values which Christ embodied, spoke and taught…when the values of honoring the Whole, at multiple levels, both the wholes within us and the wholes we are a part of; when those values rule the day the Kingdom of God is present."[32] Hell, then, is the obverse, when those values are not primary.

Prayer, in the Teal worldview, is not petitionary. "Within a nested Creation of expanding consciousness…prayer is a cell in the body of God communicating with the larger body (God)."[33]

The Integrated story, supporting Self-Actualized awareness answers our fundamental ontological questions as follows: *Who am I?* I am the Earth. I am a particular manifestation of the Earth that is conscious of itself. *Why am I here?* There is no destiny for humans outside the earth because we are a mode of this earth. I am here to be conscious of myself and all creation. I am here to gawk, as Brian Swimme says. *Where are we going?* My job is to participate with the whole to call forth the Kingdom of God. The important thing for Evolutionary Christianity is "how we live, how we love, how we relate."[34]

The emergence of the Integral worldview in the Integrated/Self-Actualized wave of development brings a renewed focus on results and the hope that perceived opposites, like science and religion, can be reconciled and the culture wars eliminated. Most importantly, our stories begin to create a meta-perspective capable of integrating all the previous waves of development and their worldviews.

• • •

The self has made it! This is as good as it gets for the ego. It is integrated; it has a deep sense of its own history and how it got here. It knows how to move in the world and create its own happiness. What could be better? But Emptiness isn't done with it. The game of hide and seek isn't over yet. Just because the self has made it doesn't mean Spirit has discovered itself. You might say Emptiness takes over here, because no good, self-respecting ego will willingly seek its own destruction. Spirit picks up the ball and says "Sorry, I'm not done with you. This wonderfully integrated self you've created is based on a lie."

Ouch!

"You've made it to the summit, now you have to take apart all that you've built … let me show you how."

And Spirit begins to show us how we have constructed this wonderful self from nothing: it's all smoke and mirrors. Ouch, again! The stories we've relied on to carry us through must all be questioned, and all of them are found wanting. All of the beliefs that have nurtured us may be untrue. Why should we confront this? Why should we take this on? Well, we don't have to. We can hang out in Integrated/Self-Actualized awareness as long as we want. But hide and seek is a very compelling game, especially when the Universe is playing it through us and we are so close. After awhile, life starts to feel like a house of mirrors. Our thoughts, our actions, our beliefs keep getting reflected back at us. Their structure is revealed, if we want to see it or not. We find we dance in the world in a whole different way. We taste what it's like to not be identified with a self; it's terrifying and exhilarating. We are drawn in.

No Belief is True:
Paradoxical/Construct-Aware (Turquoise)

Entering into the Construct-Aware wave of development, supported by a Paradoxical worldview, initiates the active deconstruction of the ego. In deconstructing the ego we step off into the abyss of meaning-making where no story is true. With the emergence of this awareness, the symbolic constructs (stories, language, concepts, and memories) with which we construct a *persona* become vividly transparent. A meaning-story to deconstruct all meaning-stories is, then, a bit paradoxical. And, paradoxically, since the individual has not yet realized the non-dual nature of reality (Unitive and beyond), a story is required: a self-destructive story to destroy all stories and send us into emptiness.

Concerning fundamental Christian categories, Alan Watts equates sin with ignorance—not the ignorance of not knowing something, but the ignorance of believing that which is untrue. Since we are born into a deluded world that obsessively demands that we see the self ("me") as real, we are born into Original Sin. What other choice do we have? Correspondingly, salvation is to wake up to our true nature: the nothingness that includes everything. The difference between Heaven and Hell turns on this one delusory belief, that there is truly a "me." To say it more precisely, we all have the sense of *I* or *me*; it is true that the I-sense exists. However, we conclude from the perception of the I-sense that there must actually be an *I* or *me*. This leap from the direct perception of an I-sense to the conclusion that a separate, bounded "me" exists is the leap from Heaven, peace, into the world of suffering, Hell. Evil makes no sense, for there is only suffering or not suffering.

For Turquoise, physical death doesn't matter. The death that matters is the death of our attachment to the false self, the ego. Preferably this happens before the physical body dies. Resurrection is our rebirth without attachment to the limited, personal self... what we call enlightenment.

Who am I? Very simply, I am no-thing, the emptiness that is everything. *Why am I here?* Well, why not? *Where are we going?* Nowhere, this and every moment is perfect. Where would we go?

What sets this understanding apart from Unitive/Trans-Personal awareness (the next stage)? For Paradoxical/Construct-Awareness insubstantiality of self is still something of a story. For Unitive awareness, it is direct knowing. The Turquoise wave of development regularly tastes, but does not have permanent, stable access to unfettered reality. So reports from Unitive awareness continue to have the flavor of story, a story lightly held.

I am not aware of any popular Christian stories supporting the Paradoxical/Construct-Aware wave of development, though a modern Gnostic Christianity founded on the Gospel of Thomas may eventually play that role. What I find are Eastern understandings adapted by Western culture. Wilber's brief characterization of Jesus represents a good first pass. For Wilber, the Turquoise view of Jesus is:

> ... *as a manifestation of the same Christ-consciousness that everybody, including you and me, can have complete access to, and thus Jesus is emblematic of a transformative consciousness that shows each person to be part of a vast system of dynamic, flowing and mutually interpenetrating process that includes all of us in its radiant sweep.*[35]

Two popular movies illuminate the theme of stepping into the abyss so characteristic of this wave of development: *The Matrix* and *Vanilla Sky*. I am particularly fond of *The Matrix* as a relevant story because it has gained a good deal of legitimacy as a cultural icon. In *The Matrix*, humans lost a war with machines and are now bred by the machines as an energy source. The matrix refers to a computer program that keeps humans from recognizing the true nature of their existence. The hero, Neo, is believed by Morpheus, a prophet, to be the chosen one who can break the power of the matrix. This scene is Neo's first, and pivotal, meeting with Morpheus.

Morpheus: *"I imagine that right now you're feeling a bit like Alice tumbling down the rabbit hole? Hm?"*

Neo: *"You could say that."*

"I can see it in your eyes. You have the look of a man who accepts what he sees because he is expecting to wake up. Ironically, this is not far from the truth. Do you believe in fate Neo?"

"No."

"Why not?"

"Because I don't like the idea that I'm not in control of my life."

"I know exactly what you mean. Let me tell you why you are here. You're here because you know something. What you know you can't explain, but you feel it. You've felt it your entire life; that there's something wrong with the world. You don't know what it is, but it's there like a splinter in your mind driving you mad. It is this feeling that has brought you to me. Do you know what I'm talking about?"

"The Matrix?"

"Do you want to know what it is?"

(Neo nods, hesitantly)

"The Matrix is everywhere. It is all around us, even now in this very room. You can see it when you look out your window, or when you turn on your television. You can feel it when you go to work, when you go to church, when you pay your taxes. It is the world that has been pulled over your eyes to blind you from the truth."

"What truth?"

"That you are a slave, Neo. Like everyone else, you were born into bondage; born into a prison you cannot smell, taste or touch. A prison for your mind. (sigh) Unfortunately, no on can be told what the Matrix is, you have to see it for yourself."

(Removing two pills from a box Morpheus continues).

"This is your last chance, after this there is no turning back.
You take the blue pill the story ends; you wake up in your bed
and believe whatever you want to believe. You take the red
pill, you stay in wonderland and I show you how deep the rab-
bit hole goes."[36]

Neo, of course, takes the red pill. He does not awaken into a world of beauty and light, but of struggle and danger. What happens, making this film particularly supportive of the Construct-Aware wave of development, is Neo awakens to the very structures keeping him imprisoned in illusion. Neo sees computer codes; the Construct-Aware sees the invisible matrix of language, concepts, beliefs and the taken-for-granted cultural assumptions that hide reality from us. Turquoise sees we are all slaves. As Morpheus says in the movie: "Like everyone else, you were born into bondage; born into a prison you cannot smell, taste or touch. A prison for your mind." Unlike the previous wave of development, which integrates the past, Turquoise is highly disruptive, looking toward Unitive/Trans-personal awareness for a new, more expansive awareness.

Yet another point in Morpheus' narrative illuminates and supports Construct-Aware consciousness. Morpheus explains, "You're here because you know something. What you know you can't explain, but you feel it. You've felt it your entire life; that there's something wrong with the world. You don't know what it is, but it's there like a splinter in your mind driving you mad." Increasingly, as an individual inhabits this wave of consciousness, it becomes clear the world is not as we thought it was. We may not have known it all of our lives, but we become increasingly aware of how the world is constructed and its ephemerality.

At some point, as with Neo, a choice is required. Neo takes the proverbial leap into the abyss when he takes the red pill. The movie *Vanilla Sky* offers another compelling allegory for this leap of faith. The closing scene of *Vanilla Sky* takes place on the roof of an extraordinarily tall building. The central character, David, has been maintained in a frozen state for 150 years, living a lucid dream managed by Life Extension, Inc. He is conversing with "tech support" in the form of a pale young man. Tech support:

Tech Support: "Now is your moment of choice. You can return to your lucid dream and live a beautiful life with Sophia or whomever you wish. Or you can choose the world out there."

David: "And you can bring me back? ..."

"... Your panel of observers is waiting for you to choose..."

"How do I wake up?"

"The decision is yours (looking over the edge of the building)."

"And I chose this scenario, didn't I?"

"Yes, to face your last remaining fear of heights...It's been a brilliant journey of self awakening..."[37]

Of course, David jumps off the building into his own awakening. Again, paradoxically, he is asked to choose with a self that is increasingly recognized as illusory and not necessarily in charge. Appropriately, awakening is always toward our fears. In David's case, his fear of heights, but more generally, our fear of death. For the Paradoxical/Construct-Aware perspective, moving to the next level requires voluntarily surrendering a self (that cannot actually be surrendered by the self) that is increasingly seen to be illusory, yet with deep roots in our psyche.

Socially, and again paradoxically, these stories and the consciousness they support give rise to concerns for the planet as a whole; concerns that extend well beyond one's own lifetime. The kind of ruthless compassion, suggested in both *The Matrix* and *Vanilla Sky*, emerge in the service of freedom, both individual and collective.

• • •

We've been on our own for a while now. It hasn't been clear where we can turn. Teachers come and go. To our surprise and embarrassment we seem to move beyond the wisest people we know or have even heard of. There really isn't anything to guide us here, except Emptiness, and that's not very comforting. The only way out is surrender. The cost of freedom is everything. And it's worth the price.

Awake:
Unitive/Trans-personal (Indigo)

While "Jesus Stories" for the Integral waves of development (Integrated and Paradoxical) are somewhat scarce and still developing, the cultural stories for Unitive consciousness are as prevalent as sand. These stories are the currency of the world's great religions. In the smorgasbord of American spirituality they fill row upon row of any bookstore. Ironically, Trans-Personal consciousness requires no story. Unitive stories are all, if you will, stories for caterpillars wanting to become butterflies.

This wave of development is something of a catch-all category for several higher orders of consciousness. Since these trans-personal perspectives are inhabited by few individuals, we have little direct research about them. Yet our discussion would be incomplete without this category since it is the goal of both religion and spiritual practice.

One thing that stands out about individuals inhabiting this wave of development is their individuality. Many appear kind (such as Adyashanti, Amachi, Byron Katie, Jitu Krishnamurti, Eckhart Tolle) while others are just rude (U.G. Krishnamurti, Jed McKenna). One commonality is they are not gentle about helping us strip away our self-delusions.

One of my favorite expressions of Indigo consciousness is Byron Katie. Katie, as she is called, is a recognized spiritual teacher with a simple, yet powerful, process outlined in Appendix E: Transformational Inquiry. You will notice in her Unitive story, and any other of this genre, she is really pointing to no story at all. This is the nature of Unitive awareness: no story, no concept, no word has any reality whatsoever. But any articulation of the experience of Unitive understanding necessarily uses language and concepts and therefore sounds like a story. Notice also, that when Katie speaks from Trans-Personal consciousness she is not really telling a story, she is simply relating reality as she see it.

Throughout her book, A Thousand Names for Joy,[38] Katie responds to passages from the Tao Te Ching. In the following passage she expresses, as best words can manage, the world seen with no concepts. Her reference point is the opening passage of the Tao Te Ching: "The tao that can be told is not the eternal Tao."

*You can't express reality in words. You limit it that way.
You squeeze it into nouns and verbs and adjectives, and the
instant-by-instant flow is cut off. The tao that can be told isn't
the eternal Tao, because trying to tell it brings it into time.
It's stopped in time by the very attempt to name it. Once
anything is named, it's no longer eternal. "Eternal" means
free, without limit, without a position in time or space, lived
without obstacle.*

*There's no name for what's sitting in this chair right now. I am
the experience of the eternal. Even with the thought "God," it
all stops and manifests in time, and as I create "God," I have
created "not-God." You can substitute anything here—with
the thought tree, I create "tree" and "not-tree"; the mecha-
nism is the same. Before you name anything, the world has
no things in it, no meaning. There's nothing but peace in a
wordless, questionless world. It's the space where everything
is already answered, in joyful silence.*[39]

Responding again to a passage from the *Tao Te Ching*, "Not-knowing is
true knowledge."

*To think you know something is to believe the story of a past.
It's insane. Every time you think you know something it hurts,
because in reality there's nothing to know. You're trying to
hold on to something that doesn't exist. There is nothing to
know and there is no one who wants to know it.*

*It's so much easier to know that you don't know. It's kinder,
as well. I love the don't-know mind. When you know that you
don't know, you're naturally open to reality and can let it take
you wherever it wants to. You can drop your identity and be
who you really are, the unlimited, the nameless. People call
me "Katie," but I don't ever believe it.*[40]

Wilber sees Jesus as the Christ-consciousness made manifest.

*[Unitive consciousness] might [see Jesus] as emblematic of
the transcendental, infinite, selfless Self, the divine consciousness that was in Jesus and is in you and in me, a radically all-
inclusive consciousness of Light, Love and Life that is resurrected from the stream of time upon the death of the loveless
and self-contracting ego, revealing a destiny beyond death,*

*beyond suffering, beyond space and time and tears and terror,
and hence found to be right here, right now, in the timeless
moment in which all reality comes to be.*[41]

The danger in this depiction of Jesus is it suggests a romance that creates yet another story. Yet the real Unitive story for the Trans-Personal wave of development is *no story at all*. Make up whatever story you want about sin, salvation, heaven or hell; they have no intrinsic meaning of their own; only you can give them meaning. They are neither true nor untrue, they just are.

In the Unitive "story," I am whatever is happening in this moment. The total and complete purpose of my life is whatever I am doing right now (talking to you, saving a drowning child, or picking my nose) because there is absolutely nowhere else to go. Life has no drama, no story; it is seamless, unitary, peaceful and free. Indigo knows this directly. This is home to the awakened; it is the goal and purpose of faith.

• • •

*There it is, Spirit's game of hide and seek is complete! It has found itself
once again. And what will it do now? Forget itself, of course.*

• • •

We have been on quite a journey. We have developed a model that, at least in theory, brings together everything there is in a coherent package. Since Spirit, or Emptiness, is the source and substance of everything, we have an appropriate map of the territory of the Integral Church. Of course, Integral Church can't do everything. So, in the next chapter I will whittle Integral Theory down to a manageable size.

Notes

1 Attributed to the great haiku master Basho Matsuo (1644 ~ 1694).

2 I am very grateful to Rev. Paul Smith for the insights he provided into the elements of worldviews. Our conversations and his wisdom are reflected throughout this chapter.

3 Matthew 17:1-8.

4 Matthew 27:52-53.

5 *The Chronicles of Narnia: The Lion, the Witch and the Wardrobe*, dir. Andrew Adamson, perf. Georgie Henley, Skandar Keynes, William Moseley, Walden Media, 2005.

6 Matthew 25:32-33.

7 Crowe, David, "Katrina: God's Judgment on America" Beliefnet.com, (originally printed in *Restore America* http://restoreamerica.org, http://www.beliefnet.com.

8 *Left Behind: TheMovie,* dir. Vic Sarin, perf. Kirk Cameron, Brad Johnson, Janaya Stephens, Columbia Tri-Star, 2000.

9 *Fiddler on the Roof,* dir. Norman Jewison, perf. Topol, Norma Crane, Leonard Frey, United Artists, 1971.

10 Wilber, Ken, *The Integral Vision: A Very Short Introduction to the Revolutionary Integral Approach to Life, God, the Universe, and Everything.* Boston: Shambhala, 2007, 143-45.

11 Some scripture citations have been excluded for brevity. Source: Chick Publications, Inc. ©1984-2008, http://www.chick.com/.

12 Living the Questions, 2007, http://www.livingthequestion.com/.

13 *Dogma*, dir. Kevin Smith, perf. Ben Afleck, Matt Damon, Linda Fiorentino, View Askew Productions, 1999.

14 "Secular Humanism is a way of thinking and living that aims to bring out the best in people so that all people can have the best in life. Secular humanists reject supernatural and authoritarian beliefs. They affirm that we must take responsibility for our own lives and the communities and world in which we live. Secular humanism emphasizes reason and scientific inquiry, individual freedom and responsibility, human values and compassion, and the need for tolerance and cooperation." Council for Secular Humanism, http://www.secularhumanism.org/.

15 Wilber, Ken, *Integral Psychology: Consciousness, Spirit, Psychology, Therapy*. Boston: Shambhala, 2000.

16 Andrew Sullivan: the Daily Dish (at The Atlantic.com), 17 Feb 2007 http://andrewsullivan.theatlantic.com/.

17 Spong, John Shelby, "Jesus for the Non-Religious", *The Washington Post,* On Faith, July 31, 2008, http://newsweek.washingtonpost.com.

18 *The Da Vinci Code*, dir. Ron Howard, perf. Tom Hanks, Audrey Tautou, Ian McKellen, Columbia Pictures, 2006.

19 Hawken, Paul, *Blessed Unrest: How The Largest Movement In The World Came Into Being and Why No One Saw It Coming*. NY: Viking, 2007.

20 Paul Hawken speaks at Bioneers 2006, http://www.youtube.com/watch?v=NzMPUKAXM7U.

21 These selections come from an article entitled "Who is the 'Jesus' of the New Age Movement?" compiled by S. E. Ray for the Pontifical Council for Culture, Pontifical Council for Interreligious Dialogue. Excerpted from the website "Eternal Path for Seekers of Truth, http://www.eternalpath.com/jesusofnewage.html.

22 *1 Giant Leap*, dir. Duncan Bridgeman and Jamie Catto, documentary, 2002.

23 Wilber, Ken, "Which Level of God Do You Believe In?" beliefnet.org, 2008, http://www.beliefnet.com.

24 Abraham Maslow was a pioneer of developmental psychology. His hierarchy of needs has been used to explain many behaviors, including economic behavior, political behavior and more. See: Maslow, Abraham H., *Toward a Psycholog of Being*, 3rd Edition. NY: Wiley, 1998.

25 Swimme, Brian and Thomas Berry. *The Universe Story: From the Primordial Flaring Forth to the Ecozoic Era*. San Francisco: HarperSanFrancisco, 1992.

26 Dowd, Michael. *Evolutionary Christianity*. DVD. http://www.thegreatstory.org/evol-christ.html.

27 Sanguin, Bruce, *Darwin, Divinity and the Dance of the Cosmos: An Ecological Christianity*. (Kelowna, BC, Canada: CooperHouse, 2007). This wonderful book recently came to my attention. It poetically weaves the Universe Story with the Christian story.

28 Dowd, Michael, "A Great Story Perspective on the UCC Statement of Faith," 1990, http://www.thegreatstory.org/.

29 Ibid,

88

30 Ibid.

31 Ibid.

32 Ibid.

33 Ibid.

34 Ibid.

35 Wilber, Ken, *The Integral Vision: A Very Short Introduction to the Revolutionary Integral Approach to Life, God, the Universe, and Everything*. Boston: Shambhala, 2007, 143-45.

36 *The Matrix*, dir. Wachowski Brothers, perf. Keanu Reeves, Laurence Fishburne, Carrie-Anne Moss, Warner Bros., 1999.

37 *Vanilla Sky*, dir. Cameron Crowe, perf. Tom Cruise, Penélope Cruz, Cameron Diaz, Paramount Pictures, 2001.

38 Katie, Byron *A Thousand Names for Joy: Living in Harmony with the Way Things Are*, (New York: Harmony Books, 2007).

39 Ibid, 3.

40 Ibid, 236.

41 Wilber, Ken, *The Integral Vision: A Very Short Introduction to the Revolutionary Integral Approach to Life, God, the Universe, and Everything*. Boston: Shambhala, 2007, 143-45.

Chapter 4
"Yes ... And" Theology:
An Integral View of Scripture

The earth is God's playground. How does She play? She plays through us and every other creature; with every thought, feeling and breath, divine Emptiness lives us. The stories we live are the context for Her life in us. Without our stories we would be like the animals, fun...but not as much fun. It's like going to an amusement park. We can ride the bumper cars, but if we really want a thrill we get on the big roller coaster; humans, and our stories, are the big roller coasters of this earthly amusement park. We each have our individual stories, and all these stories are woven together into larger and larger stories in a complex and unending web. The world's scriptures are the big stories of human life. They are the grand Myths in which Spirit plays.

All scriptures are false. All scriptures are true. No words can express the play of Emptiness. Still we try. It is our nature to try to write a great big story of how it all fits together. Every culture has its great Myths, the big stories that tell them how the world is. In the West it is the Bible. For thousands of years Emptiness has sculpted the Bible and infused it with meaning through human minds. In words, none of which are true, truth is reflected back to Spirit through human eyes. In this cosmic game of hide and seek nothing is more confusing or ennobling than the great Myths of scripture. Through them Spirit can become lost and found again. Every Bible story, infused with divine intelligence, misleads and informs; each is like an onion, layers upon layers with Emptiness at its core.

• • •

In the previous chapters I developed an expansive map for the emerging Integral Church. To repeat an important axiom: the map is not the territory. The best map, the best possible analytical tool, is never the same as reality. Spirit enters and engages the world through story. We do not see the world as it is but through the filters of our stories, the Worldviews we assume are true. If the nature of reality is Emptiness, then we are all engaged in the play of form. We construct a dream world with our stories and Spirit dances through us. Our lives are the roller coasters in the best amusement park in the universe. In this cosmic game of hide and seek, Spirit plays all the parts. Any form (say, human) will awaken when Spirit chooses to wake up to itself in that form. Ultimate awakening is in the hands of Emptiness, Spirit. But the game is not entirely on/off, black/white, awake/asleep. In the human playground there are myriad shades of gray. These are the Stages of Development we move through on our journey from cradle to Christ-consciousness. And the road map to bigger and better roller

---

Box 4-1:
Review: Stages of Development

Tribal/Magic (Purple): A world of magic
Mythic-Literal/Warrior (Red): Life is a zero-
  sum game: only winners and losers
Traditional/Conformist (Amber): One Truth
Modern/Achiever (Orange): Better living
  through reason and science.
Postmodern/Pluralist (Green): more
  perspectives reveal more of reality.
Integrated/Self-Actualized (Teal): Embrace
  paradox and ambiguity across multiple
  systems and time frames.
Paradoxical/Construct-Aware (Turquoise):
  Ruthless compassion in the service of
  freedom.
Unitive/Trans-personal (Indigo): Truth
  known directly

---

coasters is scripture. Scripture provides the blueprint for a culture's amusement park; it is a guide through the Lines of Development, the Quadrants, the States, but especially the Stages of Development. All of these are present in scripture for those with "eyes to see, and ears to hear." This chapter will walk down the Integral path through scripture.

In the art of improvisational theater one plays a variety of games to sharpen skills. One such game is entitled "Yes/And." It's very simple. One person in a group offers a few lines of a story, the next person picks it up with the phrase "yes, … and" and continues to tell the story however they see fit. It then moves to the third person and so on as a story emerges.

An integral view of scripture is similar. It begins with the Tribal/Magic perspective. "Yes," it says, "… and." Yes, the Tribal understanding of scripture is true for that perspective…and that's not the whole story. The Tribal story will be transformed, parts rejected, adapted and included in the Mythic-Literal view of the world. Yes… we now have a more expansive, inclusive understanding of scripture which is true for Warrior consciousness…and that's not the whole story either. The Mythic-Literal/Warrior story is taken up and transformed; elements are rejected, adapted and included in the larger Traditional worldview. Yes…this new understanding is true for the Conformist perspective. And, building upon that, we explore additional layers of complexity from the Modern perspective, and so on.

John 3:16

An example of "Yes…And" theology is in order. Remember, an Integral view finds in scripture meaning appropriate to each stage of the journey from Magic to Trans-personal consciousness. Here, I explore the most widely quoted Biblical reference in the West: John 3:16: "For God so loved the world that he gave his only begotten Son, that whosoever believeth in him should not perish, but have everlasting life."

From the Tribal/Magic perspective this passage is largely incomprehensible, nearly invisible. That there is a father and a son is comprehensible, but that somehow a son was given to the world so people could have eternal life is beyond the complexity of the Magical mind. John 3:16 only begins to have meaning with Warrior consciousness and the Mythic-Literal story. At this wave of development, the passage is literally true as stated: Jesus is the *only* son of God and if you believe in him you will not die. Individuals inhabiting Warrior consciousness might understand this passage slightly differently, but it would not occur to them to question the one true meaning. That one and only true meaning comes from the legitimate authority in such matters: the priest, minister, shaman or guru.

In a marvelous sermon entitled "Reclaiming John 3:16," Rev. Richard L. Smith of the First Congregational United Church of Christ in Tucson, Arizona, unintentionally walks us from Tribal/Magic through expanding understandings of John 3:16 to the level of Modern/Achiever.[1] Speaking of his youth as a dedicated Christian, Rev. Smith sought to understand what it meant to honor John 3:16.

> *Not wanting to spend eternity in a place that was even hotter than where I already lived, I tried to believe in Jesus, which meant believing certain things about him—for instance that he was the Son of God, sent from heaven to earth for the sole purpose of dying on the cross for my sins. It meant that he was not really human, but only pretended to be, that he lived a sinless and perfect life, one that I could never hope to imitate but only venerate; that he performed miracles akin to fetes of magic, and that his body literally rose from the grave, after which he was able to walk through closed doors, and then after forty days literally flew up through the sky to heaven, where he waits until the time is right for him to come back and vanquish all his foes —that is, the ones who don't believe all these things about him.*

This passage reflects a typical Mythic-Literal reworking of a Magical conception of Jesus. The Jesus who "performed miracles akin to fetes of magic" is not a human but a god in disguise. To avoid spending "eternity in a place that was even hotter than where I already lived," he must *believe* in Jesus, "which meant believing certain things about him." Taking the Jesus story literally requires believing that Jesus "was the Son of God, sent from heaven to earth for the sole purpose of dying on the cross for my sins." If one does not believe this, Jesus will "come back and vanquish all his foes—that is, the ones who don't believe all these things about him."

In the next passage, the young Rev. Smith begins the move from an unquestioning Warrior orientation to a Conformist perspective supported by a Traditional worldview. It doesn't mean that his Mythic-Literal understanding is false, just that it is limited. Here is a lovely example of a young man searching to move beyond that limited perspective and into a Traditional/Conformist understanding.

> *In Sunday school we were introduced to Jesus as a person: one who called children to his presence, who taught not so much about himself but rather what it meant to be a loving person, and whose life of love and service to others was something we could hope to imitate. He was a person we could follow, not just adore. And we were taught that loving Jesus means loving other people. I felt that love, in my family and in my church. And I was given plenty of opportunities to share that love with others...In all those years I was never once asked if I was "saved"—but many times I was asked if I would serve! I was never asked if I believed that "Jesus was the only begotten Son of God"—but many times I was asked if I would follow Jesus by putting his teachings into practice and by loving my neighbor as I love myself. So I began to suspect that to believe in Jesus meant to believe in the things he taught and the way he lived, more than to believe certain things about him [emphasis added].*

The Conformist perspective brings the first inklings of self-awareness and critical thought. Too many questions arise in the Conformist mind, especially during the teenage years, to blindly accept the literal understanding of Warrior consciousness. In Conformist awareness we become aware of the other. We see ourselves reflected in others. In this new, I/Thou understanding we relate to Jesus as a human we can emulate. Young Rev. Smith "began to suspect that to believe in Jesus meant to believe in the things he taught and the way he lived, more than to believe certain things about him."

The adolescent Smith now inhabits the Conformist wave of development supported by the Traditional worldview of conventional Christianity. The shift from Traditional/Conformist to Modern/Achiever began to occur for Rev. Smith when he discovered diversity.

Specifically, I acquired Jewish friends! They were fine people, and from what I could tell, they lived as "good" a life as I did. The only difference was that they went to Temple on Saturday mornings, they had different holidays, and they didn't use the exact religious language that I did. "They don't believe in Jesus as the Son of God," I thought. "Does that mean they are condemned?" And then I began to wonder about all the people who had never even heard of Jesus—the ones who lived before he was born, and the ones who lived in this hemisphere before the Europeans arrived, and the ones who even today have not been encountered by missionaries. And what about those who had, but who choose to remain Moslems or Buddhists or Jews, or follow their traditional spiritual paths? What about Gandhi, a Hindu, who also adopted parts of Jewish, Moslem, and Christian faith? Could it possibly be that there were other valid paths to God, other ways to be a "good person," besides the one I was born into? A very literal reading of John 3:16—and the verses which follow—would seem to say "No." Believe that Jesus is the Son of God and you'll go to heaven. Nothing else matters.

The literal understanding of John 3:16 no longer squared with Rev. Smith's understanding of Christianity. The exclusion of good people of other faiths from the Kingdom of heaven grated against his increasingly inclusive sensibilities and self-principled authority. Yet the passage from John retained a resonance and power from childhood that was of great importance to him: "…this verse remains near my heart, and that's why I want to reclaim it!" Rev. Smith has moved into a fully modern exploration of John 3:16.

One of the first questions I asked as I begin to do that is…Are these the words of Jesus? The Jesus Seminar says NO—in fact almost nothing ascribed to Jesus in the Gospel of John can be traced back to him, historically…Many interpreters and scholars believe that quotations marks were not part of the original documents, and that John never placed these words on Jesus' lips—rather they are the writer's own commentary on the meaning of the Christ-event.

Relying on modern historical analysis Rev. Smith reinterprets each phrase from John 3:16:

- *"God so loved the world" means "God is involved in an oning relationship with the creation, remains a part of it, and passionately cares for it."*

- "God's only son" is "not just a theological statement, but a political one, and a very daring, dangerous, and subversive one at that!" because it put you at odds with Caesar. Fur ther more, "son of God" is not a biological term but a meta phor. "Son of God is a wonderful image—an image that suggests a relationship, not with an impersonal force, but with a personal caring creator, like a father or a mother."
- "The point of Christian faith is not 'believe in Jesus now for the sake of heaven later', but 'trust in the vision that Jesus proclaimed and live eternal life now.'

Rev. Smith reclaims John 3:16 as follows:

> God loves this world so much that God enters the world, is in relationship with us, comes to us in the man Jesus, calls us to trust in the vision of life that Jesus proclaimed, and bids us give our hearts and lives to following and seeking and serving, and thus experiencing that quality of life called eternal.

In offering his own, internalized understanding of John 3:16, the good Reverend's transition to the Modern/Achiever perspective is complete.

Notice that, from an Integral perspective, all of the stories in this process are true, though perhaps not in Rev. Smith's mind. First, the Tribal/Magic and then Mythic-Literal/Warrior perspectives held and nurtured him through his childhood. Second, when questions arose about the magical Jesus, a new story of Jesus, as the loving servant to be emulated, became available. Third, when the exclusivity of Traditional Christianity became problematic, the Modern reframing of John 3:16 allowed Rev. Smith to include the two previous understandings in a new and more expansive interpretation that meets his current needs. Rev. Smith has built a rich and stable foundation for his faith.

To continue our Integral exploration of John 3:16, we must leave Rev. Smith. Our "yes…and" journey now explores this passage from the Postmodern/Pluralist perspective. A defining premise of the Postmodern/Pluralist orientation is that all truth is relative and the best possible approximation of truth comes when "all the voices are in the room." In other words, a broad spectrum of cultural orientations, types and faiths are most likely to approximate truth. It is important to note that Postmodern/Pluralist inclusion is horizontal, not vertical (which distinguishes it from Integral). In the Postmodern worldview, all perspectives are equally valid; there is no legitimate vertical, or meta-perspective from which to evaluate the relative truth value of each perspective, hence, horizontal. From the Pluralist orientation, Rev. Smith's final interpretation of John 3:16 is one possible understanding that must be balanced against myriad other interpretations, the sum of which approximate truth through rich narrative. From this perspective, the Mythic-Literal, Traditional and Modern stories expressed above simply reflect different viewpoints of equal value. A definitive statement of the meaning of John 3:16 is not possible because any perspective is inevitably determined by one's "social location," i.e., the confluence of age, race, class, gender, sexual orientation, etc., of the interpreter.[2]

A Postmodern/Pluralist interpretation of John 3:16 would begin with a statement of the interpreter's social location. I, for example, am a white, middle class, middle aged male living in the Western U.S. Hence, my understanding of John 3:16 is limited to the narrow set of lenses proscribed by my cultural context. Nonetheless, being a committed Pluralist, I will offer my understanding of this passage in humility knowing the inherent incompleteness of whatever I might offer. That said, I might reframe John 3:16 as follows:

> *For the Goddess so adored us, her creation, that she willingly gave the special creation of her womb that we might thrive and have life abundant here on earth and ever after. Allow the essence of this great life, which is known in different forms throughout all faiths, to seep into your soul and save you, it will as nothing else can.*

A truly Postmodern understanding of John 3:16 would see this interpretation as a mere sliver of the interpretations and understandings available from different perspectives. A Womanist perspective, an African-American perspective or a gay perspective would all make their equally valid contributions.

We now move from first tier interpretations John 3:16 to second tier, or Integral, interpretations. Recall that first tier orientations tend to see their perspectives as the only true perspective, while second tier, Integral orientations see the value of all waves of development and their supporting worldviews. Second tier perspectives are, like Postmodern/Pluralist views, susceptible to highly relativistic interpretations. After all, the Integral perspective includes and values the Postmodern/Pluralist orientation. Yet Integral is more willing to take a stand based upon a coherent meta-perspective that ascribes more truth value to some views than to others.

There are different ways of framing an Integral view of scripture. Each approach uses a different story to weave together the various levels and worldviews indicated throughout this book. The one we have just walked through is based on Integral Theory. From this perspective, all of the interpretations of John 3:16, from Magic to Postmodern, are true, but not equally true. Tribal/Magic has the narrowest understanding. It is transcended, but incorporated into the Mythic-Literal worldview. The limited truths of the Mythic-Literal worldview are surpassed and incorporated into the Traditional worldview and so on through Modern, Postmodern and Integral. Thus the Integral interpretation of John 3:16 becomes a tapestry of nested perspectives, each building upon the truths of the previous perspective.

So, what kind of statement could we make about the meaning of John 3:16 from an Integral perspective? The statement "For God so loved the world that he gave his only begotten Son, that whosoever believeth in him should not perish, but have everlasting life," expands from near invisibility for Magical eyes; to a dogma of literal, magical beliefs for Warrior eyes; to emulating Jesus at the Conformist wave of development; to Achiever belief in the potential expressed by Jesus' life; to a broadly inclusive view of Jesus as the living expression of life's generosity and abundance for the Pluralist. All of these perspectives are true and each incorporates the previous perspective. Unfortunately, what Integral Theory gains in analytical rigor it sometimes looses in poetic presentation.

Two other integral perspectives are less rigorous but more compelling as stories. The first is *The Universe Story* developed by Brian Swimme and Thomas Berry and adapted by Michael Dowd's *Evolutionary Christianity*. The second story sees through mythological lenses, as articulated by Joseph Campbell and Michael Meade.

The Universe Story and *Evolutionary Christianity* offer a 3rd person perspective on John 3:16: "For God so loved the world that he gave his only begotten Son, that whosoever believeth in him should not perish, but have everlasting life." The "Universe," or the Whole, holds the place of God in this story; like God, there is more to the Universe than we can know. The Universe has an intrinsic intelligence that gives birth to stars and galaxies and planets and worms and people. There is nothing beyond the Universe in this cosmology; it is simultaneously the impersonal source and content of everything. Love is an intrinsic quality of the Universe and, hence, the Universe loved the world as itself. "Son" has implications consistent with John 1:

> In the beginning was the Word, and the Word was with God, and the Word was God. He was in the beginning with God. All things came into being through him, and without him not one thing came into being. What has come into being in him was life, and the life was the light of all people. The light shines in the darkness, and the darkness did not overcome it.[3]

The Word does not refer to Jesus or any particular person, but to the fundamental life process emerging and evolving since the creative act we call the Big Bang. As we abandon ourselves to the evolutionary genius of the Universe ("believeth in him") we cannot perish, for we *are* the Universe itself. Implicit in this cosmology is the developmental orientation that includes all of the previous perspectives on John 3:16, Warrior, Mythic, Modern and Postmodern, since they are the evolutionary building blocks of human evolution.

A mythological understanding does not deny the evolutionary dynamic but steps out of time to tell its Integral story. In his recent book *The World Behind the World: Living at the Ends of Time*, Michael Meade speaks of Old Mind. Old Mind is eternal and it is trying to catch up with us, if only we will pause and let it. Old Mind is more personal than Universe without the implications of other carried by the word "God." As Meade says, "Whatever survives the ravages of time and the threats of extinction involves the Old Mind, the instinctive, intuitive inheritance of humankind, the primordial sense of life that permeates all of history without believing in any of it."[4] Old Mind is, of course, the Christ that emerged in Jesus and is simultaneous with the Divine, Mystery, God or whatever you want to call it. Hence, John 3:16 becomes: "Mystery so loves its creations that it imbedded itself (the Christ) in each and every aspect; if you know this, if you allow Old Mind to remind you, you shall know you are eternal".

An Integral understanding of John 3:16 includes all the perspectives presented here. Unlike the Postmodern/Pluralist perspective, Integral sees them as a nested holarchy of expanding perspectives that transcend and include each previous perspective, just as Integral is transcended and included in more expansive perspectives that follow it.

The *Bible*

This "yes ... and" orientation of Integral understanding applies to the whole of the *Bible*. Is the *Bible* the literal word of God, inerrant in every way? Yes ... and much, much more. To be "scripture," writings must meet us at all waves of development and from any perspective. The sacredness of Biblical scripture is that it does just that, meets us where we are (as do all other Holy Scriptures, whether associated with a faith tradition or not). It may not be that every scriptural passage will speak to all levels and all perspectives; rather, different passages may "light up" for us according to our need. The point is we call writings Holy Scripture because we count on them to speak to our need in the moment. Do we need hard and fast rules to hold onto in a time of fear and desperation? Then you are *commanded* to love God with all of your heart, mind, soul and spirit. Do we need a great story to make sense of our lives? The story of Jesus' selfless sacrifice is ready at hand. Do we need the courage to listen to our own council and not be swayed by others? Jesus' admonition to pray in the quiet of your closet and not show off in the public square supports us.[5] Do we need to know that all are welcome? Paul's inclusion of the gentiles[6] is readily interpreted from an inclusive, pluralist stance.

While an Integral view of scripture that includes Stages, Lines, Types, States and Quadrants is desirable, it may not always be practical. Certainly, richness unfolds in personal study of scripture when we consider all these perspectives, but it is not always practical to enumerate all of these levels all the time. Sermons, for example, that always worked through the levels would soon become dry and boring. Ideally, an Integral Church could visit each perspective and saturate itself in that orientation for, say, an entire Sunday morning. It might celebrate

Miracle Sunday (Tribal/Magic)
Praise Sunday (Mythic- Literal/Warrior)
Old Time Religion Sunday (Traditional/Conformist)
Poke Fun at Jesus Sunday (Modern/Achiever)
Interfaith Sunday (Postmodern/Pluralist).
Holy Roller Sunday (altered states)
Contemplative Sunday (1st person, Upper Left Quadrant)
Down on Your Knees Sunday (2nd person, Lower Left Quadrant)
Evolution Sunday (3rd person, Lower Right Quadrant).

Of course, this would require a broad conceptual understanding of Integral Church as a context. Even more challenging, it would demand that we celebrate each perspective with genuine enthusiasm for its contribution, with no irony or mockery.

Sunday Reflections

The following reflections, all delivered at Suquamish UCC, offer a spectrum of perspectives on scripture from an Integral orientation, without all the detail. The first piece looks at the topic of temptation and explores the story of Jesus in the desert immediately after his baptism. The second explores the idea of the Trinity from a 3rd person perspective using the Universe Story as its palette. The third takes up the Liturgical Year as an allegory of spiritual awakening and fills in the details of the myth presented in Chapter 2. The fourth brings in developmental levels in an exploration of belief and doubt. The final reflection looks at humor.

I admit to a bias in these reflections. Since I did not grow up in the church, I don't relate to God as "other," so I generally approach scripture from a 1st or 3rd person perspective. To bring balance in our church, we have a strong tradition of lay members and retired clergy preaching, primarily from a 2nd person perspective.

Temptation (February, 2008)

Matthew 4:1-11

Then Jesus was led up by the Spirit into the wilderness to be tempted by the devil. He fasted forty days and forty nights, and afterwards he was famished. The tempter came and said to him,

"If you are the Son of God, command these stones to become loaves of bread." But he answered, "It is written, 'One does not live by bread alone, but by every word that comes from the mouth of God.'"

Then the devil took him to the holy city and placed him on the pinnacle of the temple, saying to him, "If you are the Son of God, throw yourself down; for it is written, 'He will command his angels concerning you,' and 'On their hands they will bear you up, so that you will not dash your foot against a stone.'"

Jesus said to him, "Again it is written, 'Do not put the Lord your God to the test.'"

Again, the devil took him to a very high mountain and showed him all the kingdoms of the world and their splendor; and he said to him, "All these I will give you, if you will fall down and worship me." Jesus said to him, "Away with you, Satan! for it is written, 'Worship the Lord your God, and serve only him.'" Then the devil left him, and suddenly angels came and waited on him.

What a great story! In the Biblical context, the story follows Jesus' baptism by John the Baptizer. Jesus comes up from the water, takes a breath, and reality descends upon him—in the form of a dove—and a voice says, "This is my son, in whom I am well pleased." If you were Jesus, what would you do? Most of us would probably do just what Jesus did; get the heck out of there. Jesus does just that, he heads off into the desert where he fasts for 40 days and 40 nights. (By the way "40 days and 40 nights" is a euphemism—it means a long time). At the end of that time the Devil challenges Jesus to what sounds like a theological ping pong game:

> **Satan:** "Feed yourself."
> **Jesus:** "Man does not live by bread alone."
> **Satan:** "Throw yourself from the temple."
> **Jesus:** "Do not put God to the test."
> **Satan:** "Worship me and earth's kingdoms are yours."
> **Jesus:** "Get away, I only worship God."

Then the angels brought him lunch.

That's the story. The tradition seems to have taken it as literally true. I don't know if it's true or not, but it doesn't really matter. It doesn't matter if the story is literally true or allegorical. What matters is how the story serves you and your journey. This story of Jesus' 40 days in the desert is one of those grand mythical teaching stories of the *Bible*. It's not just a story about Jesus—it's a story about you. (Actually, if every story in the *Bible* doesn't include you, it's pointless).

In the West we have problems seeing this story as being about us. When someone comes to the awakening insight that "I am God," the Western tradition burns him or her at the stake (until recently, literally). In the East when someone says, "I am God," the tradition asks, "What took you so long?"

In this story Jesus comes to the realization that "I am God," not in some egotistical way, but through direct knowledge of the Divine as his true nature. Any such awakening comes with incredible opportunity and power, on the one hand, and incredible danger, on the other. Jesus does just what any responsible person would do: he "gets out of Dodge." He retreats from humanity to figure out how to deal with this revelation and new found power. In the language of the *Bible*: "Jesus was led up by the Spirit into the wilderness to be tempted by the devil."

So, who is this Devil, the Tempter, the *Bible* speaks of? Though it works for us in childhood, I'm pretty sure it's not some nasty guy with horns, a forked tail, and wings. I am confident that the Devil is *us*. In Greek, the word *persona* literally means *mask*. *Personae* referred to the masks that actors would put on to portray roles in a play. The word *persona* later got translated as *ego*. What we call "the Devil" is the *persona* that we wear. And "sin" is believing that the *persona* we wear is who we really are.

The *persona*, or the ego, knows that it is just a mask…that it has no reality of its own. The *persona* is the garment we wear so we can act in the world, because we have to have some way of interacting on the physical plane. The *persona* (the ego) is the vehicle. The problem (sin) arises when we get confused and believe the *persona* we wear is truly who we are. All suffering begins here, in believing the mask we wear is who we truly are.

The project of the *persona* is to deny its insubstantiality and convince itself, and all other egos, that it is real. That in us which is 100% dedicated to persuading us that the mask we wear is who we are is called Maya in the East. Maya is, among other things, the goddess of illusion; she has no real power except the power of confusion, illusion and deception. In the West we call Maya the Devil.

In this story, the Devil (the god of self-delusion) has just been thrown a bone of incredible power. God says to Jesus, "You are my son, in whom I am well pleased." *Cool*, responds the Devil/ego/ *persona*/Maya, *you've always thought you were special, but here's proof that you are the very son of God! You are even more special than you thought! Let's kick butt!* Others have had similar awakenings and taken the Devil's bait: Jim Jones is a contemporary example. Jesus doesn't fall for the Devil's seduction, nor does he just blow off the ego's temptation; rather, he goes into the desert (at least metaphorically) to struggle with the possibilities of this new awakening.

The first thing the Tempter does is to point out that Jesus can use his awakening to become wealthy: "If you are the Son of God, command these stones to become loaves of bread" (or, bars of gold, if you like). It's true; such awareness can be used to generate personal wealth. Perhaps, Jesus seriously considered this option but ultimately concluded: *I don't live by bread alone. I don't live by riches. That's not what my life is about. I live by that which takes my breath in and blows it out, takes my breath in and blows it out, until I die.*

Next, the *persona*, masquerading as the true self, tries a different strategy: "Throw yourself down [off this pinnacle] for it is written, 'He will command his angels concerning you,' and 'On their hands they will bear you up, so that you will not dash your foot against a stone.'" In other words, *Do some magic tricks; everyone will know you're special then.* Some gurus today do just that. I have read of one who will sit on a rock in the middle of a river and direct the water flow over him, or around him, or beside him. Another manifests ash from thin air.

What a temptation! New insights and understandings tempt us to show off. We think: *I've had this amazing epiphany! Now I really understand!* The temptation is to show off, subtly, of course, because we are *very* sophisticated: *Please notice how much more spiritual I am than you.* Or, *I am so much more humble now.* Or in the Integral Church: *how much wiser and more inclusive we are than other Christians.*

Jesus responds to the Devil's offer: "Do not test God!" Magic tricks have nothing to do with awakening. If you use awakening to do magic tricks and show off you have missed the point…entirely.

Finally, the Devil says, "All you have to do is worship me." Of course, this has nothing to do with worshiping Satan. It has to do with what we do, day in and day out. Each and every day we fall flat on our knees in front of the altar of our false self, and promise: *I will do anything to keep you alive, to believe that I am separate and above it all. Convince me that I am unique and not just normal. Show me how truly special I am, be it my greatness or my sadness, it doesn't matter!* I imagine Jesus responding, *Been there, done that; after all, I am human.*

Jesus essentially gives that same answer he has given for all of the ego's temptations: *That's not it. The point of this awakening is not about strengthening the false self that keeps me imprisoned in delusion. It is about freedom. It's not about what is seen; it is about that which does the seeing. It's not about what I hear; I am devoted to that which hears. It's not about what I taste; it's about that which tastes.*

In all of these examples, Jesus steps back and rejects the fabulous temptations that come with being a spiritually realized being—all the opportunities for the *persona* to aggrandize and set itself apart (to worship Satan). Jesus steps back into the utter simplicity of *that which is breathing me, that which is seeing through me, that which is hearing through me,* in other words, God. And in that choice, he awakens even more fully, and life itself (the angels) serves him.

Of course, this story is not really about Jesus; it's about you, it's about me. It is a story about how we awaken. It is a story of how we will choose when we come to a new understanding. Will I use my awakening to reinforce the illusion of myself as separate, unique and better or will I recognize the source as the Divine within and give thanks? I invite you to enter into this story and see if it has any truth for you. If it has a glimmer, go more deeply into it. This story has no purpose whatsoever except your spiritual awakening. It's just a story, until and unless it serves your awakening. Amen.

• • •

In the following reflection, I bring a 3rd person orientation to the idea of the Trinity. I use Brian Swimme's conception of the fundamental building blocks of the universe, *differentiation, communion* and *subjectivity,* as the lens.

Trinity (June, 2007)

Matthew 28:18

> *Go therefore and make disciples of all nations baptizing them in the name of the Father, the Son and the Holy Spirit.*

Today I want to talk about the Trinity. In these modern times, it's easy for us to think of the Trinity as something a bunch of theologians came up with so they would have something to write about, to argue about and to create a lot of whoopla about. It's certainly a topic that has stirred up controversy in the church for centuries now. If my memory of history serves, The Unitarian church broke from the Congregational church over this issue: "Is God one or three in one?"

Our tradition says that God is three-in-one persons. You all understand this, right? I haven't been a Christian for a very long time; most of my life I wasn't. I used to look at this and wonder, "What in the world are they talking about?! Why would anyone ever fight over this?" It was just inconceivable to me; mostly still is. A Princeton theologian made a comment, however, that was very helpful. He remarked that theologians did not come up with the idea of the Trinity. Rather, it was an idea that emerged within the culture when people looked around and asked, "How is God interacting with this world?" Or, even more fundamentally: "What is the nature of our world and our universe?" We in the West intuit Trinity quite naturally; it's there in the structure of our language. Not surprisingly, insights into the three-part nature of reality were conveyed in the **Bible** by a language and symbolic references that would make sense to that era. To take it literally, or to think that our era will understand that truth the same way, seems mistaken.

Today I will suggest a different way of understanding the Trinity that may be more amenable to contemporary minds. It comes from the cosmologist Brian Swimme and the philosopher Thomas Berry. I consider their "Universe Story" to be an important alternative theology grounded in science. In *Canticle to the Cosmos*, Swimme proposes three fundamental building blocks for the entire universe. The first he calls *differentiation*, a big word for something very simple: everything is different. There seems to be a propensity to the universe that says "Diversity is great! Uniqueness is wonderful!" There appears to be this great force, this wonderful playfulness, bent upon making everything different. Just as no two snowflakes are alike, no two people are alike, no two stars are alike.

Let me share a quick side story about differentiation. While in seminary, I spent one summer working at a state mental hospital (seemed like perfect preparation for parish work). There I met Paul, a young man in his 20's suffering from schizophrenia. A few years prior to being institutionalized, he had been arrested and taken off his meds while in jail. He became psychotic and tried to scratch his eyes out. We had some wonderful conversations. In these conversations Paul would often return to his conviction that "God didn't make any extra people." This was his faith: that absolutely everybody is unique, everybody is needed, everybody is worthy.

That's the human face of differentiation. No two snowflakes are alike, no two galaxies are alike, no two humans are alike. There is this exuberance to the universe that cannot be captured by any word, but *differentiation* is as good as any for expressing the dynamic of the universe that is always creating variety, always changing, always expanding.

Of course, you can't have a universe that is always differentiating, always expanding, always new and different without connecting it in some way. So, the second fundamental principle of the universe, according to this cosmology, is *communion*: everything is connected. Not just things close to each other are connected, but everything is connected to everything everywhere. John Muir, the great naturalist said it well: "When we try to pick out anything by itself, we find it hitched to everything else in the universe."[7] We cannot consider any one thing in isolation, but only in relationship. Everything is in communion with everything else.

In quantum physics, there is this astounding idea that goes under the dry scientific heading of nonlocal causality. Fundamental particles have characteristics, one of which is called *spin*. When two particles are related, one will have spin *up* and the other will have spin *down*. Once these particles are connected, one will always have spin *up* and the other will always have spin *down*. Building on this knowledge, scientists have performed a remarkable experiment. They separated two related particles far apart. Then they changed the spin on one particle from *up* to *down* and *instantaneously* the spin on the other particle flipped from *down* to *up*. There was no time between the two events. Somehow the two particles are connected in their essence, and we don't know how. The obvious implication is the entire structure of the universe is one. That's *communion*.

The third component, which we in the West find more challenging, is *subjectivity*. We all experience subjectivity. It is the sense of "I" or "me." The challenge is the assertion that *subjectivity* goes all the way down to quarks or strings. Everything has an intrinsic sense of being (though certainly not self-conscious). That's the notion of *subjectivity*.

Even though the scientific phrasing of these ideas is new, the basic intuition is not. In fact, these building blocks of the universe, *differentiation, communion* and *subjectivity*, are so basic they are foundational to the very structure of our language. *Subjectivity*, the sense of being, is first-person singular. I am in the first person singular when I speak. If I talk to you, you're the second person. When you and I have a conversation we become *We*. That's *communion*. When we talk about what a great job Kathy is doing playing piano for us today and how wonderful the choir sounds, we are speaking of them in the third person. That's *differentiation*.

I would like to suggest that the intuition that gave rise to the Trinity is grounded in exactly the same fundamentals as our language: first person, second person, and third person. And that Trinity expresses the fundamental dynamics of the universe: differentiation, subjectivity and communion. What we call The Trinity is an expression of these basic principles articulated in the language of the time. First, God the Father, the "I am that I am," points to the radical subjectivity at the very core of existence. In the East it is called *emptiness*. Second, relatedness, connection and *communion* are embodied in the Christ, the ultimate "we" connecting all with all. Third, the Holy Spirit, typically spoken of as flame, ghost, or spirit, points to *differentiation* (the ultimate It), the third person.

This may sound a bit convoluted, so let me suggest its relevance. The Trinity clearly points to something essential about the universe. It's not just another one of those "silly Christian ideas" we walk away from as we grow up and say it just doesn't make sense anymore. Rather, it points to something fundamental for our daily lives. As we explore together how to draw the Christian story bigger, how to make it fuller while honoring our tradition, we can actually look at the Trinity as one of those incredibly expansive stories that makes God internal to me, brings me into loving relationship with the Divine, and connects me intimately with everything in the universe. May you know that directly and with love. Amen.

• • •

In the following commentary on the Liturgical year, I step back and look at a tradition of the church and explore it with new eyes. I suggest that the Liturgical Year is a different way of looking at our personal and spiritual development.

Allegory of the Liturgical Year (February, 2007)

Do not seek to follow in the footsteps of the wise. Seek what they sought.[8]

"What's the Liturgical Year?" I asked my mentor, Ken, at the beginning of my church internship in seminary. He graciously pointed to a very cool calendar on the wall that correlated the calendar year with Jesus' life…such was my naiveté. Interesting, but pointless I thought, just another anachronism of the early church.

Now that I have hung out in ministry for a few years, I have come to a different opinion, though not the conventional one. The conventional explanation is that we focus on the seasons of Jesus' life as a form of worship for our Savior. I have a deep respect for that understanding and support it. However, since I don't really worship Jesus, such an interpretation makes little sense to me. I relate to Jesus as a loving friend who might help me realize my own divinity and dance in the Kingdom now. So, when I look at the Liturgical Year, I see an institutionalized allegory of Jesus' life as a metaphor for our own awakening, for our salvation. This, of course, does not invalidate the traditional view of the Liturgical Year. I hope my contribution makes it richer by adding a 1st person dimension.

This view of the Liturgical Year came to me as I reflected upon the Ox Herding Pictures of Zen. I often make sense of Christianity through Zen eyes. The Ox Herding Pictures depict the path to enlightenment from the Zen perspective. It occurred to me that the Liturgical Year outlines a similar path; one that recurs in larger and smaller cycles throughout our lives. It goes like this:

"Wuz happenin'?" (Advent)

Advent represents the dawning of awareness. It is the first glimmer that things are not as we thought. It is symbolized by Mary's pregnancy and the expectation that something wonderful is happening:

Now the birth of Jesus the Messiah took place in this way.
When his mother Mary had been engaged to Joseph, but be-
fore they lived together, she was found to be with child from
the Holy Spirit.[9]

Full of hope and excitement at the dawning of this new awareness, Advent compels us to search more deeply. Mary, seeking to better understand what was happening to her and the implications of her pregnancy, seeks wisdom from Elizabeth.

In those days Mary set out and went with haste to a Judean
town in the hill country, where she entered the house of
Zechariah and greeted Elizabeth. When Elizabeth heard
Mary's greeting, the child leaped in her womb. And Elizabeth
was filled with the Holy Spirit and exclaimed with a loud cry,
"Blessed are you among women, and blessed is the fruit of
your womb.[10]

Advent happens in any number of ways. You may notice that it is not really "Saturday" or "Monday" but that it is actually just today; or you notice for the first time that you are lost in your personal drama and return to the present moment to suddenly discover that there is no problem. Whatever sparks awareness changes us. Advent offers the merest taste and is likely to slip away for days or years; but once you have glimpsed differently you must eventually search.

"Oh, WOW!" (Christmas)

Christmas follows Advent in the Liturgical Year. As I see it, the birth of Jesus represents that breakthrough comprehension that begins to change everything. It is as if we are seeing for the first time. It can be as small as some concept we have been trying to wrap our minds around and suddenly understand; or as grand as a mystical vision that fundamentally shifts our perception of reality. With Jesus birth, as with any birth, there is a wholeness, a finality, to it. What has been birthed cannot be sent back. This genie cannot be put back in the bottle.

He went to be registered with Mary, to whom he was engaged
and who was expecting a child. While they were there, the
time came for her to deliver her child. And she gave birth to
her firstborn son and wrapped him in bands of cloth, and laid
him in a manger, because there was no place for them in the
inn.[11]

In the process of personal awakening, the glimpse offered by Advent may motivate you to turn your attention inward. Christmas is your reward for beginning that inward journey. Advent offers you a glimpse; Christmas brings self-validating proof. The Christ child has been born in you. Wow!

"Look at This!" (Epiphany)

The fundamental shift in perception born at Christmas begins to reveal a whole new world. This new world is symbolized in the season of Epiphany by the Magi and the gifts they bring:

> *In the time of King Herod, after Jesus was born in Bethlehem of Judea, wise men from the East came to Jerusalem, asking, 'Where is the child who has been born king of the Jews? For we observed his star at its rising, and have come to pay him homage.'*[12]

As we begin to see with new eyes, with a new mind, great treasures unfold before us. This can be an ecstatic journey as we explore the implications of our new awareness. Instinctively, we seek to maintain the epiphanies of our new awakening. This is symbolized in the flight to Egypt:

> *Now after they had left, an angel of the Lord appeared to Joseph in a dream and said, Get up, take the child and his mother, and flee to Egypt, and remain there until I tell you; for Herod is about to search for the child, to destroy him.*[13]

"Holy S_ _t!" (Lent)

It is, perhaps, our greatest hope that Epiphany will last forever, but Lent is just around the corner. Eternal Epiphany is the principal promise of today's spiritual marketplace. Yet, it is only the first movement of spiritual awakening. Advent, Christmas and Epiphany have an "additive" flavor as more insights are added to our understanding. But spiritual awakening, salvation, requires *subtraction*. Lent begins the process of subtraction. The positive, wonderful revelations of Epiphany confirm our sense of self, the building up of identity; but salvation requires the stripping away of the self. "Again I tell you, it is easier for a camel to go through the eye of a needle than for someone who is rich to enter the kingdom of God."[14] In Lent, we journey into the shadows...the hell we have avoided. In Lent, we challenge everything we thought was true. It is our journey into the desert:

> *Jesus, full of the Holy Spirit, returned from the Jordan and was led by the Spirit in the wilderness, where for forty days he*

was tempted by the devil. He ate nothing at all during those
days, and when they were over, he was famished.[15]

The point of Lent is not further understanding; it's not about more answers to more questions. Lent begins the process of destroying the questioner. In Epiphany we believe there is a separate *me* who has now become very cool and spiritual because of its new way of knowing. As we grow accustomed to this new way of knowing, we discover we are still deeply attached to the perceiver of these new truths. We can, of course, stop here and be really cool, spiritual folks. But if we have the drive to push further, it becomes clear that that which seeks answers to the questions must also go. We are required to take a "leap of faith" right into emptiness. This is death for the sense of self, or the *me* we have identified with all of our lives. That *me* must die.

How does the *me* die? It dies by being recognized for what it is, a construction of the mind. It does not die by an intellectual explanation of how it is constructed, but by recognition that it simply has no substance. How is this accomplished? There are many practices, my favorite is the inquiry, "Who am I?" which is perhaps better articulated as "What am I?" or "What is me?" or "To whom does this thought arise?" or "What is thinking this thought?" or "What is having this feeling?" Through the process of inquiry the *me*, that which seeks, is revealed as insubstantial, as not real. And slowly or suddenly, awareness dawns that I am not what I thought I was. Nor am I the higher self I imagined my true self to be. Rather, that which I am is no self at all. I do not discover my higher self, "I" discover that there is no self…and off the cliff we fall.

"Oh My God!" (Holy Week)

The fundamental insight of Lent is not that there is light at the end of the tunnel, but a cliff. Passion or Holy week symbolizes the final destruction of the ego, our illusory sense of a separate self. God does not want most of us; God wants all of us, stripped naked and simple. At the culmination of Lent we must voluntarily walk off the cliff. This is symbolized at the beginning of Holy Week by Jesus' paradoxical return to Jerusalem, paradoxical because it is simultaneously celebratory and sad. We know it ends in death. During this week the persona Jesus is beaten, humiliated, battered and broken. By the end of Holy Week Jesus must surrender fully. The ultimate expression of "the cliff" comes from Mark: "and Jesus cried out…'My God, my God, why have you forsaken me?'"[16] Even our last concept of God must be forsaken in our disidentification with the I-sense (ego).

We've been on an incredible rollercoaster ride! We begin our climb with the faintest glimmer of understanding in our season of Advent (Wuz happenin'?). Our glimmer blossoms into the birth of understanding at Christmas (Wow!) and expands through Epiphany (Look at This!). But what goes up must come down. Lent (Holy

S_ _t!) is the vehicle. All that we thought we'd escaped with our epiphanies must be confronted. Confronting our inner demons in Lent eventually leads us to our own Jerusalem, Holy Week (Oh My God!). Our utter surrender brings the greatest surprise, not oblivion, but new life … Easter. This is the great promise of Christianity.

"Ahhhhhh" (Easter)

The incredible discovery of Easter is that what we most feared does not come to pass. Who I always thought I was has died, yet I exist, but not as the "I" I thought I was (language is not our friend here!). Not only do "I" exist, but I inhabit a realm of freedom, of spaciousness, I never imagined possible:

> After the Sabbath…Mary Magdalene and the other Mary
> went to see the tomb. And suddenly there was a great earth-
> quake; for an angel of the Lord, descending from heaven,
> came and rolled back the stone and sat on it…But the angel
> said to the women, "Do not be afraid; I know that you are
> looking for Jesus who was crucified. He is not here; for he has
> been raised."[17]

Easter represents the full awakening of the Christ within. The limited self, born of fear, is fully transcended. "The Father and I are One," as Jesus said. From an Eastern perspective, the best translation of Nirvana is "Ahhhhhh," a deep sigh of release and relief. Such is the nature of Easter. Such is resurrection.

I have stated this process in its most dramatic form as symbolized by Jesus' life, death and resurrection, but if you pay attention you will see the process repeating itself at all levels of our daily lives.

"Who's Gonna Clean Up This Mess?" (Pentecost)

We're not done yet. The all important season of Pentecost is about integrating the transformations from Advent through Easter. In the symbolism of the Liturgical Year, we are now on our own. It is up to us to integrate the changes we have been through. No one can do it for us. But it's OK. Through the spiritual awakening symbolized by the Liturgical Year, we have now internalized, to greater or lesser degree, the Christ-consciousness. We call it the Holy Spirit.

> When the day of Pentecost had come, they were all together
> in one place. And suddenly from heaven there came a sound
> like the rush of a violent wind, and it filled the entire house
> where they were sitting. Divided tongues, as of fire, appeared

among them, and a tongue rested on each of them. All of
them were filled with the Holy Spirit.[18]

Salvation, resurrection, enlightenment mean nothing until they are brought back into everyday life and that is the task of Pentecost. No surprise, it is the longest season of the Liturgical Year.

• • •

In the next reflection I explore the relationship between belief and doubt in the context of increasingly expansive worldviews.

Belief and Doubt (October, 2008)

John 20: 24-29

> *But Thomas (who was called the Twin), one of the twelve, was not with them when Jesus came. So the other disciples told him, "We have seen the Lord." But he said to them, "Unless I see the mark of the nails in his hands, and put my finger in the mark of the nails and my hand in his side, I will not believe."*
>
> *A week later his disciples were again in the house, and Thomas was with them. Although the doors were shut, Jesus came and stood among them and said, "Peace be with you." Then he said to Thomas, "Put your finger here and see my hands. Reach out your hand and put it in my side. Do not doubt but believe." Thomas answered him, "My Lord and my God!" Jesus said to him, "Have you believed because you have seen me? Blessed are those who have not seen and yet have come to believe."*

Thomas is one of the bad guys of scripture, mostly because of this passage. Clearly the writer of the Gospel of John had an agenda. The Biblical historians in the Jesus Seminar say this reading was not likely to have been part of Jesus' words, but those of an evangelical community formed nearly 100 years after Jesus' death. What did they have to say? They said *believe*. If you believe then you will see and then you will be saved. What a message—believe and you will be saved.

I feel compelled to defend Thomas, perhaps because I am his namesake. Imagine that Susie comes to me and says, "I just saw Martin Luther King, and he was alive!" Or, "I saw Elvis alive! Really!" Shall I believe her? Shall I believe that Martin

Luther King or Elvis is actually alive, or I should ask for evidence? Personally, I'm going for evidence. Now, put yourself in Thomas' position. The request in the Gospel of John is to believe, and the way it's framed by the evangelist is, *you are wrong if you doubt.* What you need to do is believe and not question. But I think Thomas was right to doubt. I imagine that Thomas felt something like this, "Nothing is more important to me than whether Jesus is dead or alive. I chose to abandon everything to follow this man. Now you tell me that, even though I saw him die, he's alive. I'm not going to go through this again. I'm not going to give my heart again without proof." So he says, "I want to know, I want to see for myself."

The church has followed John's admonition not to ask for evidence; just believe. I think Jesus would have said just the opposite: "Yea Thomas, don't believe a bunch stories. Find out for yourself! Faith is not about believing what other people believe. It's not about their life; it's your life that's on the line. Don't take someone else's word for something that affects your life so profoundly. Find out for yourself."

Yet, paradoxically, belief is essential if we are to move ahead. How then, do we balance belief and doubt? When I think about belief, it has a forward motion that carries me into possibility. In the state of belief those possibilities open and they open and they open. Doubt provides the container. Doubt keeps us from just believing everything and anything. If we believe everything, we don't get anywhere. We don't get any closer to what Jesus was about if we just believe everything. This seems especially pertinent in our current era.

Looking back, the church has long been the authority on what to believe or not. If you sought evidence for a particular belief, like when Galileo invited folks to look through his telescope, the church would respond, "Sorry, evidence doesn't agree with our beliefs so it can't be true."

What we call the Enlightenment slammed into the church like a freight train. As popular consciousness became increasingly rational, people questioned. As science emerged, the response of the modern mind to the church was no more myths, no more lies; if you want to tell us this stuff you've got to prove it! Well you can't prove God; no empirical proof is possible. No scientific experiment can prove that there is or is not a God. Rationality, reason, and doubt hammered the church over the next three centuries as modern reason demanded evidence. It concluded there was no concrete evidence for believing in miracles or in God.

Now, there is something really interesting about humans. We seem to be hardwired to make meaning out of our world. We don't live our lives as if they were just a bunch of events that happen willy nilly. We string them together in a story and say, "Oh! There's a purpose to my life, there's meaning, it has continuity." The things I have done in the past connect with the things I'm doing now and what I plan to do in the future." We're hardwired to think in this way. When doubt comes along in the form of science and reason, it offers a really lousy story to make meaning from. It says we are nothing but a mistake, a fluke of the universe, the result of random particles crashing together haphazardly until they create life. The modern story tells us life is very complex, so what you think of as important and spiritual and godly is just a byproduct of the complexity of your brain. Go snuggle up with that when you feel lonely and afraid! It is no surprise we yearn for more. It is no surprise we are moving beyond this modern story.

Our movement beyond modern reason creates a conundrum. The emergence of modern reason over the past 300 years has brought miracles greater than the church ever imagined. We live twice, three times as long as people even 200 years ago. We fly around the world, we go to the moon. We do things that were inconceivable. How is this possible? Because we doubt, because we reason, and because we question. The sterile story that we don't want to snuggle up with when we're lonely and afraid also gave us our material wealth and benefits. The story doesn't serve my soul, but it certainly serves my body.

In the 1960's, we witnessed the emergence of a new way of knowing. We call it postmodernism. "Postmodern" means we don't really know what it means yet, just that it comes after modern. We are in the midst of this revolution of consciousness. We are caught in it as a culture.

A great realization of postmodern consciousness is that science and reason are not the end of evolution. Postmodern understanding realized our minds are not the sole source of good information. Our emotions and intuitions will tell us important things also. We discovered that groups we'd ignored before, women, minorities, the elderly, the young, native peoples, also have truths.

The idea that truth depends upon who you are and the culture that formed you exploded upon the scene in the 60's. For all its great insights, postmodernism came with a fatal flaw. When we open the door and claim that everyone has a piece of the truth, what leaps in is the relativity of all truth: "My truth is my truth, and your truth is your truth; it's all relative dude!" Whatever I want to believe, from big foot to alien abductions, I am free to believe whether it has any grounding in the world or not. Evidence doesn't matter, because all evidence is suspect because we have discovered its cultural context.

Look at a New Age magazine. Notice all the advertisements for gurus and spiritual types? What do they promise? They promise if you follow their teaching you will become awakened or enlightened. If their promises were true, we should be up to our necks in enlightened people by now. But we aren't. We don't even bother to ask for evidence of their success, we simply soak it in. Ask these great spiritual teachers, "How many of your students have actually awakened by following your process?" Are there hundreds? Dozens? Is there one person that you would hold up and say, "Look this guy attained what Jesus attained, so can you." My point is that, without some evidence, we are lost in believing everything that comes our way.

In our leap into postmodernity we made a huge mistake—we rejected reason. When we recognized the limits of reason, we inadvertently threw the baby out with the bathwater. Since reason can't give us everything it promises, we conclude it has nothing to offer. We now find ourselves immersed in this mish-mash of beliefs with no compass. The central belief of postmodernity is "You believe your thing and I'll believe mine." In its extreme form it becomes, "If you want to fly a plane into some tall building that's your thing, not mine." In recapturing our spiritual sensibility we have, inadvertently, resurrected the pre-Enlightenment Church's stance that belief trumps doubt.

I suggest we hear the wisdom of Thomas and discover for ourselves the balance between belief and doubt—that we allow *both* deeply into our hearts. At the extreme I would say *believe everything, doubt everything*. Allow belief to open you, then doubt what is open; believe again, then doubt everything you see. This is not my idea. It is my expression of a well worn path of awakening. The great spiritual traditions call it *inquiry*. In inquiry we open to something, then we question it fundamentally. Then we attend to what emerges from the fire of inquiry. This is the wisdom of Thomas: *I'll believe it, but I want to see for myself. Don't mess with me; I'm going to doubt it all. And what emerges from this caldron of belief and doubt is what I will base my life on.* I say Amen.

• • •

Playfulness is core to the Integral Church. Creating a culture supportive of Integral Church requires humor, playfulness and a reverent irreverence. Great joy and humility emerge when we no longer take ourselves seriously—sincerely, but not seriously.

Man Plans, God Laughs (February, 2008)

Ecclesiastes 7: 3-4

> Sorrow is better than laughter; it may sadden your face, but
> it sharpens your understanding. Someone who is always
> thinking about happiness is a fool. A wise person thinks about
> death.

This quote from Ecclesiastes is about as humorous as our *Bible* gets. The philosopher, Alfred North Whitehead once commented, "The total absence of humor from the *Bible* is one of the most singular things in all of literature."[19] This is in stark contrast to other faiths who consider humor and laughter integral to the spiritual life. The title for this sermon, "Man Plans, God Laughs" comes from the Jewish tradition. Aiya did some research and found this great article for me, "Holy Laughter or Strong Delusion," by Warren Smith. In it, Mr. Smith reports the results of a *Bible* search that found 42 references to laughter. Twenty-two refer to scornful laughter: "They laughed us to scorn" (Nehemiah 2:19). Seven refer to Abraham and Sarah's disbelief when they found her pregnant at 90 years old. Most of the rest have to do with Job's friends' mockery of him and Solomon's council to prefer sorrow over mirth as in our scripture reading. Even Jesus counsels against laughter: "Woe unto you that laugh now! For ye shall mourn and weep."[20]

Clearly, the question of humor is no laughing matter. Someone as serious as Aristotle asked, what makes us uniquely human? Or, in Christian terms, what about us is created in the image of God? Aristotle concluded that what sets humans apart is our ability to laugh, because no other animal laughs. Is that true?

I recently listened to a radio interview with a professor from Washington State University who researches how rats play. He wondered why the normally vocal rats made no noise when they played. One of his graduate students suggested that rats, like bats, might make sounds we can't hear. With the appropriate technology they discovered that rats do make sounds at a frequency too high for us to hear when they play. The researchers went a step further and started tickling the rats. Lo and behold, the rats made a sound that could only be described as laughter. So much for this conceit of human uniqueness.

Still, there *is* something that does set us apart from other creatures, something truly in the image of God. It appears we are the only species capable of thinking about our thinking. That's not the divine part; what is truly divine is that when we peacefully reflect upon ourselves, the only thing we can do is laugh. We are most godly when laughing at ourselves.

You have to wonder why this didn't make it into the *Bible*. If this is really central to our divinity, why isn't it in the *Bible*? I suspect that laughing at yourself was politically inexpedient. You don't control people and consolidate an empire by saying that life is a lark. You consolidate an empire by scaring people. Religion is a great way to tell people that if they don't behave they'll burn in hell.

Imagine Jesus. Here is a guy who is wide awake and has seen life as it really is. Those who have awakened consistently say things like "Don't worry, be happy." Or "There is nothing to lose but your hell." All we really have to lose is our fear, our pain, our sorrow. Life and reality are far more gentle, kind and forgiving than all of our thoughts about it.

I find it hard to imagine Jesus mournfully shuffling down the road saying, "Hey guys, anybody want to slog on over to Capernaum and save some souls?" Would you follow a guy who never laughs? My favorite depiction is of Jesus having a great big belly laugh. Most representations of him are sad, inert, peaceful, or boring. These are nice, domesticated versions that work fine for our domesticated spirituality, but it doesn't have anything to do with a Jesus that I want in my life.

Human life is a gas, so why take it seriously? We have inherited the image of a big daddy God in the sky with his finger on the "SMITE" button just ready to nail us. My preferred image portrays God as a big golden retriever puppy playing a game. What's the game? Hide and seek, of course. I am God, playing a game and pretending I'm *not* God. You are God, playing a game pretending you're *not* God. And how much fun is it to be on earth and play this game together? What else would God do? God knows there's nothing to lose. There's nothing to achieve. There are no t's that need to be crossed or i's that need to be dotted. There is no death...really. There is nothing to be lost. Jesus said it clearly: "The Kingdom is inside of you, and it is outside of you."[21] The kingdom of heaven *is right here*, open your eyes. You don't have to do anything, you don't have to ask anything, there is nothing you have to do for the kingdom of heaven but receive it.

Here is the main point: If you're not laughing, you're probably missing the Christian story. If life isn't absurd to you, you're probably missing the point. If you don't think it's about laughter, look in the mirror. Tell me God doesn't have a sense of humor! I wake up and I look in the mirror, if I don't scream, I usually get a good laugh. If we take ourselves seriously, we're probably missing the point.

Now, I can't say I always live fearlessly with a continuous chuckle in my heart. But I spend enough time with a humorous God to know that any religion telling us to take ourselves seriously is bunk. This may offend some, but I have tasted this truth. Jesus says, "You will know the truth, and the truth will make you free."[22] What is the truth to make you free? That truth cannot be spoken, but the consequence of knowing it can only be a profound belly laugh, right from the depths of your soul. If that's not the truth, then spare me the truth. I can only conclude with a joke.

Three departed souls were standing at the gate of heaven. Saint Peter asked them, "What is the meaning of Easter." The first said, "That's when the family comes together to enjoy a turkey dinner and count their blessings." Peter pointed down and that first soul was gone.

The second said, "That's when people decorate a pine tree and place presents under it." Again, Saint Peter pointed down, and the second was gone.

The third said, "It's about a man who came two thousand years ago. People in the temple became angry at him and put him to death. After three days, he came out of his tomb." Saint Peter was beginning to think this one had it. Then the soul added, "And then Jesus saw his shadow and we had six more weeks of winter."

One final comment: I hear they found a new beatitude in the Dead Sea Scrolls. It goes like this:

Blessed are those who can laugh at themselves, for they will never cease to be amused.

Amen

Notes

1 All quotes from Smith, Richard L. "Reclaiming John 3:16," (Whosoever.org, date unknown), http://whosoever.org/. I say that Rev. Smith's description is "unintentional" because I see no evidence that he is using a developmental frame for his presentation. The developmental frame is something I impose upon this delightful presentation of his personal journey.

2 As suggested here, the Postmodern/Pluralist perspective does a great job of including, and legitimating, previously unheard and marginalized voices (women, Native American, black, Latino, gay/lesbian). At the same time, its radical inclusivity engenders a "treading on thin ice" mentality that avoids critique, except on the grounds of exclusion: what voices have been left out? This leaves little for the Pluralist to say. My observation is that, in concrete settings like a church, where folks want to hear something substantive and normative, one orientation will come to dominate, be it politically progressive, feminist, liberationist, or gay/lesbian.

3 John 1:1-5.

4 Meade, Michael, *The World Behind the World*. (Portland, OR: Greenfire Press. 2008) 8.

5 Matthew 6:5-6: "And whenever you pray, do not be like the hypocrites; for they love to stand and pray in the synagogues and at the street corners, so that they may be seen by others. Truly I tell you, they have received their reward. But whenever you pray, go into your room and shut the door and pray to your Father who is in secret; and your Father who sees in secret will reward you."

6 Acts 10:34-35: Then Peter began to speak to them: "I truly understand that God shows no partiality, but in every nation anyone who fears him and does what is right is acceptable to him."

7 Source: http://www.brainyquote.com.

8 Matsuo Basho, famous 17th century Japanese haiku poet.

9 Matthew 1:18.

10 Luke 1: 39-42.

11 Luke 2:1-8.

12 Matthew 2:1-2.

13 Matthew 2:13.

14 Matthew 19:24.

15 Luke 4:1-2.

16 Mark 15:34.

17 Matthew 28: 1-6.

18 Acts 2: 1-4.

19 Source: http://www.brainyquote.com. Original source unknown.

20 Luke 6:25.

21 Gospel of Thomas, Chapter 3.

22 John 8:32.

PART II

INTEGRAL CHURCH IN THE WORLD

Chapter 5
Application of Integral Theory
to the Integral Church

Before we apply Integral Theory to the Integral Church we must ask, why? Why go through the trouble of creating a new kind of church? The answer is soul, and it is best answered in myth.

• • •

Every Great Story, every myth that nurtures our spirits, must tell us where we come from and what happens to us when we die. One reason people have grown weary of the Enlightenment Myth, the story that maintains modernity, is that it says we begin when we are born and disappear when we die. This, of course, makes good rational sense based on the information we have, but it doesn't account for continuity. By continuity I mean the intuition that there is more than this—that, when we settle back into the Silence, we sense we are continuous, eternal. The Zen folks speak of our original face, the one we had before our parents were born. The Tibetans, those great scholars of death and dying, speak of the eternal drop that migrates from lifetime to lifetime. Christians speak of eternal life after death in either heaven or hell. No matter the story, every faith recognizes we are more than just this life. This is not some philosophy or comforting belief as rationalists would tell us; it is a compelling realization that arises from attending to the Silence within.

Of course we can't know what we were before we were born or what we will be after we die. Continuity only tells us we continue. Does every aspect of our persona dissolve away as our bodies return to dust? Or is there something about us that persists, something we might call the soul?

The soul has an important place in our Great Myth, for Life and Intelligence are phenomenally conservative. The Universe saves every successful experiment, builds multiple copies, and adapts it. Spines, toes, noses and brains have been evolving and developing over eons; so too has consciousness.

The Tibetan's say the "eternal drop" of who we are returns to earth-

ly existence until it learns its lessons and escapes reincarnation. I prefer a gentler story. This one has my soul, the consciousness created over eons of development, hanging out observing life on earth. When something on earth piques my interest, I am drawn into physical existence. I become a person. I don't come back with the same personality or skills I might have had in a previous life, but there is some essential continuity (which we sense throughout our lives). I incarnate with the body, the personality and the life situation that will allow my soul to do whatever it came for. The soul has its own agenda; it has no interest in pleasing the person I call "me." What serves the soul does not necessarily serve the personality created by the mind. In fact, what serves the soul may be very different from what serves the mind. The mind wants clarity; the soul thrives on ambiguity. The mind wants certainty; the soul needs paradox to evolve and pursue whatever attracted it in the first place.

Our Bible tells the human story using Adam and Eve, the first people. Mythically, they represent what makes us human. Initially they were naked and hung out with the animals. They were at one with God. The Bible says they were thrown out of Eden when they ate of the Tree of Knowledge of Good and Evil. In modern language, human minds got complex enough so we could think about ourselves; we became self-conscious. Adam and Eve became self-conscious so they put on clothes. Becoming self-conscious ejected us from the Garden of Eden, not because God was angry at us for disobeying, but because we now imagined we were separate from God. The Bible says we have been kept away from the Garden's Tree of Life lest we partake of its fruit and become immortal like the gods. I'll tell you a secret. There aren't really angels with flaming swords guarding the gates to the Garden of Eden; there are only our thoughts, our beliefs and our stories. But these are much more powerful than any flaming angels because our thoughts, beliefs and stories keep us from the actual Tree of Life, which is within us. The actual Tree of Life is that continuity we all sense but can't grasp. It is the simple feeling of being pervading all that that we are. It is so simple it is always relegated to unimportance.

This is the great spiritual secret: there is no secret! As St. Francis said, "What you are looking for is what is looking." The enlightened consciousness we are pursuing is that which is looking out through our eyes at this moment, reading this sentence. Religion has nothing to offer that we don't already have; yet we typically need something like religion or spirituality to awaken to this truth. That's what happens when we live in the world of paradox, right and wrong, good and evil, left and right. Faith offers the mind the courage to stand in the tension of opposites and be transformed, for transformation is the path of the soul. Churches don't offer this because *it's not what the mind wants (so people won't pay for it); the mind wants clarity and assurance.*

In the Great Myth guiding this book, we continue and we abide, not as egos or personas, but as souls. Soul is not some magical or religious term but something present in this moment. It's not the same as the Emptiness that observes everything; soul is more active, it wants to do something, it incarnated to do something. The something soul wants to do may have little or nothing to do with the plans we construct with our minds. But soul always wins. If our minds conform to the direction of soul, we are happier and more peaceful, our purpose discovered. And this is where Integral Church fits into this Great Myth. The point of Integral Church is to create a context in which our soul's desire can unfold with the least resistance because all resistance comes from the mind. Keep the mind happy and the soul's purpose can unfold. Teach the mind to listen and it will assist the soul's journey. Open up possibilities in a safe environment and the soul will blossom. That's the point of Integral Church.

How Can Integral Theory Guide the Integral Church and Help Susan and Bob?

Bob was raised Catholic, but abandoned the church in his teens. In college he majored in biology, and moved further from the idea of a creator God. Bob and Susan met in college. Susan was raised in a fairly conservative church. They became friends, lovers, and gladly married during their senior year when Susan became pregnant. They weren't stressed about this. Both had good job prospects, they were in love and were delighted by the idea of a child. They didn't even consider a church wedding, knowing that they would not be accepted by their traditional faith communities. They went to the justice of the peace for a civil ceremony, followed by a big party with their friends and family.

Bob and Susan had a great community of friends, they were professionally successful and both had loving, supportive families. Their life appeared idyllic, so friends and family were surprised when, a decade later, Susan filed for divorce. Bob was both surprised and bereft. In his mid-30's, he found himself adrift. Family and friends cared for him; he continued to be involved with his children. He and Susan managed an amicable divorce, but something essential was missing, not just a partner but something deeper. He tried returning to the Catholic church of his youth, but that was a disaster. He visited various Protestant churches and explored Eastern faiths and meditation. He learned much, but yearned for more. His childhood in the Catholic Church and his daily work as a scientist were at war within him. He needed a new story to weave his life around, but everything he encountered left him empty and more confused. Churches demanded he set aside his reason so that he could belong to the community of the faithful; his work in science mocked the stories of the church. It felt like a wasteland to Bob. He couldn't return to a faith that rejected what he had learned from science. He couldn't stay in a barren world of random chance. He had no idea how to proceed forward. I'd like to say that Bob found solace in an Integral Church, but there wasn't one for him to find. Bob continues to search.

When Susan met Bob in college, she knew they were a perfect match. They shared common interests in the sciences and they both wanted to make a difference in the world. Life was good for many years. They had a comfortable home, capable and happy kids, a circle of friends from college and supportive families. But Susan felt something was lacking. It wasn't Bob. She loved him and was pleased their romance of earlier years had matured into a comfortable and nurturing partnership. The problem wasn't Bob, it was their whole life. They had all the trappings of success and yet it felt hollow. Even though she knew it wasn't Bob, Susan couldn't see another way out of her stultifying life. In divorcing him, she was casting herself out of an enviable life of friends, family and comfort, but she saw no other option. That she had reached the pinnacle of her life, and it was this empty, was unbearable. So she stepped off the proverbial cliff into the unknown. The question is, will she be caught? And could she be caught and supported by an Integral Church?

From the perspective of Integral Theory, Susan and Bob reached the limits of the orientations they have lived within for many years—the Modern/Achiever wave of development. Susan reached the limits of Achiever some time before Bob. Bob was thrust up against the limits of this perspective by Susan's decision to divorce. Bob, unprepared for such fundamental change, might eventually find refuge in his Catholic roots. He might overcome his rational doubts and scientific questions and be included in a community and a story that gives his life coherence.

Susan is looking for a different way of being: one that renews wonder, awe and reverence in her life. If she doesn't find it, she may retreat to her more traditional roots. Or she may discover an aspect of New Age spirituality, Buddhism, or Native American spirituality in which to immerse herself. Such a move would thrust Susan into a new way of seeing, into what I call the Pluralist perspective. She might discover a whole new world opening up to her, new friends and a new life; but at what cost? Did she need to divorce Bob and break up her family to change? Could an Integral Church have supported her and Bob by respecting Bob's perspective and allowing Susan the changes her soul demanded? These are some of the questions we must answer.

In applying Integral Theory to Integral Church and to Bob and Susan's situation, the first thing we notice is *the map is not the territory*. Reality is far more complex than any map and theory's clarity quickly becomes a quagmire in practice. This, of course, is just as it should be. We would never want life to be lived with the sterility of theory; and we don't want to forget that theory is just a map, not reality. With this in mind, we ask, what role does Integral Theory play in the messy processes of real life churches? How could it help Susan, Bob and their children?

We begin with a clarification. To be an Integral Church does not mean all practices are Integral or everybody inhabits an Integral perspective. What I call Integral begins with the Self-Actualized wave of development: second tier. This is the first perspective that truly embraces all the previous levels in the overall spiral of development. This Stage is the first to deeply recognize the complexity of human spiritual evolution and seeks to nurture the full spectrum of that spiral. Likely, one or more individuals within the church will find the Integral map appealing or Integral Church would have no traction at all. But moving in the direction of Integral Church does not require a large contingent of folks to inhabit Integral consciousness. It does help if the pastor or some legitimate authority in the church inhabits Self-Actualized or Construct-Awareness but if not, it is sufficient that folks desire to become integrally informed and use this map as a bootstrap to becoming an Integral Church. Being integrally informed simply means applying the insights of Integral Theory to the church as a whole.

How might an Integral Church support Susan, Bob and their children during their time of need? In general, an effective Integral Church will recognize their needs and support them just where they are while offering possibilities for further development. In particular, Bob could find a story and friends who are nurtured by a modern revisionist take on Christianity. A Modern, scientific understanding of Christianity could reconnect him with his Catholic roots while respecting his scientific mind. Or he might enjoy the "heresy" of *The Da Vinci Code* as a way of humanizing Jesus. Or he might find that he could be overtly agnostic or atheist and still be welcomed.

Susan would find her emerging Pluralist perspective supported in an Integral Church. Her heart might be drawn to environmental issues, questions of justice or interfaith expressions of the divine. If Susan had been in an Integral Church, she might have discovered common ground with Bob. Together, they might have realized Bob shared her environmental values and his Achiever perspective brings practical financial and technical skills to the service of saving the earth. Meanwhile, their children could have been nurtured in an environment that recognized their developmental needs and supported their ongoing development.

In general, the Integral Church's mission is to serve people as fully as possible on their journey of awakening or salvation, which includes all the crises of life we identify as distinctly human. Currently, churches and denominations tend to serve folks at a particular wave of development. Fundamentalist churches primarily serve the Magic and Warrior waves of development. The mainline churches typically serve Conformist stages. The Achiever wave is served by secular humanism, scientism, and some progressive churches. Most progressive, New Age and Unitarian Universalist churches serve Pluralist development. An Integral Church is required to integrate these perspectives into a unified whole.

This means that when an individual begins to reach the limits of a particular developmental perspective, they are often confronted with either the painful choice of leaving their church community or denying their own development. Without an Integral Church, Susan and Bob must find different spiritual communities to support them.

The Integral Church endeavors to do three things in response to a dilemma like Bob and Susan's.

- First, all Stages of Development are celebrated and each level's valuable contribution to spiritual awakening is recognized. When an individual finds how they understand changing, they need not leave the church to find meaningful challenge and support. They can participate in activities nurturing different ways of knowing.
- Second, a home is provided for those who are running up against the limitations of any particular Stage of Development and want to continue to grow within expanded Christian perspectives.
- Third, an expansive new understanding of the Christian faith is supported having the potential of carrying the church into a new, vital role in American culture.

In addition to helping the Bobs and Susans of the world, the Integral Church seeks to move beyond the value-relativity of the Pluralist/Postmodern wave of development that plagues many progressive churches. To be a postmodern, progressive church is not a bad thing, of course. In fact, it is a phenomenal achievement to be radically inclusive of different cultural perspectives, of different sexual orientations, and of different worldviews. But this achievement also creates a trap that Integral Church seeks to overcome. The trap of Pluralism is not that every perspective has truth, but the premise that every perspective is *equally* true. Incorporating the wisdom that previously marginalized voices, such as women, minorities, and different cultures, is a stellar achievement. The problem is with the assumption that each voice has equal "truth value."

To suggest some voices and perspectives have more truth value than others will, of course, have the Pluralist screaming "foul!" Any self-respecting Pluralist must ask of me, "How can you possibly, as a middle aged, middle class, white male, judge the validity of *any* other view? Aren't you just resurrecting patriarchy after so many battles have been fought to free marginalized people from its tyranny?" But the radical relativism of the Postmodern/Pluralist view is precisely where the progressive church gets stuck. To be consistent with the commitment of radical inclusivity, the postmodern perspective must not judge the values and beliefs of any people because "truth" is relative to the cultural context. At the extreme, this means that the values of the Klu Klux Klan have as much merit as the values of Gandhi; or that the 911 terrorist attacks cannot be criticized because the individuals flying the planes held values consistent with the culture in which they were nurtured. In their cultural context… they are heroes.

Integral Theory and the Integral Church do not deny that "truth" and values are culturally conditioned as revealed by Pluralist awareness. The integral perspective merely challenges the assumption that relativism (or radical inclusivity) is *the* last word on truth or values. Integral Theory does not move "backwards" toward patriarchy or modernity to find viable explanations. Instead, Integral Theory and the Integral Church move forward into a more inclusive meta-perspective.

Again, Pluralist awareness says this is impossible. The Pluralist argument is that any kind of meta-theory or meta-perspective is hierarchical and thus inherently marginalizing to some groups. Or a meta-perspective is just patriarchy in a new guise (never mind that the judgment "no hierarchy is better than hierarchy" is a hierarchical judgment). A problem for the progressive church arises from its commitment to radical inclusivity. It must strive to please everyone all the time and agree with every idea or philosophy, no matter how goofy. It's no wonder when folks exhaust the fruits of radical inclusivity and want clearer guidelines for action; their only alternative in the Christian landscape is the traditional church they sought to escape… or the rejection of religion all together.

Let me reiterate. I am not disparaging the vast achievements of the progressive church with its center of gravity in the Pluralist wave of development and the Postmodern story. On the contrary, my commitment is to propel the church forward as the inherent limitations of the postmodern orientation become obvious. The purpose of the Integral Church is to point beyond postmodernity in a manner that preserves and furthers the gains of the Pluralist stage as exemplified in progressive churches.

With this commitment in mind, and the dilemmas faced by Bob and Susan, the following sections lay out a basic map to guide an emerging Integral Church. There are no prescriptions for how an Integral Church will look, since each church will create its own distinct culture. What Integral Theory offers is a large conceptual framework and a spectrum of questions to guide the evolving Integral Church. In the following chapter I will flesh out the map with examples from my own church in Suquamish.

Questions from Integral Theory

If Integral Theory is to provide a helpful road map for the Integral Church and for Susan and Bob, it will do so through the questions it inspires. In the following sections I explore some of the fundamental questions that emerge from Integral Theory that can help guide the Integral Church.

The Lines that Matter

In Chapter 2, I listed some of the more important Lines of Development or "intelligences." While these lines, and more, are involved in the delightful complexity we call human, all are not equally relevant to the role of the church. I consider the following Lines of Development central to the Integral Church's primary task of supporting the entire spectrum of human development.[1]

- Cognitive: What am I aware of?
- Self: Who am I?
- Values: What is significant to me?
- Moral: What should I do?
- Interpersonal: How should we interact?
- Intrapersonal: What do I see when I look inside myself?
- Spiritual: What is of ultimate concern?
- Needs: What do I need?
- Emotional: Wow do I feel about this?

Being an Integral Church, or an integrally informed church, does not mean you will focus on all of these "intelligences." But awareness of their existence is important for how you will focus the energies of the church. Some questions to guide you:

- What Lines of Development are most important for your church to help develop?
- Does your church tend to focus on some "intelligences" and ignore others?
- Do you focus on the attributes of each line at a particular wave of development? In other words, are the values, morals and explanations couched, say, in Pluralist or Achiever terms? Do traditional morals or "shoulds" dominate conversations, such as how to save the earth?
- There are likely very good reasons for an emphasis on some lines. What are those lines and why are they emphasized?
- Presumably those reasons were valid at earlier times, does the reasoning still hold under current circumstances?

As suggested by Bob's and Susan's search for a different way of making meaning in their lives, an emphasis on values could help them find common ground. It's hard to imagine a church that doesn't include values as an important line of development. The question is "what values?" Are Bob's Achiever values paramount, or Susan's Pluralist values? Can both be celebrated? For example, can you celebrate saving the planet and making money? Can you simultaneously support the vision of God as loving Father, the intelligence of the universe, and Cosmic Prankster? Can you celebrate a deep sense of personal insight (intrapersonal) alongside social ineptitude (interpersonal)? Bob and Susan are likely to require validation for all these ways of seeing on their journey from one wave of development to the next.

Of course, the vibrant diversity of humankind ensures this complexity will be available in almost every church. The question is, is the complexity acknowledged and affirmed? Is human complexity understood as just that, complexity, and not sin or failing? The great value of Integral Theory for Integral Church is an explicit, conceptual framework; a map acknowledging the importance of this complexity.

States of Consciousness

In becoming an Integral Church, it is useful to note the things we can change and those we cannot. Some dimensions of human development and spiritual awakening can be changed; others are beyond our influence. Since the Integral Church hopes to provide a conveyor belt for consciousness through increasingly expansive ways of being and knowing, understanding what we can influence is essential. The church cannot, for example, change the mix of intelligences (Lines of Development) folks bring to the church, nor can it significantly influence the Types of individuals who show up. The Integral Church can, however, employ States of Consciousness and Worldviews to support the evolution of individual consciousness. I will explore this more fully under Room to Roam, later in this chapter.

Altered States of Consciousness offer powerful experiences of the Divine. By altered states I mean the experiences of expanded awareness, feelings of oneness or caring, or deep understanding or joy. In Chapter 2, I described States of Consciousness as expanding from Gross (body) to Subtle (mind) to Causal (soul) to Witness to Non-Dual. We live most of our lives in various forms of Gross and lower Subtle consciousness. That is, most of our attention is absorbed by bodily sensations and the chatter of our mind. More expansive States, in the higher Subtle[2], Causal, Witness and Non-Dual, are generally experienced as altered, in that they are less common for us. These States often have a self-confirming reality that speaks of the Divine. Altered or expanded States of Consciousness (ranging from contemplation to ecstasy) are often downplayed in progressive or mainline churches as compared with Charismatic or Pentecostal Churches. But expanded States can play a vital role in an emerging Integral Church. I invite you to explore the following questions as a beginning.

- Does your church foster altered or expanded States of Consciousness?
- If so, how are those altered states interpreted?
- Is it safe to experiment with expanded States of Consciousness?
- Are some altered states considered taboo, like speaking in tongues or entheogen[3] induced states?
- Are there opportunities and support for contemplative practices?

Generally, expanded States of Consciousness are what bring folks to church. They come for their "God fix," as some would say. Folks come to be moved in some way that suggests divine presence. In mainline Protestant churches, this comes via the sermon, music and prayers in emotional and rational forms (both Subtle States). Charismatic churches go directly for ecstatic emotion. In the mystery of the Latin Catholic mass, I have tasted Causal awareness. Taize (chanting) can open dream-like states in the upper Subtle. What will actually carry folks into more expanded States cannot be known for sure. It's common in my church for folks to tell me it was a good (or bad) service for wildly different reasons. Sometimes the perspectives and States of Consciousness expressed are so diverse I wonder if I was in the same service!

For Bob and Susan, worship-inspired altered states can create experiences that bind them together. Pentecostals and Charismatics clearly understand this. They are masters at creating altered states, like speaking in tongues, swooning, elation, and faith healings. Some of these States are very expansive. The downside is they are explained through very restrictive Worldviews (more about this later). Mainline and progressive Protestant churches are far more demure, but still offer altered states— glimpses of the divine—as confirmation of the existence of God. The Integral Church offers Susan and Bob tastes of expanded awareness and expansive explanations. Understanding that glimpses of the divine are always filtered through the lenses of our personal stories, offers a common ground for Bob and Susan to understand how they can touch the same reality yet experience it very differently.

Stages of Development

If an Integral Church is to provide a caring context for spiritual evolution through all the waves of development, then it must offer programs and activities that support and challenge individuals at each Stage of Development. In the following chapter I will present a variety of examples of programs from my church in Suquamish but, first, some general questions for consideration by your church.

- Is the full spectrum of levels of development represented … in programs? … in worship?

- Are there opportunities to experience faith from the perspective of each wave of development?
- Is there an appropriate balance of challenge and support to progress through the spectrum of consciousness?
- What programs support and nurture each wave of development? Magic? Warrior? Conformist? Achiever? Pluralist? Self-Actualized? Construct-Aware?
- Are some waves of development accepted more readily than others (some progressive churches have a very difficult time with the traditional orientation)?
- How can less honored developmental perspectives be respected?

If an Integral Church is to offer Susan and Bob support, it must provide a spectrum of opportunities to explore. This can be quite challenging, particularly for smaller churches. My church, for example, is relatively small with about 130 members and 70 to 80 active individuals. Despite our size, we provide a surprisingly expansive menu of opportunities to experience different perspectives. This is intentional. I have led from an Integral orientation since my arrival in 2002; but our expansive programming also reflects pre-existing structural components. Some of the intentional pieces include interfaith services, a modern/progressive bible study, and integral discussion groups. But it also includes more traditional practices like rummage sales, Thanksgiving and Christmas baskets, traditional hymns and a traditionally structured worship service. Bob and Susan would likely find discussion groups that would meet their different needs and aspirations. Over time, they would discover that worship moved across and celebrated different developmental perspectives.

Types

Gender, race, social class, sexual identity and personality can all shape the cultural mix of a church. The gay churches I have attended have a distinct character to them. African-American churches are conspicuously different from Anglo churches and upper-middle class churches are very different from working class churches. Churches have been referred to as the most segregated places in America on Sunday morning, not just by race, but by class and sexual identity as well. Some are even more extroverted than others (extrovert is a Type). This is not surprising. We look to our churches to support and confirm us in the most fundamental ways. It is natural to gravitate to those places that resonate with the cultural stories of our families that, in turn, are closely connected to race and class and, more recently, to sexual identity. This is not a bad thing. While much is gained by sharing across gender, class, race and identity lines, we also need to affirm our differences. Churches serving particular Types can still be Integral; and every church will include different Types. Imagine that Bob is African-American and Susan is Anglo. Can the church genuinely acknowledge the multitude of issues confronting Susan and Bob? The challenge of an Integral Church is to be inclusive of the Types that are present.

Types cut across the levels of development, Quadrants and Lines of Development. Men and women, as described previously, go through the same developmental stages, but women do so with an orientation toward relationship while men do so with an orientation toward autonomy. Similarly, a gay or lesbian individual will have a distinctive take as they move through the full developmental process. Looking at distinct populations within your congregation can help focus attention on populations that are underserved. Consider the following questions to help highlight populations you are serving well or possibly missing.

- Do you account for different perspectives based on gender, race, social class, sexual orientation, age, or personality type (e.g., Myers-Briggs or Enneagram)?
- Do you tend to emphasize some orientations more than others? For example: extravert? Gay? Elderly?
- Why do you emphasize some Types?

Quadrants and the 1-2-3 of God

In Chapter 2, I presented the Quadrants as the Big Three of I, We and It or the first, second and third person perspectives inherent in every event, activity or thought. If we are to use Integral Theory as a road map for the Integral Church, how do the Quadrants, or the Big Three show up and what questions do they demand? One way is in what Wilber calls the 1-2-3 of God: that is, relating to God as:

- Self: the core of my being, my true and essential nature (first person)
- Other: God as the great "Other" with whom I can be in relationship (second person)
- Nature: God as universe, the physical manifestation operating according to consistent laws of nature (third person)

If, as an Integral Church, we want to comprehend God as fully as possible, then at a bare minimum, we must consider God from these three perspectives.

Similarly, the Quadrants help raise questions with respect to programs. Does your church provide adequate opportunities for understanding and experiencing the Divine from first, second and third person orientations? Most churches do a great job of creating community and relating to the Divine as "Other." The language of traditional theology is theist and relating to God as "Other" is supported by both music and liturgy (Lower Left Quadrant). See Figure 5-1. Churches have also become socially active (Lower Right Quadrant) and emphasize action in the world. And most churches have some standard of behavior for their members (Upper Right). Ironically, the interior of the individual (Upper Left) is often neglected, in both traditional and progressive churches. This is the first person realization of oneness with the Divine ("the Father and I are one"). Until recently, the claim "I am God" would get you burned at the stake, literally or metaphorically. The point of being integrally informed as a church is to examine whether these different ways of encountering the divine are present. Choosing to emphasize one area over others is entirely up to your church; the point is to do so with full knowledge of the choices being made.

Below are some general questions organized by Quadrants (using all four Quadrants rather than the Big Three).

Upper Right Quadrant (Behavior: "It")

- What expectations for behavior do you hold?
- How are these expectations different for children, youth, teens and adults?
- Are programs or opportunities available for individuals to practice different kinds of behavior?

Figure 5-1: The Quadrants

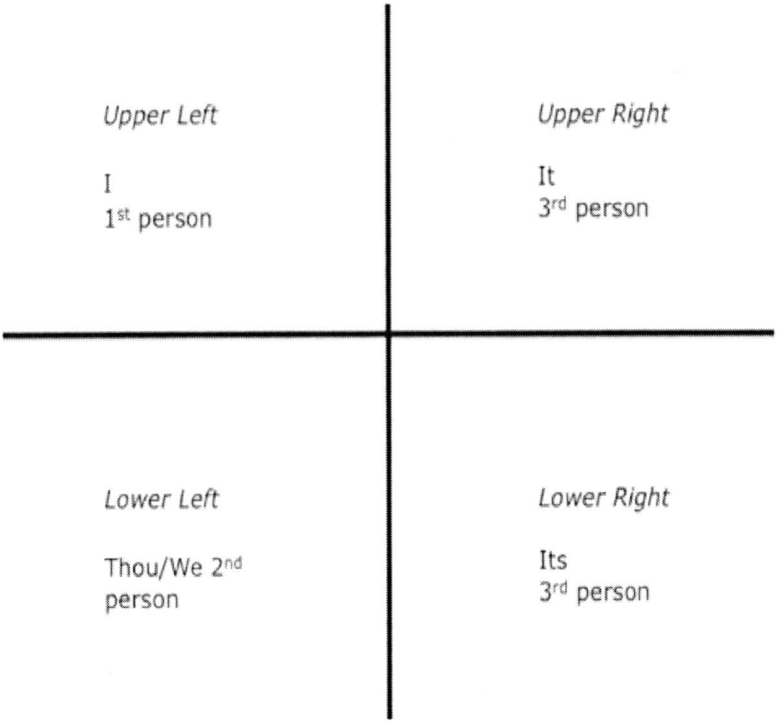

Upper Left	*Upper Right*
I	It
1st person	3rd person
Lower Left	*Lower Right*
Thou/We 2nd person	Its
	3rd person

For example:

- Personal health and fitness?
- Yoga
- Helping the elderly with household tasks?

Lower Right Quadrant (Social: "How the 'Its' fit")

- Does the church engage in social action?
- If so, what kind of social action do you engage in?
- Are some kinds of social action (e.g., peace marches) more acceptable than others?

Lower Left (Cultural: "We/Thou")

- What stories of Jesus are legitimate in your church?
- Are some stories more acceptable than others?
- Are faith stories of other religions welcomed in your church?
- How far from the mainstream can these stories deviate before they are considered unacceptable?

Upper Left Quadrant (Intention: "I")

- Do you engage in exploration of the individual interior?
- What techniques do you use?
- Is there encouragement for personal risk taking?
- What programs support personal exploration and development?

These questions are pivotal for Susan and Bob as they each seek to negotiate a new orientation in the world. Are there opportunities for Susan to investigate shadow dimensions of herself she previously avoided? As she uncovers dimensions of herself previously consider "unacceptable," are cultural and community stories available to support her? Do these stories have legitimacy within the church community? What actions are implied by these new understandings? Are there avenues for their expression?

Specifically, Susan may discover that (through the 3-2-1 process of Integral practice or Transformational Inquiry[4]) she studied the sciences because of family pressure to succeed in a predominantly male world. Perhaps, in the process of self-exploration, she rediscovers a passion for art previously considered trivial or unproductive. Is balanced community support available for her to follow through on this discovery? Such discoveries could motivate a variety of responses. Will she abandon her current career to pursue artistic endeavors? Will she retain an unfulfilling job just to support herself and her children? An integral orientation recognizes the importance of both paths. It understands the soul's drive for expression in art and the body's ongoing need for food, clothing and shelter. The Integral Church holds a story that supports this dilemma, not as a problem to be solved toward one polarity or the other, but as a reflection of our intrinsic complexity. Ideally, an Integral community would support Susan to stay in the paradox and allow an inclusive wisdom to emerge. That meta-story includes the Achiever dimension that wants prosperity and success for the family, and the Pluralist craving for unique personal expression.

In a similar fashion, the Integral Church does not deny Bob's Catholic roots, but offers an expansive story of the universe consistent with his scientific orientation. Brian Swimme and Thomas Berry's *The Universe Story* may provide a context supporting Bob as he sorts out a different way of understanding his world.

Creating a Map

If the church is to respond to Bob and Susan's needs, and others in need of understanding and direction, the church requires a map. In this section, I offer a simplified map of Integral Theory to help explore your church from an Integral perspective. It will help answer this question: Does your church offer the depth and breadth of programs, groups, activities and events to support folks in this complex and rapidly changing world?

In Figure 5-2, I have combined the Upper Right and Lower Right, "It/Its" Quadrants. To avoid undue complexity, the map includes only the Quadrants (as the Big Three: I, We, It/Its), Levels of Development and States of Consciousness. Combining these three components of Integral Theory offers a big picture for the church seeking to become more integral. Deeper insights can be added by looking at Lines of Development and Types that are served by your church. These are explored in the following section.

I hope you will use this map to consider your programs and how they contribute to the over all spiritual and personal development of your church community. In the next chapter I provide examples of how this map has been applied in the emerging Integral Church I pastor in Suquamish, WA. Remember that, while the map is useful, the real jewel is the conversations and understanding it elicits.

How to Fill In This Map

To be integrally informed, a church would generally want a good balance of programs across the full spectrum of development (Magic to Construct-Aware) and the Quadrants (I, We, It/Its), or, if it is not balanced, an understanding of why that is. This last point is important. An integrally informed church may not want to offer everything; it may want to focus, say, on social action or personal development. The map simply demands that the church be fully aware of the choices it is making. The Progressive church, for example, has emphasized social action, often at the expense of personal or spiritual development. I have heard Progressive Christians referred to as "Democrats with prayer."[5] This is not bad, per se, but social action is less effective if conducted without awareness of what is being sacrificed. At the other extreme, a Fundamentalist church may focus on personal development up to a particular Stage, say Warrior, then discourage movement beyond. In the unlikely event that such a church decided to become integrally informed[6], it would have to explain why it didn't encourage development beyond Warrior consciousness.

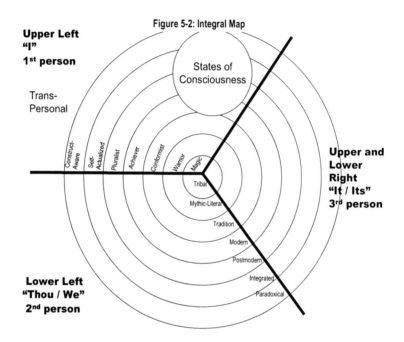

Figure 5-2: Integral Map

This map will help your church become more integrally informed. Populating it is quite simple. Let's walk through it, step by step.

First, take a look at each program, activity or event in your church. Begin by asking where it fits in the Big Three. Does it primarily serve the spiritual or psychological development of the individual, the interpersonal dynamics of the community or the broader society as a whole? Most programs will, of course, be relevant in more than one "Quadrant." A class on dynamic marriage, for example, will not only improve interpersonal relations ("We" Quadrant) but will also affect the personal understandings, emotions and identity of the individuals involved ("I" Quadrant). While any program will have relevance to each Quadrant, the map is most helpful if you place each program where it is *most* relevant. Thus, a class on dynamic marriage would go in the lower Left, interpersonal Quadrant, even though it has implications for the other realms.

Second, consider the developmental level or levels a program best supports. As an example, consider Christian education for young children, say ages four to six. Children inhabit a magical order of consciousness at this age. It is therefore developmentally appropriate to teach the basic faith stories as literally true: Moses parting the Red Sea, Jonah in the belly of the whale, and Jesus walking on water. These stories are primarily about the cultural stories guiding us as we collectively make meaning. Therefore, elementary Christian education belongs in the Lower Left Quadrant ("We"). And since it is appropriate to children at Magical consciousness, it is located in the innermost circle (purple, if we had color).

At the other end of the spectrum of development, consider a program focusing on personal development of the individual—say a class in faith formation. Such a program would be situated in the Upper Left Quadrant. Any program is likely to touch on two or more developmental levels depending on the nature of the class and the individuals involved. For example, a class focusing on the personal meaning of scripture interpreted by Modernist theologians (e.g., Marcus Borg and John Shelby Spong) would likely touch on the Conformist and Pluralist Stages of Development, but its center of gravity would be Achiever. We have such a class at my church. You will notice, on the map in the following chapter, it spans from upper Conformist to lower Pluralist.

Third, some programs or events don't really fit into the developmental schema as they are not intended to inspire permanent change. One example is a drumming circle. Collective drumming generally induces an altered State of Consciousness that fades when the drumming is over. Even though entering altered states can support emergence into new waves of development, the primary point of drumming is the expansive awareness experienced in that moment. As such it would be mapped in the States of Consciousness bubble in the Upper Left Quadrant.

As you map programs and events you will likely discover two important things. The first is success. You will quickly discover how much you are actually offering that is important to people's lives. Second, you will see the gaps in the overall integral picture. You may or may not want to fill all the gaps, but knowing where they are will bring greater integrity and coherence to the overall mission of your church. In the following chapter you will see the gaps we discovered at my church in Suquamish. The concluding chapter indicates how we are filling those program gaps.

How to Explore Types and Lines

Bringing in the greater specificity of Types and Lines helps refine your programs, events and even worship for the needs of your congregation and community. Consider, for example, mapping programs according to the line of development or intelligence on which they focus. Do programs cluster around a particular intelli-

138

gence? Perhaps your programs are mostly intellectual pursuits that emphasize the cognitive (thinking) line of development. Or maybe they are mostly "touchy feely" programs that emphasize the emotional line.

Similarly, you can evaluate the Types to which you cater. Are you primarily an upper, middle or lower economic class congregation? Are you predominantly black, white, Asian or of mixed races? Are you a young or old church? Are you a gay or straight church? More subtly, do you cater more to extroverts or is there a contemplative dimension that is appealing to introverts?

As mentioned, churches are often highly segregated, not just by racial Type, but by a variety of Types. This is not surprising since we are all drawn to our own Type when we want comfort; and we all want comfort in our church.[7] Being an Integral Church does not mean we have to cater to all Types; that is the blessing and curse of the Progressive church. Rather, being an integrally informed church requires cognizance of the Types of individuals we can best serve and not presuming that we can or should serve all Types[8].

Since every individual encompasses a variety of typologies, it is worthwhile to identify which Types dominate in your church so you can best serve your congregation and explore how greater (or lesser) diversity might serve your church community. Are you predominately a white,

---

Box 5-1
Review: Lines of Development

Differentiated Intelligences:

- Cognitive: *What am I aware of?*
- Self: *Who am I?*
- Values: *What is significant to me?*
- Moral: *What should I do?*
- Interpersonal: *How should we interact?*
- Intrapersonal: *What do I see when I look inside myself?*
- Spiritual: *What is of ultimate concern?*
- Needs: *What do I need?*
- Emotional: *How do I feel about this?*
- Kinesthetic: *How should I physically do this?*
- Aesthetic: *What is attractive to me?*
- Psycho-sexual: *What is the nature of my sexual identity?*
- Nature: *What is my relationship to the natural world?*
- Worldview: *How do I see the world around me?*

elderly upper class community? How might younger or poorer members be served while serving the larger congregation? Are you a gay church? How might more straight folks enrich your community? Are you trying to serve too many demographics? Would you be better off focusing on a particular Type and serving them better?

These are the questions and issues that emerge when we map the Integral Church. In the following chapter, I describe a number of programs from my own church and how this mapping shows up in a concrete situation.

Box 5-2
Review: Types

Horizontal difference at each level of development.

Examples:

- Race
- Gender
- Ethnicity
- Personality type
- Sexual orientation
- Class
- Lines of Development

Room to Roam and Integral Church

As mentioned, the church has limited tools to promote personal evolution through increasingly expansive Stages of Development. While we can offer programs that facilitate personal development, generally only a small percentage of churchgoers participate in these programs. And these programs are more effective if set within a broader context of support. That broader context is created in the church's ability to produce different States of Consciousness and articulate different Worldviews (Jesus Stories) appropriate to different Stages.

With this in mind, I now adapt the metaphor of *Room to Roam* to indicate how an Integral Church can more effectively support personal development and spiritual awakening. I have argued that the Integral Church has a particularly important role to play in the formation of consciousness in our world. In the West, the Christian church "owns" the great myths that create the context for development of our individual consciousness. As such, the church could have a vital role in offering and legitimating more expansive worldviews to support the evolution of individual awareness. This doesn't mean that action in the world isn't important. It is, but the distinctive role of the church primarily involves individual and collective consciousness[9]. Expansive States of Consciousness offer glimpses of the Divine. To the degree that the church creates opportunities to experience these expansive States, it encourages personal evolution through more embracing waves of development.

Given this orientation, I have modified Dr. O'Fallon's conception of *Room to Roam* (Figure 5-3, page 153) to highlight the tools available to the Integral Church in its endeavor to support personal development and spiritual awakening. Instead of Stages of Development on the left hand portion of the "V," I have listed the Worldviews that support the different Stages of Development. We are all on a journey from cradle to Christ-consciousness, and the way we get there is through increasingly expansive waves of development. The church has limited ability to shape those developmental waves directly, but we can create an environment that nurtures the evolution of individual awareness. We do this, of course, by offering "Jesus Stories" for different stages of the journey and by offering, encouraging and legitimating different States of Consciousness.

Using this model, we can illustrate the orientations of different churches (See graphics, pages 152-154). A Charismatic church, for example, can generate quite expanded States of Consciousness. These States are then translated through Mythic-Literal Stories such that the Room to Roam for an individual is as depicted in Figure 5-4 in the shaded area.

As reflected in Figure 5-5, a more conventional, mainline Protestant church will offer and legitimate a more expansive worldview (Traditional) but is likely to be much more circumspect in fostering altered States of Consciousness. An individual's Room to Roam in a Traditional, mainline church will be comparable to the Charismatic but have a significantly different profile as indicated in the shaded area.

A progressive church will have yet a different profile. The orientation of radical inclusivity shifts the Worldview toward Postmodern; but most progressive churches are even less comfortable with non-rational States of Consciousness than even the Traditional church as indicated in Figure 5-6.[10]

Why does this matter? The room where individual consciousness can roam is limited by the confluence of Worldview and State of Consciousness. Individual development is, on one hand, encouraged up to the limits of the shaded area on the graphs. On the other hand, development is discouraged beyond the shaded area. In the example in Figure 5-5, Pluralist personal development is encouraged by the Postmodern worldview, but not beyond. Without an Integrated Jesus story an individual is discouraged from developing beyond the Pluralist perspective. Similarly, when only Subtle (mental) States of Consciousness are supported and legitimated, transmental, mystical experiences will be discounted or denied. Since both Worldviews and States of Consciousness create the context in which personal development can occur, the more expansive the Room to Roam the greater the possibility for personal evolution.

In contrast to Charismatic, Traditional and Progressive churches, the potential of the Integral Church is greatly expanded as indicated in Figure 5-7. Ideally, the Integral Church fosters and supports the full spectrum of personal and spiritual development by offering both expanding Worldviews and States of Consciousness.

This *Room to Roam* map offers yet another tool for exploring opportunities to become a more integrally informed church. Try placing your church on the left wing of the V in the realm of the Worldviews you offer and validate. On the right wing of the V, indicate your church's comfort with different States of Consciousness.

We now have some basic tools for exploring how Integral your church may be at present. These tools are, as yet, quite abstract. In the next chapter I flesh out this model by applying it to my own church in Suquamish.

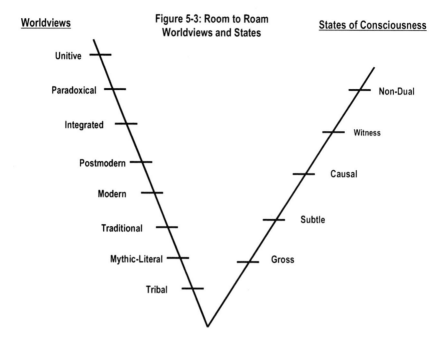

Figure 5-3: Room to Roam
Worldviews and States

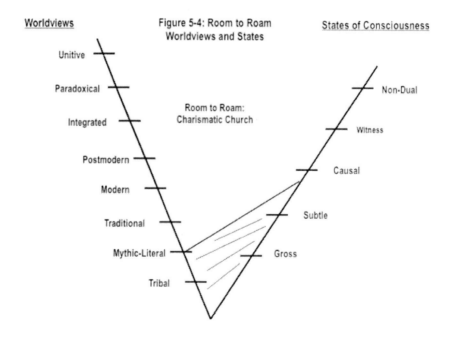

Figure 5-4: Room to Roam
Worldviews and States

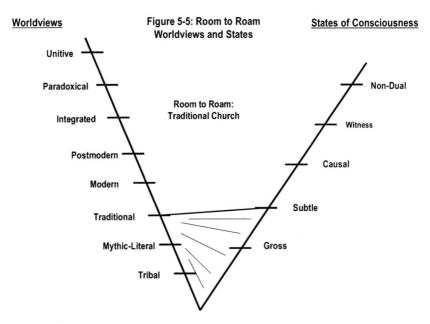

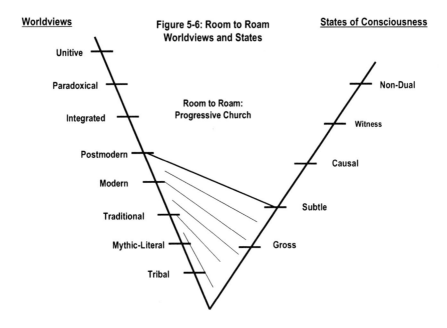

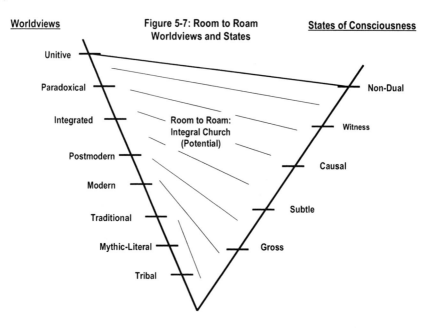

Figure 5-7: Room to Roam
Worldviews and States

Worldviews

- Unitive
- Paradoxical
- Integrated
- Postmodern
- Modern
- Traditional
- Mythic-Literal
- Tribal

Room to Roam:
Integral Church
(Potential)

States of Consciousness

- Non-Dual
- Witness
- Causal
- Subtle
- Gross

Notes

1 Wilber, Ken, *Integral Spirituality: A Startling New Role for Religion in the Modern and Postmodern World.* (Boston: Integral Books, 2006) 60.

2 The Subtle State of Consciousness includes the entire mental realm. We are normally quite accustomed to our emotions, thinking, and dreaming. I call these the lower Subtle. The higher Subtle would include psychic experiences, perception of archetypes, or lucid dreaming.

3 Entheogens are psychoactive substances used by indigenous, and other, cultures for millennia to open the doors of perception on the divine.

4 See Appendix E

5. Source unknown

6 I say it is unlikely that a fundamentalist church would want to become integrally informed because the Myth-Literal perspective sees in black and white terms, not systemic. Something like Integral Theory would be off the radar screen of the Mythic-Literal perspective.

7 In 1963 Dr. King gave a speech at Western Michigan University. During a question and answer session with the University President, Miller, Dr. King was asked, "Don't you feel that integration can only be started and realized in the Christian church ... ?" Dr. King's response in part was, "We must face the fact that in America, the church is still the most segregated major institution in America. At 11:00 on Sunday morning when we stand and sing and Christ has no east or west, we stand at the most segregated hour in this nation. This is tragic. Nobody of honesty can overlook this." This segregation continues today. See Racism Review: http://www.racismreview.com.

8 I am not suggesting that we should not welcome all Types. Rather, I am pointing to the practical dimensions of actually serving all Types. The Progressive church can fall into the trap of trying to serve everyone, then serving no one well. An Integral Church would certainly welcome all Types and encourage them to organize and flourish under its banner, but would avoid spreading itself too thin.

9 I'm probably getting myself in trouble with liberation theologians here who emphasize praxis: reflection and action. I agree that action is essential to the formation of consciousness. Still, I believe the church has a comparative advantage in personal and collective consciousness formation and hence should focus there.

10 The New Age movement tends to keep the Postmodern Story while simultaneously embracing non-rational, altered states, some of which are post-rational, others that are decidedly pre-rational. To the degree that the New Age promotes genuinely more expanded States of Consciousness the Room to Roam expands.

11 I'm probably getting myself in trouble with liberation theologians here who emphasize praxis: reflection and action. I agree that action is essential to the formation of consciousness. Still, I believe the church has a comparative advantage in personal and collective consciousness formation and hence should focus there.

12 The New Age movement tends to keep the Postmodern Story while simultaneously embracing non-rational, altered states, some of which are post-rational, others that are decidedly pre-rational. To the degree that the New Age promotes genuinely more expanded States of Consciousness the *Room to Roam* expands.

Chapter 6
Permission and Possibilities:
The Experience of an Emerging Integral Church

Are you afraid of new things? Well, take courage, we live on the playground of the Infinite…and the Infinite is always new. Remember how Emptiness has nothing to lose because it has no space, or time, or anything? It's just empty in ways we can't comprehend. While we take our lives seriously, Emptiness, Spirit, God does not. We're afraid of new things because we take ourselves seriously. We have this idea there is something to lose. We have this sense of self (which is real) and conclude that having a sense of self means we really are a self, separate from everything else. This creates all kinds of problems. Mostly, it scares us so we don't let ourselves play; we avoid new adventures. When we believe our self-sense is really an actual self, we think we have to protect who we are. We must show how capable we are, how athletic, how smart, how beautiful, how talented. We dare not look stupid unless it makes us popular. We can't look ugly unless it makes us look smart or cool. We don't try new things because we might look foolish.

The irony of human existence is we __must__ create this "self" that's afraid and doesn't want to play. We create it until it's time to dismantle it. We spend years becoming a self only to discover we have to take ourselves apart. By then, of course, that's the last thing we want to do! The point of building a self-sense is to take it apart. Such is Spirit at play!

When we're afraid we don't change, individually or collectively. We don't want our institutions to change, especially the ones we count on, like the church. We want our churches to preserve the wisdom of the past. And well they should…but not at the expense of the playful, ever-expanding present.

• • •

Now, more than ever, the West needs a *mature* Christianity. One that contributes moral and spiritual guidance in a world facing a multitude of crises: from terrorism to financial collapse, from poverty to global warming, from oil depletion to incessant war. Why? We are by nature spiritual and no solution suffices without including the spiritual. However, a spirituality, a religion, enmeshed in literalisms and dogma cannot serve this role. The church can only speak to these crises by offering increasingly expansive perspectives on our lives and the issues of the day. The religious traditions are best suited to inspire these expanding perspectives because they grew up with humanity and only these traditions have the legitimacy to point beyond themselves.

I invite you to envision church leaders standing side by side with leading scientists, artists, multinational executives and government leaders all proffering enlightened perspectives on the issues of the day. Imagine our most visible religious spokespersons *not* condemning the modern world from atop backward-pointing magical-mythical pulpits, but pointing forward as respected advisors in matters of the utmost importance. Imagine congregations across the country actively challenging Christianity to "grow-up" into its modern, postmodern and integral possibilities. Imagine a catechism leading the way into increasingly expansive ways of knowing and leading in the world. There's a startling vision for the 21st century church!

Our destiny is Christ-consciousness. The awakened ones tell us the realization of our Christhood, our Buddha nature, the Tao, is inevitable. That's good news, but not for the ego. The good news for the ego is that how we get there matters. Paradoxically, the *persona* we create on our journey to eventually disidentify with our *persona* is integral to our full awakening in and as the Christ. No step into more expansive consciousness is complete without that consciousness manifesting in the world. And everything we manifest in the world is mediated by the *persona* we have constructed. To use Wilber's analogy of a guitar we may pluck the strings of Spirit (taste the divine), but their resonance depends upon the quality of the sound box (our *persona*).

The Integral Church is the vehicle for nurturing our journey from infancy into our Christhood. It does so by creating a conveyor belt for the evolution of consciousness[1]. The Integral Church supports us through more expansive ways of knowing and being by creating a legitimate context for our personal and collective spiritual development, by offering and legitimating stories for all phases of the journey, by creating programs and experiences that offer tastes of consciousness beyond our current comprehension, by creating safe places to take chances, by offering a map by which we can orient ourselves, by helping us to laugh at ourselves and by encouraging us to play. In these ways the Integral Church nurtures us all along our journey from cradle to Christ.

• • •

In this chapter, I explore how the church I pastor in Suquamish is exploring the possibilities of Integral Church. This is a truly humbling endeavor. While there is tremendous need in our culture for faith voices to move beyond tradition and carry us through all the stations of life, we are just scratching the surface of what an Integral

Church can be. Despite having an outstanding map in Integral Theory, we find our church in new territory very quickly. It feels like we are scouts exploring a new path of faith in the Christian terrain. The attitude we bring to this endeavor is of the utmost importance, for it creates the context in which an Integral Church emerges. We describe that attitude as "permission and possibilities." I will explore this in the next section, but first some context.

Suquamish Community Congregational United Church of Christ is located in northwestern Washington, just across Puget Sound from Seattle. It is a medium sized church located in a low to middle income community. The town is woven together with the Port Madison Indian reservation and the Suquamish Tribe. Until recently, the tribe was poor and scattered, but a successful casino is rapidly altering the community. The tribe is very civic-minded as it seeks to improve both the wellbeing of tribal members and the community as a whole. Suquamish, the ancestral home of Chief Seattle, is an anomaly as it is surrounded by commuter communities ranging from upper middle income to very wealthy. The church is 90 years old and has roughly 130 members; half are actively involved. We are predominantly Caucasian, highly educated with many in the teaching and healing professions. It is a very progressive church in a conservative region. Consequently, we draw from a large area, with some folks traveling 40 miles or more every Sunday. As this community becomes more prosperous, more folks are attracted locally. The congregation is predominantly in their 50's to mid 60's with a wonderful contingent of younger families and wise elders. More than two-thirds of the members are women: strong, independent and highly capable.

The church has a deep sense of continuity. Some members have been there 50+ years, many for 15 to 30 years. The previous pastor was there for 22 years, his predecessor for 14 years. As of this writing I have been pastor for seven years and hope to continue for many more.

My orientation to church and faith has been deeply shaped by the integral perspective. I have used the lens of Integral Theory as a guide since my arrival in 2002. In 2007, I formally introduced the idea of Integral Church and it was well received by the congregation. As with any fundamental shift, the ideas have become sufficiently integrated to stir questions, doubt and enthusiasm simultaneously. I consider this to be just the right context in which probing questions can be asked and the reality of Integral Church explored.

The Dynamics of an Integral Community

A wonderful metaphor from systems theory illuminates the dynamics of this community, but first a useful distinction is in order. The distinction is between *com-*

plicated systems and *complex* systems. A *complicated* system has lots of rules to guide it. Governments, schools, corporations, the legal system and medicine are *complicated* systems. In contrast, a *complex* system has a few very dynamic rules. Every institution (and every church) is a mix of both *complicated* and *complex* systems.

As an Integral Church, we are interested in both the *complicated* and *complex* systems that comprise the whole. That is, both the dynamic meaning-making culture (the *complex* system) and the institutional structure of constitutions, bylaws and committees (the *complicated* system) are essential. That said, my focus in this section is on the dynamics of the culture that support changes in the institutional structure as the Integral Church emerges. What implicit rules maintain a *complex* system while the institutional form is evolving?

The metaphor I use for the *complex* system that guides the church is a flock of geese flying in a V formation[2].

A flock follows three pretty simple rules:

- Fly to the center
- Match your speed to the goose next to you
- Don't hit another goose

These simple, dynamic rules are sufficient for a flock to fly together, to shift leaders, and to move ahead. The analogy to Integral Church is obvious:

- *Fly to the center*: Attend to the Divine—the center of our being. As Jesus said, "Seek ye first the kingdom of God…"
- *Match your speed to that of another goose*: Be present. As Crosby, Stills and Nash said in the 70's, "If you can't be with the one you love, love the one you're with."
- *Don't hit another goose*: Don't take yourself seriously. Have you noticed when you're dealing with a rigid person, and you both take yourselves seriously, it's like crashing into one other? But if you deal with someone who knows the fiction of *me* to be a fiction and they don't take themselves seriously, it can be a delightful dance.

Not surprisingly, these three dynamic rules mesh beautifully with the great commandment: "Love God with all of you heart, mind and spirit, and your neighbor as yourself."[3] To love God with all our heart, mind, soul, and spirit is to fly to the center. To attend to the Divine at the center of your being. The next part of the commandment blends two of our rules, match your speed to the goose beside you (be present) and don't hit another goose (don't take yourself seriously). These are summarized in the injunction to "love your neighbor as yourself." In being fully present to whomever you are with and not taking yourself seriously, love of neighbor emerges spontaneously.

Hence, the practice of Integral Church begins with attention to the dynamics of community that will sustain it as moves more intentionally toward integral. Again, these are:

- Attend to the Divine (*fly to the center*)
- Be present (*match your speed to that of another goose*)
- And, above all, do not take yourself seriously (*don't hit another goose*).

When we keep these dynamic *complex* rules at the center of our attention, the complicated institutional rules emerge gracefully and appropriately. These dynamic rules are the core of our culture of "permission and possibilities."

The culture of permission and possibilities shows up at Suquamish Church as a broadly based and deeply ingrained sense of playfulness. Individuals are readily encouraged to take personal risks, whether by stretching their talent in choir or musical performances, preaching before the congregation, exploring hidden assumptions or confronting deeply engrained beliefs. There is a profound sense of safety in this culture primarily, I believe, because most of us are able to step back and laugh at ourselves. The living example of individuals being sincere, but not serious, gives permission for others to experiment with possibilities in their lives. So, as we have embarked on this journey into Integral Church, we are supported by an expansive orientation to the divine, a surprisingly widespread willingness to listen to one another and a good sense of humor.

Mapping Programs

Figure 6-1 repeats the map created at the end of Chapter 5. (See pages 178-181 for figures 6-1 through 6-5.) We will fill in this map for Suquamish Church as I describe the different programs we offer.

One of the great potentials of the Integral Church is its capacity to offer programs that span the Stages of Development, utilize and support different Developmental Lines, allow different Types to contribute, experience different States of Consciousness and to experience God as self, other and nature. In practice, any particular program will tend to span several different levels, engage different Lines and appeal to various Types. In using the integral model we both celebrate our achievements and identify gaps in our offerings. The goal is to offer a full spectrum of programs, activities and practices to accommodate folks on their spiritual/human journeys. In the following pages, I outline the programs at Suquamish Church and how we are beginning to fill in the Integral Map (Figure 6-1).

There are two major benefits of creating this map. One benefit is a map's capacity to demonstrate existing strengths of the church while highlighting missing elements. A more significant benefit of an Integral Map is the conversation it motivates. The mere discussion of a program's placement on the Integral Map expands awareness and a community becomes more integrally informed.

As you explore placement of your church's programs on the Integral Map, it becomes obvious each program or event touches a variety of elements across the Quadrants, Levels and Lines. I encourage you to place a program in only one place on the map. Find the center of gravity or primary focus of the program by its Quadrant and place it there. For example, we placed the choir at the traditional level in the It/Its or third person Quadrant because it is part of the church's social practice having deep roots in our Christian tradition (Figure 6-2). At the same time, choir members report how singing requires them to stretch beyond their comfort levels and how they have grown from this experience; I also hear how choir enhances relationships and nurtures a deeper "we" space (Lower Left Quadrant). This highlights both the strength and weakness of any map. Any experience, like choir, has correlates in all Quadrants and our placement is somewhat arbitrary. Placing a program in all Quadrants would, of course, negate the purpose of a map. The demand to place a program in only one Quadrant confers important benefits. First, it motivates thoughtful conversation and invites greater integral awareness. Second, forcing each program into only one slot quickly illuminates where the focus and gaps are in an Integral Church program. Our mapping of Suquamish Church has motivated a whole new outreach discussed in the concluding chapter.

Box 6-1
Review: Developmental Lines

- **Cognitive:** *What am I aware of?*
- **Self:** *Who am I?*
- **Values:** *What is significant to me?*
- **Moral:** *What should I do?*
- **Interpersonal:** *How should we interact?*
- **Intrapersonal:** *What do I see inside myself?*
- **Spiritual:** *What is of ultimate concern?*
- **Needs:** *What do I need?*
- **Emotional:** *How do I feel about this?*

In the sections below I will describe a number of programs at Suquamish Church and how they fulfill the larger goal of Integral Church to provide a full spectrum of opportunities to grow in the first, second and third persons of God. A few points to remember as we make use of the map developed in the previous chapters:

1. The concentric circles represent the Stages of Development, the perspectives, available to us on our journey.
2. The map is divided into Quadrants reformed into the Big Three: the Upper Left ("I" or 1st person perspective); Lower Left ("We" or 2nd person perspective); and the Right Hand Quadrants (the Upper Right and Lower Right Quadrants combined; 3rd person perspective or "It/Its").
3. Space is included for programs intended to initiate more expanded States of Consciousness.
4. Lines of development (intelligences) are indicated in parentheses as they apply to a particular program.

You will notice that worship is absent from this map. Worship serves a spectrum of roles in the church and must span all the Quadrants, Stages and Lines in some manner. I will address worship in the Appendix. It is also clear that small and medium sized churches are limited in their programming. An Integral Church balances competing demands. On the one hand, clarity of purpose and close attention to relative strengths will help focus energies as revealed by mapping your church. On the other hand, a church of any size can retain the flexibility to allow congregants to self-organize and birth new programs.

TAGS

An important program in the Suquamish Church is called TAGS: Talking About God Stuff. The format of TAGS is very simple. We watch a video, stop it whenever an interesting point arises and see where the conversation goes. The most popular videos come from cosmologist Brian Swimme. Swimme, along with philosopher Thomas Berry, is author of *The Universe Story*. These videos, *Canticle to the Cosmos*[4], and *Powers of the Universe*[5] offer incredibly rich material for discussions of the interface between science and religion, the nature of our universe, and our personal meaning cosmologies. Swimme's is the finest example of a third person discussion of God I have encountered.

Though a year may be spent on a series by Brian Swimme, TAGS has met weekly for nearly six years, in two different groups, and explored a variety of teachers. Theologians Marcus Borg and John Spong bring a contemporary, progressive, second person orientation to Deity. The popular spiritual teacher, Eckhart Tolle and Zen teachers Adyashanti and Genpo Roshi bring first person perspectives and mythologist Joseph Campbell offers yet another second person perspective. Our conversations span faith stories, good and evil, the nature of time, free will and much more, and generally connect with wisdom from the Christian tradition. The fundamental spirit of the group is playful trust that allows deep questioning. For more about this very successful program see Appendix D. When it comes to placing TAGS on the map of the Integral Church, there are a number of considerations. Our conversations are primarily intellectual, so it clearly serves development of the cognitive line. Even though conversations focus on cosmology, the natural sciences and brain research, which are all third person orientations to the Divine Mystery (God as impersonal object), we are actually refining and critiquing the stories that give our lives meaning. This situates TAGS in the Lower Left Quadrant.

Box 6-2
Review: Quadrants as the Big Three

Upper Left Quadrant
- Interior of the Individual
- What is it like to be me?
- Intention
- 1st person perspective: the view from inside the individual

Lower Left Quadrant
- Interior of the Collective
- Who are we together?
- Culture
- 2nd person perspective: the view from within the group

Rifht Hand Quadrants
- Combines Upper Right and Lower Right Quadrants
- Exterior of the individual and the collective
- What is It? How do the Its fit together?
- Behavior and nature
- 3rd person perspective, the view from outside the individual and the group
- Types are not specifically mapped since they tend to cut across all the dimensions with their particular flavor. They are indicated when relevant to particular programs.

A remarkable depth of thought emerges from TAGS conversations. Much of it begins from a scientific, rational orientation (Achiever/Modern) and quickly expands to questions about the reliability of rationality as the primary means of knowing, which leads to questions from cultural or ecological perspectives (Pluralist/

Postmodern). Eventually, the question will be raised about how all these issues fit together in a global perspective and the conversation shifts to the Self-Actualized wave of perception. It is not uncommon for a collective intelligence to emerge where we momentarily taste Construct-Awareness. As these explorations generally include implications for caring and compassion, the spiritual line is also engaged. In Figure 6-3, I placed TAGS in the Lower Left Quadrant, spanning developmental stages from Modern/Achiever (Orange) to Paradoxical/Construct-Aware (Turquoise). Notice that I have included the cognitive and spiritual Lines of Development in parentheses.

TAGS: primary orientations

- Line(s) of Development: cognitive, spiritual
- Quadrant: Lower Left, 2nd person
- Level(s) of Development: Modern/Achiever, Postmodern/Pluralist, Integrated/Self-Actualized.
- State(s) of Consciousness: predominantly gross and subtle
- Types: neutral

Transformational Inquiry

Four years ago we began a program of personal development we called Transformational Prayer (later expanded to Transformational Inquiry). We adapted the work of Harvard developmental psychologists Robert Kegan and Lisa Laslow Lahey (*How the Way We Talk Can Change the Way We Work*[6]) into a powerful contemplative process for personal change. The Kegan/Lahey process involves four steps of discovery of our Big Assumptions. Big Assumptions comprise the implicit structure of our personal meaning-making system, the source of our identity. They are called Big Assumptions because: 1) they are generally invisible to our conscious awareness, 2) they are unexamined because they are considered true, and 3) they are *Big* because they generally run our lives. Using language as our vehicle for self-exploration, we first ask, "What frustrates you?" Or, "What complaint do you have?" Or, "What is something you would like to change?" The first shift is to recognize you wouldn't complain or want to change if you didn't have a deeply held *positive* commitment. The second question asks, "What do you do or not do that keeps this commitment from being fully realized?" In other words, what is your personal responsibility, i.e., what actions do you take to keep your positive commitment from happening? Unlike most self-help programs, which stop with the discovery of personal responsibility, the Kegan/Lahey process moves deeper into our human complexity to ask, "What else might I be committed to?" Typically, these competing commitments are self-protective commitments we don't tell others about (like "I am committed to having things my way" or "I am committed to avoiding conflict at all costs"). Going still deeper, we mine these competing commitments for the Big Assumptions upon which they rest…the foundational beliefs forming our identity. While Kegan and Lahey use this approach to uncover invisible Big Assumptions and initiate a process of slowly altering those assumptions, we use the discovery process itself as a transformative practice. Essentially, we spread each step into a weeklong practice that elicits many valuable insights.

Transformational Inquiry is an expansion of Transformatioal Prayer. Transformational Prayer is generally a six or seven week small group process. Inquiry involves a weekly commitment for six months. We add to Kegan/Lahey the immensely powerful work of Byron Katie[7]. Katie's deceptively simple process asks four questions about any stressful thought: Is it true? Can you know with absolute certainty that it is true? How do you react when you hold the belief that this thought is true? And who would you be if you couldn't have the thought? Then turn the thought around by exploring different forms of its opposite. Katie's four questions are then focused on the Big Assumptions unearthed by Kegan/Lahey. In particular, these questions are focused on the *evidence* for the truth of the Big Assumption. See Appendix E for a full explanation of Transformational Inquiry.

Permeating this six-month endeavor is a westernized spiritual practice that I developed based on my work with a Native shaman. It is very simple: do some kind of exercise each day while listening to a recording of an awakened person. We use Eckhart Tolle's *The Power of Now*[8] as the primary tool and Katie's *Loving What Is*[9] during that portion of the class. Participants are asked to listen to the recordings all the way through, and repeat listening all the way through, over and over. It is not so much the content as the experience of being drawn into a higher order of consciousness that is transformative.

The work of Transformational Inquiry and Prayer is focused directly on the first person experience of the Divine. As we investigate and inquire into the mental/egoic structures that filter the world for us, the world opens. Increasingly we come to see the world as it is, with fewer and fewer filters. This is one effort to "not do as Jesus did, but to see what he saw." For all these reasons, Transformational Inquiry is mapped in the Upper Left Quadrant, spanning Achiever to Self-Actualized levels of development (See Figure 6-4). I invite you to study Appendix E so that you can use Transformational Inquiry in your church.

Transformational Inquiry: primary orientations

- Line(s) of Development: self, values, intrapersonal, emotional
- Quadrant: Upper Left, 1st person
- Level(s) of Development: Modern/Achiever, Postmodern/Pluralist, Integrated/Self-Actualized.
- State(s) of Consciousness: subtle to causal
- Types: neutral

Faith Formation Study Group

We are very fortunate to have a retired UCC minister as a dedicated member of our congregation. Every Sunday morning, Ed Evans teaches in the tradition of contemporary progressive theology to about dozen people. Using theologians like Marcus Borg, John Dominic Crossin and Bishop John Shelby Spong, Ed offers the Modern/Achiever perspective on biblical literature. This does not mean folks in this group are *at* the Achiever level, rather it is a story from this developmental perspective that individuals inhabit while they participate in this class. This perspective is wonderfully summarized in a series of programs entitled *Living the Questions,* which we have also used in TAGS. The orientation, keeping with the orientation of the historical church, is strongly second person: God as other. We consider this a vitally important addition to the integral programs we offer. While this group explores personal values, its focus on the meaning stories of the Modern perspective recommends it to the Lower Left, "We" Quadrant, Modern level. This is one of those programs that could also be attributed to the Upper Left, "I" Quadrant. See Appendix C for more complete discussion of our Faith Formation Study Group. This and the following programs are indicated on our church's comprehensive map (Figure 6-5).

Faith Formation Study Group: primary orientations

- Line(s) of Development: cognitive, spiritual, values
- Quadrant: Lower Left, 2nd person
- Level(s) of Development: Modern/Achiever
- State(s) of Consciousness: gross and subtle
- Types: neutral

Call to Care

Call to Care is a group dedicated to caring for others. They respond to people in crisis or those just needing some loving support. Call to Care is particularly important because it fulfills a traditional and vital role of the church that is not part of my calling or strengths. By inhabiting this traditional perspective and living its richness, this group offers essential services, meets personal needs and offers a realm of traditional practice very meaningful to the congregation.

Call to Care: primary orientations

- Line(s) of Development: interpersonal
- Quadrant: Lower Left, 2nd person
- Level(s) of Development: Traditional/Conformist
- State(s) of Consciousness: causal
- Types: neutral

Another traditional practice that serves the church and the community is the Rummage Sale. This is a bi-annual event engaging more than a dozen members of the congregation. It is significant because the Rummage Sale attracts folks who are not attracted to other church programs. For about a week our social halls are filled with clothes, household items, electronics, you name it, all at bargain prices. The church makes money, folks on limited income in our community find deals on things they need and individuals give of their time and gifts. This is one of those lower right Quadrant activities, action in the world from a traditional/conformist orientation. This does not mean that the folks who participate find their center of gravity at traditional/ conformist, only that they choose to inhabit this perspective during the time of the Rummage Sale, perhaps to renew that dimension of their life.

Rummage Sale: primary orientations

- Line(s) of Development: interpersonal
- Quadrant: Right Hand, 3rd person
- Level(s) of Development: Traditional/Conformist
- State(s) of Consciousness: gross
- Types: neutral

Many Stories ... One Community

What we call "Many Stories ... One Community" is an explicitly Postmodern/Pluralist endeavor. It involves periodic, interfaith services with Native American, Buddhist, Baha'i and Jewish faiths and Dances for Universal Peace. The Native shaman (who is also a Christian minister) may tell a Christian story from the native perspective. The Buddhist monk loves to sing African-American spirituals. The Baha'i share prophesies and a Middle Eastern perspective. And the Jews tell fabulous stories. Dances for Universal Peace brings folks into various circle dances from different faiths. "Many Stories ... One Community" offers a different set of faith stories (lower left Quadrant) from the postmodern/pluralist perspective. Inevitably, after each event, someone will come to me and say "Now that's church!"

Many Stories...One Community: primary orientations

- Line(s) of Development (Intelligence): interpersonal, spiritual
- Quadrant: Lower Left, 2nd person
- Level(s) of Development: Postmodern/Pluralist
- State(s) of Consciousness: gross to causal
- Types: neutral

Earth Stewardship ... Graciously Green Group

Earth Stewardship again represents the Pluralist perspective, but this time from the lower right, social action Quadrant. Recently, this group created a Green and Global Faire that was a great success in our community. Projects are still flowing from this endeavor.

Earth Stewardship: primary orientations

- Line(s) of Development: cognitive
- Quadrant: Right Hand, 3rd person
- Level(s) of Development: Postmodern/Pluralist
- State(s) of Consciousness: gross and subtle
- Types: neutral

Medicine Wheel

Our church is surrounded by the Port Madison Indian Reservation, so cross cultural issues are a constant presence. Since 2002, we have been host to the on-going teachings of the Medicine Wheel. Ironically, this teaching is not associated with the Suquamish Tribe but the Cowlitz tribe a hundred miles to the south. It offers a wonderfully different cultural meaning story (Lower Left Quadrant) at both the postmodern and integral levels. Grandfather Roy Wilson weaves together wisdom from Christian, Native, Jewish and Muslim faiths through the metaphor of the medicine wheel.

Medicine Wheel: primary orientations

- Line(s) of Development: cognitive, emotional,
- Quadrant: Lower Left, 2nd person
- Level(s) of Development: Postmodern/Pluralist
- State(s) of Consciousness: subtle
- Types: neutral

Women's Book Club

The Women's book club consists of women meeting monthly to discuss an agreed upon book. It is highlighted here because it is directed specifically to a *Type...* women. A comparable event, though not as sophisticated, is the Sages breakfast, where a handful of old farts get together every two weeks to solve the world problems.

Women's Book Club: primary orientations

- Line(s) of Development (Intelligence): cognitive, interpersona
- Quadrant: Lower Left, 2nd person
- Level(s) of Development: Modern/Achiever, Postmodern/Pluralist
- State(s) of Consciousness: gross and subtle
- Types: female

Meditation

A small group meets each week to meditate together. Each individual engages in his or her own practice after a brief ritual. The intent is to be still and directly experience what is. Some folks use techniques learned elsewhere, others merely listen within. It is typical for individuals to experience inner peace and expanded states of awareness, though this is not necessary for a successful meditation. The premise of our meditation is the more often one experiences expanded or higher States of Consciousness, the more readily they move from one level of development to the next. Since expanded States of Consciousness experienced in meditation are transient they are placed in the States of Consciousness circle in the Upper Left Quadrant.

Meditation: primary orientations

- Line(s) of Development (Intelligence): spiritual
- Quadrant: Upper Left, 1st person
- Level(s) of Development: inclusive
- State(s) of Consciousness: subtle to non-dual
- Types: all

Choir

Our choir offers a much loved tradition for worship. Therefore, it is an activity in the world (Right Hand Quadrants) at the level of Tradition. Some use choir and its related activities, like talent shows and concerts, as an opportunity for personal growth by stepping out of their comfort zone for an audience of friends and strangers alike. Several report expanded States of Consciousness as they engage the music, particularly during performances.

Choir: primary orientations

- Line(s) of Development (Intelligence): interpersonal
- Quadrant: Right Hand, 3rd person

•Level(s) of Development: Traditional/Conformist
• State(s) of Consciousness: subtle and causal
• Types: all

Enlightenment Intensive

Enlightenment Intensives, as the name suggests, are not part of the traditional church venue. They emerge from an Eastern tradition and are led by friends of the church with our support. In a retreat setting, individuals practice an intensive reflection process for three, sometimes up to seven, days. In dyads, folks explore one of the following questions for the entire retreat: *Who am I? What am I? What is another?* These are the vehicles for entering expanded States of Consciousness and increasing the possibility of a direct experience of the Divine. Again, since the states attained during the Enlightenment Intensive are transient, it is placed in the States of Consciousness circle in the Upper Left Quadrant.

Enlightenment Intensive: primary orientations

• Line(s) of Development: cognitive, intrapersonal, emotional, self, spiritual
• Quadrant: Upper Left, 1st person
• Level(s) of Development: inclusive
• State(s) of Consciousness: subtle to non-dual
• Types: all

Christian Education

We seek to make our Christian education (CE) programs developmentally appropriate for all our children. The primary task of CE is the enculturation of our youngsters into the foundational stories of the faith. It is all about coming together to create collective understanding and shared meaning that will guide our lives, hence it is indicated in the Lower Left, "We" Quadrant. All of our CE programs focus on the same Lines of Development: cognitive, interpersonal, values, moral and spiritual. Where the programs vary is according to the developmental stage of the children. Our youngest children are taught the stories of the *Bible* in all their magical, miraculous splendor. Stories are taught as literally true, just as we tell our young children that Santa Claus and the Tooth Fairy are real. As they enter middle school age, they begin to question the stories, just as they begin to doubt Santa Claus. Their questions are not discouraged, nor are they encouraged; they are merely present in the class setting. The focus in middle school years (Mythic-Literal/Warrior) is on appropriate behavior. As our children move into their teen years, more questions arise and these are supported. In the liberal context of our church, the questions often revolve around the miraculous events and authenticity of the Bible. While the questions ring of Modern/Achiever, they emerge from the milieu of peers and typically reflect the overwhelming desire of teens to fit in. So, even though the questions sound modern in their orientation, teens are nonetheless deeply engaged in the appropriate developmental tasks of their age, becoming socialized in their cultural milieu, a Traditional/Conformist orientation.

Young children (4-7): primary orientations

- Line(s) of Development (Intelligence): cognitive, interpersonal, values, moral, spiritual
- Quadrant: Lower Left, 2nd person
- Level(s) of Development: Magic
- State(s) of Consciousness: gross
- Types: all

Middle Children (7-11): primary orientations

- Line(s) of Development (Intelligence): cognitive, interpersonal, values, moral, spiritual
- Quadrant: Lower Left, 2nd person
- Level(s) of Development: Warrior
- State(s) of Consciousness: gross
- Types: all

Teens: primary orientations

- Line(s) of Development (Intelligence): cognitive, interpersonal, values, moral, spiritual
- Quadrant: Lower Left, 2nd person
- Level(s) of Development: Conformist
- State(s) of Consciousness: gross into subtle
- Types: all

Mapping Quadrants, Stages and States

All of this information comes together in two comprehensive maps and a table. The first map (Figure 6-5) uses Quadrants, Stages of Development, and States of Consciousness to give a bird's-eye view of the distribution of programs at Suquamish Church. Lines of Development (e.g., cognitive, moral, spiritual) are indicated in parentheses then organized by Intelligence in Table 6-1. The Room to Roam diagram (Figure 6-7) indicates the developmental space supported by Suquamish church.

Several things stand out in this map. First, there is only one program in the Upper Left Quadrant, the realm of personal development. Even though Transformational Inquiry is a far-reaching program, the map reveals it as the only program aimed directly at personal change. The map clarifies that efforts to become more integrally informed are focused primarily on presenting and legitimating Jesus stories (Lower Left Quadrant). In other words, our focus is on creating context rather than directly taking on personal evolution.

Second, the programs that create this context are concentrated in the Modern/ Achiever and Postmodern/Pluralist waves of development. In particular, the Traditional/Conformist perspective is lacking. And, like many progressive churches, we find it difficult to integrate this perspective.

Third, our actions in the world (Right Hand Quadrants) have been sparse and focused on traditional activities. This is largely intentional as the congregation wanted to back off from social justice work to nurture their individual interiors. Still, it presents a challenge for us as we seek to be more Integral.

Mapping Lines of Development

Table 6-1 indicates how various programs of Suquamish Church align with different Lines of Development. Two Lines stand out: Values and Morals. One would expect a church to say a lot about values and morality, most Mythic-Literal and Traditional churches do. The Progressive church, in contrast, finds the imposition of values or morals repugnant. The Integral Church emerges from the Progressive church and struggles with the value relativism so characteristic of the Postmodern/Pluralist wave of development. An important challenge for an emerging Integral Church is moving beyond this relativism to articulate values and morals consistent with Integral awareness.

Room to Roam

As I have indicated, a primary objective of the Integral Church is to create psychological, emotional and spiritual space where individual consciousness can evolve. We do this, in part, by articulating and legitimating Worldviews (Jesus stories) to support each wave of development from Magic to Trans-personal awareness. We also do this by offering tastes of the divine in expanded States of Consciousness. As indicated by the crosshatched area in

Table 6-3
Lines of Development

Cognitive, thinking: *What am I aware of?*	TAGS, Faith Formation, Earth Stewardship, Medicine Wheel, Women's Book Club
Self: *Who am I?*	Transformational Inquiry, Enlightenment Intensive, Meditation
Moral: *What should I do?*	Christian Education
Interpersonal: *How should we interact?*	Many Stories … , Call to care, Rummage Sale, Women's Book Club, Christian Education, Choir
Intrapersonal: *What do I see when I look inside?*	Transformational Inquiry, Enlightenment Intensive
Spiritual: *What is of ultimate concern?*	TAGS, Faith Formation, Many Stories … , Meditation, Enlightenment Intensive, Christian Education
Needs: *What do I need?*	Earth Stewardship
Emotional: *How do I feel about this?*	Transformational Inquiry, Medicine Wheel, Enlightenment Intensive

Figure 6-6, the Integral Church seeks to offer a vast and well-supported space for consciousness to roam.

How is my church in Suquamish doing? We were not surprised to find a rather lopsided configuration (Figure 6-7). As I have led this church from an Integral orientation since my arrival, we celebrate a full spectrum of Worldviews in worship, in programming, and in special events. However, like most Protestant denominations we are decidedly uncomfortable with altered states, especially if they look Charismatic or Pentecostal. I don't know if we can change worship significantly, though we may make strides in developing more contemplative practices.

With these maps, and the information they summarize, we have very powerful tools for becoming more integrally informed. In becoming integrally informed we create the best possible setting for our congregations to evolve personally and, hence, collectively. As we become more Integral, we reclaim our rightful role as purveyors of the divine from cradle to Christ-consciousness.

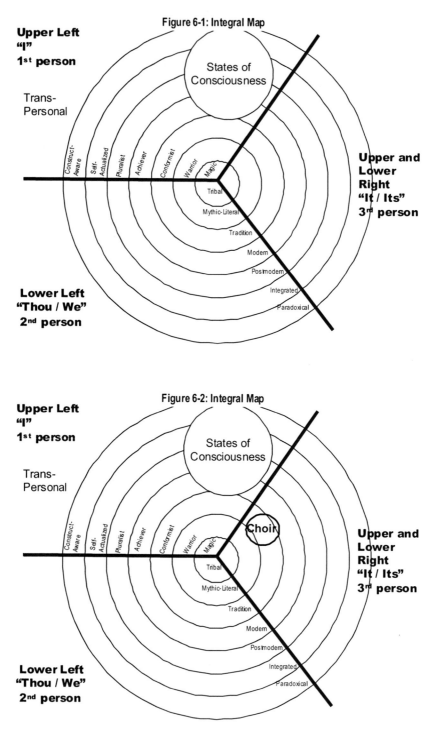

Figure 6-1: Integral Map

Figure 6-2: Integral Map

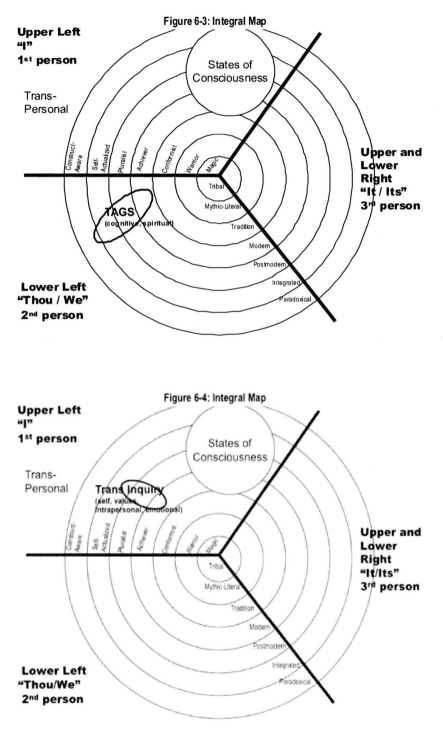

Figure 6-3: Integral Map

Upper Left
"I"
1st person

Trans-
Personal

Upper and
Lower
Right
"It / Its"
3rd person

Lower Left
"Thou / We"
2nd person

States of
Consciousness

Construct-Aware
Self-Actualized
Pluralist
Achiever
Conformist
Warrior
Magic
Tribal
Mythic-Literal
Tradition
Modern
Postmodern
Integrated
Paradoxical

TAGS
(cognitive, spiritual)

Figure 6-4: Integral Map

Upper Left
"I"
1st person

Trans-
Personal

Upper and
Lower
Right
"It/Its"
3rd person

Lower Left
"Thou/We"
2nd person

States of
Consciousness

Trans Inquiry
(self, values,
intrapersonal, emotional)

Construct-Aware
Self-Actualized
Pluralist
Achiever
Conformist
Warrior
Magic
Tribal
Mythic-Literal
Tradition
Modern
Postmodern
Integrated
Paradoxical

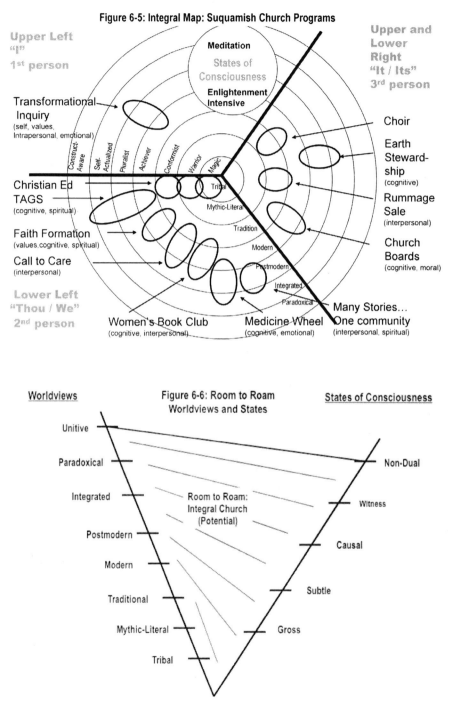

Figure 6-5: Integral Map: Suquamish Church Programs

Upper Left
"I"
1st person

Upper and
Lower
Right
"It / Its"
3rd person

Meditation
States of
Consciousness
Enlightenment
Intensive

Transformational Inquiry
(self, values,
Intrapersonal, emotional)

Construct-Aware
Self-Actualized
Pluralist
Achiever
Conformist
Warrior
Magic

Tribal

Choir

Earth Steward-ship
(cognitive)

Christian Ed
TAGS
(cognitive, spiritual)

Rummage Sale
(interpersonal)

Mythic-Literal

Faith Formation
(values,cognitive, spiritual)

Tradition

Call to Care
(interpersonal)

Modern

Church Boards
(cognitive, moral)

Postmodern

Lower Left
"Thou / We"
2nd person

Integrated

Paradoxical

Many Stories...
One community
(interpersonal, spiritual)

Women's Book Club
(cognitive, interpersonal)

Medicine Wheel
(cognitive, emotional)

Figure 6-6: Room to Roam
Worldviews and States

Worldviews

States of Consciousness

Unitive

Paradoxical

Non-Dual

Integrated

Room to Roam:
Integral Church
(Potential)

Witness

Postmodern

Causal

Modern

Traditional

Subtle

Mythic-Literal

Gross

Tribal

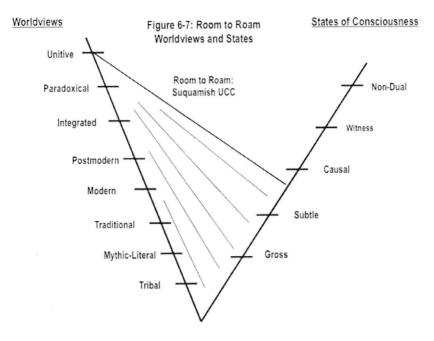

Figure 6-7: Room to Roam
Worldviews and States

Notes

1 Wilber, Ken, *Integral Spirituality: A Startling New Role for Religion in the Modern and Postmodern World*. Boston: Integral Books, 2006, Chapter 9.

2 My friend Molly Gordon shared this metaphor with me. It comes from a computer scientist named Craig Reynolds who created a computer program to model the flocking behavior of wild birds. See Waldrop, M. Mitchell. Complexity—The Emerging Science at the Edge of Order and Chaos. (Source: Gordon, Molly. *The Way of the Accidental Entrepreneur*. Suquamish, WA: Shaboom Inc., Live could be a dream ... , 2008, 18.)

3 See Matthew 22: 34-40.

4 Swimme, Brian, *Canticle to the Cosmos*, DVD, 12 hours. San Francisco, Center for the Story of the Universe, 2002, http://www.brianswimme.org.

5 Swimme, Brian, The Powers of the Universe, DVD, 9 hours, (San Francisco, Center for the Story of the Universe, 2004) http://www.brianswimme.org

6 Kegan, Robert and Lisa Laskow Lahey. *How the Way We Talk Can Change the Way We Work: Seven Languages for Transformation*. San Francisco: Jossey-Bass, 2001.

7 Katie, Byron. *Loving What Is*. New York: Three Rivers Press, 2003.

8 Tolle, Eckhart. *The Power of Now: A Guide to Spiritual Enlightenment*. Novato, CA: New World Library, 1999. Audio version.

9 Katie, Byron. *Loving What Is*. New York: Three Rivers Press, 2003. Audio Version: Audio Literature.

Chapter 7
A Revolution of Caring...
One Church at a Time

Integral Church is our vehicle for our spiritual journey from infancy into our own Christhood. It offers a conveyor belt for the evolution of consciousness. The Integral Church carries us through increasingly expansive ways of being by creating a context for our personal and collective spiritual development, by offering and legitimating stories for all phases of the journey, by recognizing where we are on the path, by creating programs and experiences that offer tastes of consciousness beyond our current comprehension, by providing safe places to take chances, by offering a map to guide us, by helping us to laugh at ourselves and by encouraging us to play. In these ways the Integral Church nurtures us all along our journey from cradle to Christ-consciousness.

In a recent book entitled *The Tyranny of Dead Ideas,* Matt Miller argues that our long term economic viability depends upon moving beyond some basic assumptions that have formed our choices but are no longer true.[1] In a similar vein, with different proposals, David Korten argues in *Agenda for a New Economy* that we need a "New story for a new economy."[2] The premise of their arguments is that the stories we tell, both individually and culturally, fundamentally shape the world we live in. I agree. The fundamental question then is, "How do we change the foundational stories that shape our world?" We do not need more information or knowledge; we already have plenty of that. We need new ways of *comprehending* the knowledge we already possess, in other words, new modes of consciousness. This feels like dangerous ground because the core of our personal identities is built upon the assumptions and premises we receive from our culture. Challenges to the cultural stories we believe are perceived as direct threats to our personal safety. Yet the world we live in demands that we change these foundational stories in profound ways. Again, the question is how?

Colleges and universities are the only institutions that regularly challenge fundamental social assumptions, but their role is limited. Their central purpose is the dissemination of existing knowledge and their primary audience is twenty-something individuals. While challenges that emerge in colleges help shape the views of young adults, transformation of our foundational assumptions must be more broadly based. This is where the church, especially the Integral Church, plays its pivotal role.

Elemental changes in the beliefs that shape our lives are spiritual in nature. The stories that guide our lives are deeply imbedded in the religious stories of who we are, where we come from and why we are important. We do not need more theories, cosmologies or religions; we need a place where we can investigate the stories that hold us and challenge their veracity. We need a place where we can become vulnerable to profoundly different ways of seeing without being threatened. This is not about teaching a new ideology, but about investigating *all* ideologies.

Integral Church is just such a place, an institution where core ideas and beliefs can be fundamentally challenged with safety and support. Challenging the basic stories of our culture may seem antithetical to the purpose of the church. For centuries the church has sought to inculcate its particular story of "how it is." But inculcation of a particular story is not the point of Christianity. Jesus said "you shall know the truth and the truth will make you free."[3] This does not mean you will be set free by the particular story of a particular church at a particular time. It means that in knowing truth directly, you shall be freed of all stories. This is beautifully expressed in the poetic words of Walt Whitman:

> *Long enough have you dream'd contemptible dreams,*
> *Now I wash the gum from your eyes,*
> *You must habit yourself to the dazzle of the light*
> *and of every moment of your life.*
>
> *Long have you timidly waded holding a plank by the shore,*
> *Now I will you to be a bold swimmer,*
> *To jump off in the midst of the sea, rise again,*
> *nod to me, shout and laughingly dash with your hair.*
>
> *I am the teacher of athletes,*
> *He that by me spreads a wider breast than my own*
> *proves the width of my own,*
> *He most honors my style who learns under it to destroy the teacher.[4]*

Here then is the paradoxical vision and possibility of the Integral Church: to be the cultural institution dedicated to offering Stage-appropriate stories while questioning all beliefs, all stories and all theories in pursuit of the truth. This is not some relative truth, but the truth that can be known directly yet never spoken—in Christian language, knowledge of God. As the institution where Stage-appropriate stories are legitimated, while all beliefs are simultaneously open to challenge, the church's mission becomes the pursuit of that quality most lacking in contemporary culture, wisdom. The church becomes more sacred as it questions all that is sacred. It becomes more reverent because of its irreverence. It is holy in its commitment to that which is whole. Our questioning and our reverent irreverence conspire to help us

take ourselves less seriously so that we may join fully in that most holy endeavor...
play.

• • •

In writing this book, I hoped to learn more than I taught. I have not been disappointed. As I have applied Integral Theory to my church in Suquamish, unforeseen needs have appeared and new programs are emerging to meet those needs. To create a tool and have it change my own setting is a powerful experience. Rather than rewrite the book, I present the new possibilities that are emerging in one church seeking to become more Integral. As we at Suquamish UCC looked at our Integral Map, it was clear we were lacking programs for personal and spiritual development (the Upper Left Quadrant). The response has been a new initiative we call Sound Spirit. The mission of Sound Spirit is "To awaken and nurture the deepest yearnings of the human spirit through events, classes and conversations in a supportive community." Sound Spirit reaches out to the spiritual but not religious folks in our community who are likely allergic to church, Christianity or both. While this initiative will include new stories for our time, its primary focus is on the spiritual and personal development of participants.

In response to the 2009 recession a different set of programs emerged. To my delight, they were not initiated by me. In fact, they were well on their way before I knew much about them. The first is a community garden. We now have half a dozen garden plots growing vegetables for our community. The second is a community kitchen, which provides a fabulous free meal to the community the last Wednesday of each month, just when welfare money and food stamps are running out.

The community garden and kitchen have inspired exploration into yet another initiative. While Sound Spirit focuses on the Upper Left Quadrant (personal and spiritual development), this new initiative focuses on the Lower Right Quadrant: action in the world. I believe that focusing on personal and spiritual development in a context of permission and possibility calls forth social action that is both timely and relevant. At Suquamish UCC, we call this program Local Living Economies. It is inspired by an article by Sarah van Gelder in Yes! Magazine entitled, "31 Ways to Jump Start the Local Economy."[5] The article includes suggestions like "rent out a room in your home," "fix things," "form a dinner club," "do home work parties" and "start a local currency." Our initiative is to create a clearing house and educational program to help these things happen in our community.

The Sound Spirit and Local Living Economies initiatives inspire a re-visioning of Integral Church as a Revolution of Caring. Integral Church is a Revolution of Caring because it cares for the full spectrum of our human possibility. It values the full range of our development from infancy to awakening. It offers stories to nurture us as we work through the challenges and successes of our development. And it provides relevant work in the world as we each evolve. Furthermore, an Integral Church responds to the variety of intelligences present in a congregation. It nurtures different Types and provides State changes to re-enliven our sense of the divine. From this broad perspective, caring gains new meaning and practicality.

No one church is likely to meet the full spectrum of needs illuminated by Integral Theory. But by being integrally informed, we discover the gifts we can offer in the broad context of what is needed for individual journeys from Magic to Transpersonal awareness. In doing the things we do best and offering them with awareness of the full spectrum of needs, we care more effectively. We take our desire to serve and channel it where it is most appropriate, knowing where and why we can't serve in other areas. This is a grassroots Revolution of Caring informed by the most expansive understanding available.

In this vision, Integral Church provides the conceptual umbrella articulating and organizing three complementary initiatives (the Big Three of Integral Theory). This is how the Revolution of Caring is showing up at Suquamish Church.

- Personal and Spiritual development (Upper Left Quadrant).
    - Sound Spirit: personal and spiritual development for the spiritual but not religious
    - Church programs focusing on personal and spiritual development in a distinctly Christian context
    - Programs and events focused on temporary tastes of the divine (States of Consciousness) such as enlightenment intensives and meditation
- Worldviews and Cultural Stories (Lower Left Quadrant)
    - Suquamish Church worship services
    - Christian Education
    - Interfaith programs
- Action in the World (Upper and Lower Right Quadrants)
    - Local Living Economies
    - On-going programs of the church

These programs are summarized in Figure 7-1.

There is a concept in economics called "comparative advantage." It is very simple. Focus your energy where you have the resources and ability to be better than others. The church has both a comparative advantage and little other choice in supporting the evolution of consciousness in individuals. As my friend John Forman rightly argues, the church in the U.S. historically had four principal functions.

- To help the poor
- To be the conscience of society
- To be the center of family life
- To provide spiritual formation

Figure 7-1

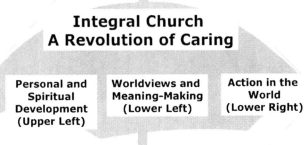

Integral Church
A Revolution of Caring

Personal and Spiritual Development (Upper Left)	Worldviews and Meaning-Making (Lower Left)	Action in the World (Lower Right)
Sound Spirit Church programs States of Consciousness	Worship services Christian Education Interfaith programs	Local Living Economies On-going church programs

Today, most of these functions are better handled by other institutions. Government and specialized agencies are better able to care for the poor. Society is more pluralistic and we no longer expect everyone to share Christian values. As traditional churches have defined "family" more narrowly; alternative family constellations are excluded. This doesn't mean the church doesn't contribute in these areas, but our role is now far more limited. This leaves spiritual formation the remaining domain where the church has a comparative advantage. I am glad to see this for I am convinced it is the true heritage and purpose of church. Integral Church reclaims that heritage and carries it into the 21st century. I hope you will join us.

Notes

1 Miller, Matt, *The Tyranny of Dead Ideas: Letting Go of the Old Ways of Thinking to Unleash a New Prosperity*, (New York: Times Books, 2009) 2.

2 Korten, David C., *Agenda for a New Economy: From Phantom Wealth to Real Wealth*. (San Francisco: Berrett-Koehler, 2009) 102.

3 John 8:32

4 Whitman, Walt, "Song of Myself."

5 VanGelder, Sarah. "31 Ways to Jump Start the Local Economy." *Yes! Magazine* (Bainbridge Is., WA, Summer 2009 Issue 50) 46.

Appendix A
Leadership

What is required to lead an Integral Church? At a bare minimum, either the pastor or a core of lay leaders must desire to create an integrally informed church. Any church can follow the model developed in this book to their benefit. But to embody the practices of Integral Church, at least a few individuals must be able to model and express (with passion) the possibilities of Integral Church. Ideally, the pastor and core leaders will have their center of gravity at the Integral waves of development (Self-Actualized and Construct-Aware). They will then embody the possibilities of Integral Church in a variety of ways that enhance its appeal.

This said, I do not believe it to be an absolute prerequisite to have any leaders at the Integral Stage of Development. Many progressive churches find themselves bumping up against the limits of the Postmodern/Pluralist perspective. These churches find themselves welcoming a broad diversity of individuals but not having an orientation that allows them to differentiate among the relative values and worldviews of those many perspectives. It is one thing to say you welcome folks wherever they are on life's journey; it is another to recognize where they are on that journey and how the church might support them. Without some meta-perspective like the one offered in this book, progressive churches can offer a genuine and heartfelt welcome, but have no idea how to really meet and serve folks where they are. As leaders of progressive churches encounter the limits of the Postmodern/Pluralist perspective they may find the Integral Church orientation useful. Keep in mind, a center of gravity at Pluralism only reflects our comfort zone; we are not limited to it. Individuals centered in Achiever and Pluralist Stages of Development have access to the integral perspective (especially intellectually) and will understand its value. For this reason, Integral Theory, and the map developed here, can help churches "bootstrap" their way into more expansive ways of serving their congregants.

Integral leadership is not easy to describe, except to say it is flexible and flowing. This does not mean it is relativistic or passive. An Integral leader is not blown about by the whims of the congregation but listens carefully to deeper movements. There is a rational, Achiever orientation to this that includes taking surveys, and finding out what most of the people want. But it's not like politics, where you alter your position to appeal to the majority. The Pluralist dimension listens to the unheard voices of minorities without preferring them. Both of these orientations are included in the larger Integral frame. Intellectually, we may discuss the balancing of majority views with those of minority views to understand the breadth of our offerings. But the critical factor for integral leaders is listening; not just listening to the voices around us, but to the voices within. In theological language, listening for the voice of God is essential.

If we were raised in a specific tradition, the voice of God is likely to be filtered through the logic of our theology. Integral leadership demands an honest and ruthless investigation into our most precious belief structures. It does not demand that we change our foundational beliefs. It does demand that we inquire into them in a manner that reduces our identification with them. This is a dynamic and paradoxical position to hold.

Integral leadership also demands profound trust; trust that things will work out as needed. Let me give an example from my church. Early in my tenure we committed to not burning people out on church work. In our church, like others, once successful programs had continued long after their effectiveness had passed. Folks felt obligated to continue the projects because "we have always done … (fill in the blank)." Energy was wasted flogging a dead horse when it could be used in new and vital ways. Our challenge was to allow, even encourage, projects to die. This was surprisingly difficult in some cases; but a new freedom was discovered. We found small groups could initiate new projects without fearing they would be saddled with them forever. The leadership challenge has been to allow things to remain undone until appropriate projects emerged. By *not* leaping into new projects, the congregation gained permission to listen deeply into what they really wanted and who had a genuine commitment to those new projects.

The central demand on folks who want to lead an Integral Church is to engage in a deep reflective process:

- Listen to teachers that challenge your view of the world (see Talking About God Stuff below).
- Inquire into your foundational beliefs (see Transformational Inquiry below).
- Engage in some form of meditation or contemplation that helps you to experience more expanded States of Consciousness.
- And listen courageously.

Finally, an Integral Church needs a fool, not a normal fool, but a holy fool. This is someone in a respected leadership capacity that can take public risks and fail, laugh at themselves and generally create an atmosphere of playfulness. The holy fool tells the congregation that life is not serious, that the risks of trying are low and the costs of failure are even lower. The holy fool creates an atmosphere of safety by regularly demonstrating that failure *is* the path of spiritual development. Blessed is the church with many holy fools.

Appendix B
Worship

A variety of elements set Integral worship apart from more conventional forms of worship. Since worship is simultaneously a collective celebration, a communal prayer, and a public presentation, it carries many demands. Three elements stand out as essential to an Integral Church service: the 1-2-3 of God, Levels of Development, and States of Consciousness. These elements need not be present in every service but would likely show up in relatively equal proportions over time.

By its nature worship will be distinctive in every Integral Church. I will use my church in Suquamish as one example of Integral worship. Using these three elements you can create an integral service to meet your church's needs.

The 1-2-3 of God

The 1-2-3 of God refers to the Divine as self, other and nature. In intentionally Integral worship services the Great Mystery will be encountered as:

- *Self*. "God as Self" refers to a 1st person orientation that recognizes our intrinsic divinity. It acknowledges with Jesus that "the Father and I are one." This, of course, is fairly far from the traditional Western Christian orientation and may need to be introduced slowly in some settings.

- *Other*. "God as Other" is the traditional 2nd person orientation of most Western churches. The divine is seen as Father (sometimes Mother), Son and Holy Spirit, all of which are distinct from humans. We worship and devote ourselves to the divine Other. We pray to God the Father. We ask assistance from the Holy Spirit. We worship the Son.

- *Nature*. God as impersonal "it," a 3rd person orientation. The notion that science is a form of theology carried out from an objective stance is becoming increasingly popular. As quantum physics, string theory, the New Biology, and the New Cosmology have revealed the vast webs of interconnection in an intrinsically intelligent universe this 3rd person perspective has gained wider acceptance.

At Suquamish Church the traditional, 2nd person perspective of "God as other" is deeply imbedded in both the structure and the music of the church. Traditional hymns, for the most part, see us in various forms of relationship with the divine. Our Prayers of the People also reflect this 2nd person orientation: we pray to a God who is other.

God as self or nature is often explored in the reflection or sermon. "God as self" is intrinsic to the mission of Integral Church as it offers a conveyor belt through increasingly expansive waves of development. My invocation or pastoral prayer will often refer to the awakening of the Christ within.

The "God as Nature" perspective is reflected in hymns like "For the Beauty of the Earth." "God as Self" hymns are less available within the Christian tradition. We often turn to more New Age music; the music of Linnea Goode, a Canadian artist, is particularly useful. The Beatles "Let it Be" is a wonderful integration of both a 2nd person perspective ("Mother Mary comes to me") and a 1st person perspective ("let it be").

Levels of Development and Worldviews

Progressively expansive waves of development, and the worldviews that support and nurture them, are an essential component of Integral worship. There are a variety of ways to integrate levels of development and worldviews. It is important to ground levels and worldview in the tradition. Conventional Christianity sees God as Other and has a structure celebrating that relationship. The very word *worship* signifies the divine is other. Our order of worship is quite conventional with three hymns, prayers and a message. We include at least one hymn, and often two, with a traditional 2nd person orientation. The Lord's Prayer is always included as part of the Prayers of the People. This structure provides a safe environment in which to explore more adventurous areas; it tells people who have been raised in the Christian tradition that this is a familiar place. The safety of this structure permits broad ranging exploration in other dimensions of worship. In the message I examine a broad range of topics from a variety of perspectives (see Chapter 4 for some examples). In particular, we are able to offer very different interpretations of scripture, as well as wisdom from other faiths, as legitimate worldviews to support individuals at different waves of development. Increasingly, we offer alternative services that replace our regular venues. Interfaith services are welcomed and services of music and poetry are well received.

States of Consciousness

As indicated in my discussion of "Room to Roam," a goal of Integral Church is to provide the widest possible expanse in which individual consciousness may roam

(See Figure B-1). This is not a relativistic wasteland, but a well structured and expansive configuration of legitimate "Jesus Stories" and States of Consciousness (see Chapters 2, 3 and 4 and the graph above).

As indicated, most Protestant churches (mine included) are quite uncomfortable with Christian forms of altered States of Consciousness, like speaking in tongues. We have discovered, however, that folks are enthusiastic about different venues, many from other faiths. Taize comes from our own tradition and involves repetitively singing simple phrases. I have recently created video presentations set to music that play for about 10 minutes prior to worship and create a more contemplative setting. Our interfaith services include dances from other cultures. Sufi and other dances are intended to induce a more expanded state of consciousness and are enthusiastically engaged by church members. Our self analysis of our *Room to Roam* (Chapter 6) has motivated us to include more of these state expanding practices as part of worship.

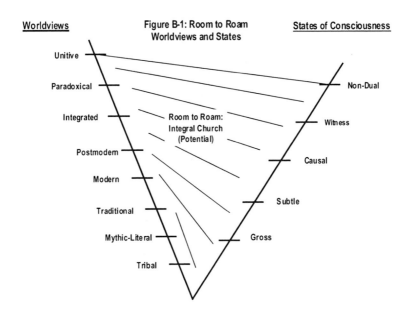

Figure B-1: Room to Roam Worldviews and States

Appendix C
Faith Formation and Scripture Study

As Suquamish Church seeks to offer a full spectrum of perspectives on the Christian story, we are fortunate to have Ed Evans as one of our teachers. Ed is a retired UCC minister and drives an hour on Sunday mornings to teach about a dozen folks before worship.

Ed's class offers a modern perspective on scripture. Two considerations give this class a modern orientation. First, it is rational and historical. Modern theologians are committed to discovering the actual words of Jesus and what they have meant in the context of his time. This is an orderly investigation. It not only seeks the historical context but, through careful textual analysis, uncovers the larger structure of the written text and how the parts fit together. These are all hallmarks of the modern scientific orientation of discovering the best possible interpretation of the Bible.

Second, discussion questions point us back to our own authority. We may look to the Bible for wisdom, but we are responsible for the interpretation. We may listen to the insights of various scholars and authorities, but we are the ones who must choose according to our own value systems and principles. We are our own moral authorities, the authors of our lives, and we must constantly reflect to bring our actions into alignment with our values.

Just because this class takes a modern perspective on scripture, it doesn't imply that participants find their center of gravity at the Modern/Achiever wave of development. Folks may participate because the class represents a new and enticing way of understanding the Bible; others may seek to fill in a more comprehensive understanding of Christianity; and still others may find that this class meets them where they are and speaks to just how they need to understand their faith.

Ed's notes give the flavor of this class and how you might structure a similar program at your church.

FAITH FORMATION DISCUSSION AND SCRIPTURE STUDY NOTES

Notes compiled from a variety of sources, including http://www.textweek.com and **The New Interpreter's Bible.**

November 2, 2008

TWENTY-FIFTH SUNDAY AFTER PENTECOST—YEAR A

Theme: We Constantly Give Thanks
Sermon: We Have So Much to Thank God For
Liturgical color: Green

Matthew 23:1-12

> *Then Jesus said to the crowds and to his disciples, "The scribes and the Pharisees sit on Moses' seat; therefore, do whatever they teach you and follow it; but do not do as they do, for they do not practice what they teach. They tie up heavy burdens, hard to bear, and lay them on the shoulders of others; but they themselves are unwilling to lift a finger to move them. They do all their deeds to be seen by others; for they make their phylacteries broad and their fringes long. They love to have the place of honor at banquets and the best seats in the synagogues, and to be greeted with respect in the marketplaces, and to have people call them rabbi. But you are not to be called rabbi, for you have one teacher, and you are all students. And call no one your father on earth, for you have one Father—the one in heaven. Nor are you to be called instructors, for you have one instructor, the Messiah. The greatest among you will be your servant. All who exalt themselves will be humbled, and all who humble themselves will be exalted.*

Context of the Text

The words of Jesus here are spoken to potential and actual followers. They destabilize more than one standard human assumption. They challenge the incoherency between human speaking and acting; they attack the motivation behind religious piety, and they replace human hierarchical thinking with a paradoxical alternative.

Eugene Boring ("Matthew," New Interpreters Bible) writes: "The crowds represent potential disciples who are still positive toward Jesus. Whereas the Sermon on the Mount contains blessings, this speech of Jesus contains woes—the opposite of blessings. Both the Sermon and chapter 23 stress the importance of inward attitudes in contrast to outward actions."

As this chapter is read, we need to remind ourselves that it is not addressed to the "scribes and Pharisees" who are "woed" in the later verses, but these are words addressed to the "crowds and disciples." Rather than attacking the Jewish religious leaders, Matthew uses these words of Jesus as a warning against the Christian leaders. Within Matthew's understanding, we would do well to try and apply these words to ourselves.

Thoughts (and Questions) to Ponder

Have we become like those whom we despise? (Johnny Carson once quoted someone who said: "Choose your enemies carefully, for you become like them.")

A key issue here is who has the authority to interpret scripture? (Even today, often what divides the conservatives, fundamentalists, liberals, main-liners, etc., is their approach to scripture and the interpretations that come out of their individual approaches.)

One of Matthew's critiques of the religious establishment was that "they say, but do not do." Can that be said of you? Of our congregation?

In the same manner, Matthew is suggesting that "they burden others while failing to act themselves." As a congregation, do we "heap burdens" upon our people, asking them to give more of their time while taking time away from their families or their private devotional life? How often do clergy fall into the trap of burdening themselves (or allowing the congregation to heap their burdens upon him/her?)

Matthew is also suggesting that religious acts that are done for the purpose of making an impression on others are wrong. What might that say to people who have Christian bumper stickers or a fish symbol on their car? Or clergy who wear collars? When are such "externals" part of our calling to be separate from the world, to be witnesses to the world, to be "holy" - that is different from what is common? When are such externals just a pious show?

Who among us has not at some point, on a greater or lesser scale, held others accountable for things or behavior which we do not expect of ourselves?

Reflections/Points to Ponder

Robert Capon: "The church is not in the morals business. The world is in the morals business, quite rightfully; and it has done a fine job of it, all things considered. The history of the world's moral codes is a monument to the labors of many philosophers, and it is a monument of striking unity and beauty. As C.S. Lewis said, anyone who thinks the moral codes of mankind are all different should be locked up in a library and be made to read three days' worth of them. He/she would be bored silly by the sheer sameness.

What the world cannot get right, however, is the forgiveness business -- and that, of course, is the church's real job. The church is in the world to deal with the Sin which the world can't turn off or escape from. The church is not in the business of telling the world what's right and wrong so that it can do good and avoid evil. The church is in the business of offering, to a world which knows all about that tiresome subject, forgiveness for its chronic unwillingness to take its own advice. But the minute the church even hints that morals, and not forgiveness, is the name of the game, the church instantly corrupts the Gospel and runs headlong into blatant nonsense.

The church becomes, not Ms. Forgiven Sinner, but Ms. Right. Christianity becomes the good guys in here verses the bad guys out there. Which, of course, is pure tripe. The church is nothing but the world under the sign of baptism. ["Hunting the Divine Fox," pp. 132-133.]

Appendix D
TAGS: Talking About God Stuff

At Suquamish Church, we have developed two important programs aimed specifically at the developmental levels I call Integral. The first, Talking About God Stuff (TAGS), takes an intellectual approach to faith. The second, Transformational Inquiry (described in Appendix E), develops tools for expanding consciousness through increasingly expansive waves of development.

The format of TAGS is very simple. We watch a video, pause when something interesting is mentioned, then see where the conversation goes. We may watch 15 minutes or 15 seconds of a program before the conversation takes off. Discussion is open ended. Video presentations have a great advantage over book discussions because no one is ever behind.

TAGS has met weekly for more than six years and has a dedicated following. Close to half of the participants consider themselves part of our church, even if they never attend regular worship services. These folks find "church" in the intimacy and exploration that occurs in a group of roughly 10 to 15.

The leader's role is to create a safe space for wide-ranging discussion. This requires that the leader not be defensive or dogmatic on any topic. In fact, an effective facilitator will bring up controversial topics and raise questions others might not broach. In our TAGS group, I am often challenged and will propose controversial ideas. By questioning my beliefs and not responding defensively I, in the role of pastor, give permission to explore foundational beliefs. Individuals' foundational beliefs may be challenged but they are never attacked. They may be questioned for clarification and others may articulate a different view, but attack is not permitted. Simply by articulating invisible unexamined beliefs faith becomes more expansive and inclusive.

The great value of TAGS is the creation of a forum where foundational beliefs can be articulated and examined. Topics such as good and evil, free will, time, God and Jesus, the nature of the self, and the history of the universe are all included in an expansive discussion. The following commentary reflects the kind of thinking through of issues that emanates from TAGS. This is one view, not a consensus opinion…which makes it all the more fun.

Of Time, Free Will and Non-Duality
(Ed Frodel, Ph.D.)

TAGS conversations seem to revolve around, and I do mean revolve around, the issue of transcendence of the ego. Our conversations wade through a plethora of personal stories and opinions, ranging from humanity's outer alignment with the creative, evolutionary process of allurement in the universe (Agape—the path of descent and compassion) to the emotional and physical forces from higher levels of energy that impose upon humanity's inner capacity to make choices (Eros—the path of ascension and wisdom).

Whether Eros or Agape, humanity lives in a dualistic universe, the implicate and the explicate (the spiritual and the material), rarely, if ever, is the question asked, "Where do my thoughts come from?" Or, perhaps more poignantly, "Who or what is witnessing my awareness at the moment?" And I should add to the conundrum whether or not humanity actually has free will if it is superseded by a higher self of the implicate realm. Inherent to this discourse, of necessity, is the concept of time, for humanity is continuously reaching out to the future from a position of being in the now, which by definition, includes the evolutionary past. So, in our lifetime do we have freedom of choice in our effort to become one with a Higher Self, the Christ Energy, or whatever?

Given the age composition of the TAGS group, I suspect that the experiences and the maturity of the group lends itself to explore the possibility that each person has had an awakening to the belief that there is a creative process to which he/she has become aware and, what's more, that he/she is an integral part of that creative process. (See Cohen, Andrew and Wilber, Ken, "A Relationship with Eternity," WHAT IS ENLIGHTENMENT, Feb.-Apr., 2008) It is that very awakening to a higher consciousness that draws each member of the group into further, and deeper, dialogue; thus, both Eros and Agape are inherently manifest in each member.

As a result, we are being pulled into greater complexity as a group (an awakened creative impulse) while steadfastly holding to our own personal, emotional and physical life energy (life is living us). So, yes, I believe we have free will to choose to be seeking a higher self in relationship with others (our humanity) and, while in the same frame of mind, to sense the existence of a higher self within (the Universal Consciousness).

This dualistic story of humanity is a glorious metaphor of the tragic, the absurd, the wonder of cosmic consciousness in evolution. Humanity has within itself all the same energy and matter that existed at the beginning of time, thus, we are folk of eternity. Heaven and hell, as such, do not exist out there; they exist at the highest and lowest levels of personal intent. And we are called to account for our choices. Jesus said, "Do not judge, so that you may not be judged. For with the judgment you make you will be judged, and the measure you give will be the measure you get." (Matthew 7:1-2) And John 8:7, "let anyone among you who is without sin be the first to throw a stone ..." Every action carries with it a result with a moral condition. For example, treating others as you would want to be treated is a choice. This is a karmic struggle, "As you sow, so shall you reap." It is this freedom of choice that is the bondage of humanity.

Only by awakening to a union with a higher state of consciousness are we potentially able to experience a true freedom from our bondage of choice. The connection with a higher consciousness eases, if not removes, the burden of free choice. "For my yoke is easy, and my load is light." (Matthew, 11:30) With this, Jesus is saying that the Karmic struggle will not exist in union with God...

Some very big questions remain to be answered, if ever. What if God's plan is really a stochastic pathway, leaving life to the quantum whims of cosmic evolution? But what if there is no plan at all? And can we even assume that Homo Sapiens is the highest life form to evolve in God's random cosmic plan? Are humans destined to be replaced by a life form with a higher consciousness level? Or is humanity stuck, so to speak, in a struggle to rise above duality, constantly knocking on the door of evolution only to find behind that door more duality? Or is extinction humanity's fate in a cosmos, currently in expansion at an increasing rate, 94% of which is composed of dark energy and dark matter?...

Think of it this way. The relative unfolding of consciousness requires of us only that we develop a pluralistic mindset in order for individuals or collective minds to move toward a postmodern stage and then into an integral consciousness. We at TAGS experience a reshuffling of ideas that can move us in and out of an awareness of a higher level of thought that is conducive to a connection with what I refer to as the Universal Consciousness or Christ Spirit. We must first look inward (Jung) to free the Self and then seek to connect the Self with the Creative Evolutionary Impulses of the Cosmos (Chardin). Having done so, and with the help of such as Tolle's Awakened Doing (acceptance, enjoyment, enthusiasm), the Karmic struggle of the choices we make, we will have achieved a consciousness awakening akin to Spirit in Action. This is our Passion of Hope.

Resources for TAGS

<u>Brian Swimme</u>

Over the years we have worked through many programs. Some will take a year or more to complete, others we tire of quickly. It is important to pay attention to the group's energy around particular teachers. In our groups we have had great success with two Brian Swimme programs: *Canticle to the Cosmos* and *The Powers of the Universe*. Swimme is a mathematical physicist and cosmologist who worked closely with the eco-philosopher Thomas Berry. Together they wrote a book entitled *The Universe Story*.

Canticle to the Cosmos was produced in 1992 and is a bit dated. This turns out to be an advantage, because most folks who attend TAGS will not have much background in cosmology. Swimme has a wonderful energy, but is somewhat tentative. His ideas are not yet perfected and the ambiguity invites exploration and open-ended dialog. *The Powers of the Universe* represents Swimme's mature statement of his cosmology. It offers a more refined, clear and precise understanding. I strongly recommend using *Canticle* before *Powers*.

Since we tend to spend a long time discussing Swimme's cosmology I periodically break it up with other videos. *Thomas Berry: The Great Story* is a wonderful compliment to Swimme and offers a philosophical perspective that balances Swimme's more scientific orientation. In *The Elegant Universe,* Brian Green offers a popular and comprehensible explanation of string theory. And *What the Bleep Do We Know* provides pure entertainment. The science in *What the Bleep* is suspect, but it does tap into an increasingly popular worldview of how our consciousness shapes the world around us (also popularized in *The Secret*).

Resources

Swimme, Brian. **Canticle to the Cosmos**. 10 programs. San Francisco: New Story Project 1990.

Swimme, Brian. **The Powers of the Universe**. 7 programs. San Francisco: Center for the Story of the Universe. http://www.brianswimme.org. 2003-08.

Thomas Berry: The Great Story; The Life and Work of The Famous Eco-theologian. Oley, PA: Bullfrog Films, http://www.bulfrogfilms.com. 2002.

Green, Brian. **The Elegant Universe; superstrings, Hidden Dimensions, and the Quest for the Ultimate Theory**. Boston: NOVA, WGBH Boston, 800.949.8670. http://www/shop.wgbh.org. 2003.

What the Bleep Do We Know. Beverly Hills, CA: Twentieth Century Fox Home Entertainment. 2004.

Evolutionary Christianity

We have recently begun watching an application of Swimme's cosmology to Christianity. Rev. Michael Dowd has done an excellent job of translating the Universe Story into Christian language. As explored in Chapter 3, Dowd takes fundamental categories (sin, salvation, heaven, hell, resurrection) and sets them within a cosmological framework resonant with Swimme. While Swimme takes a predominantly 3rd person perspective, Dowd adds a 2nd person perspective that resonates with folks raised in the Christian tradition.

Because Dowd speaks quickly and energetically, he can be difficult to follow for those who are not familiar with the topic or those with hearing difficulties. I recommend *Evolutionary Christianity* only after viewing one or more of Swimme's programs.

Resources

Dowd, Michael. *Evolutionary Christianity*. http://www.thankgodforrevolution. com.
Dowd, Michael. *Thank God for Evolution*. http://www.thankgodforrevolution. com, 2008.

The World's Religions

Any conversation in TAGS would be incomplete without an exploration of the world's faith systems. Conversations often lead into comparisons of Christian beliefs with those of other faiths.

Joseph Campbell sees myths grounding and connecting all the world religions; they are archetypical in the Jungian sense. Karen Armstrong and Huston Smith are both great scholars of the world's religions and walk us through their complexities with remarkable clarity. Bede Griffiths was a Catholic Priest who moved to India to become Hindu holy man. His first person accounts of the blessings of both Christianity and Hinduism are powerful and touching.

Resources

Moyers, Bill. *Joseph Campbell and The Power of Myth*. Cooper Station, NY: Mystic Fire Video, Inc., 1986

The Moyers Collection . *The Wisdom of Faith, with Huston Smith*. Public Affairs Television, Inc., 1996.

Westar Summer Institute. ***Karen Armstrong: What is Religion?*** Santa Rosa, CA Poleridge Press, http://www.westarinstitute.org. 2007.

The Wisdom of a Prophet, with Bede Griffiths. Perth, Australia: More Than Illusion Films; Dayananda Foundation for the Renewal of Contemplative Life. 1992.

Spirituality

Spirituality and spiritual practices are remarkably absent from Western Protestantism. Centering prayer, developed by Father Thomas Keating, is making its way into some denominations, but generally we have to look to other traditions for spiritual practices. Because of his success on Oprah, Eckhart Tolle now seems to be everyone's favorite spiritual teacher. The video listed here is only one of many available at http://www.eckharttolle.com. His gentle manner makes his powerfully challenging message quite palatable.

My favorite Zen teacher is Adyashanti. Adya has a very simple and direct approach to awakening, or salvation. The Gangaji Foundation offers a variety of videos with a similar message and a more feminine touch.

Though TAGS is primarily a discussion group, there are times when we want to engage in spiritual practices. Byron Katie offers a very simple methodology for discovering who we truly are. I provide greater explanation in Appendix E: Transformational Inquiry. Genpo Roshi is another Zen teacher who invites us to converse with our different interior voices and take a journey into Big Mind.

Resources

Adyashanti. Being Alone and Association with Truth. Los Gatos, CA: Open Gate Publishing, http://www.adyashanti.org., 2004-5.

Gangaji: ***Revealing Strategies of Ego***. The Gangaji Foundation. http://www.gangaji.org.

Katie, Byron. *Loving What Is*. NY: Three Rivers Press, 2003. http://www.thework.com.

Roshi, Genpo. **Big Mind.** Boulder, CO: Integral Institute. http://www.integralinstitute.org. 2005.

Tolle, Eckhart. ***The Flowering of Human Consciousness: Everyone's Life Purpose.*** Boulder, CO: Sounds True, http://www.soundstrue.com, 2001.

Contemporary Biblical Scholarship

Even though we have a regular Sunday morning group exploring contemporary biblical scholarship, we have used a video format in TAGS to generate different conversations. *Living the Questions* brings together well known biblical scholars and theologians to present a progressive understanding of basic Christian principles. The downside of this video is that it is expensive and not well produced.

Resources

Living the Questions: A Program for Christian Exploration and Spiritual Formation . http://www.living the questions.com, 2005.

Integral Theory

We have explored Integral Theory in various formats in the church. In TAGS we have gone more deeply into Integral Theory. The **AQAL Framework** (All Quadrants, All Levels, All Lines...) presents a variety of conversations with Ken Wilber explaining various components of Integral Theory.

Resources

Wilber, Ken **The AQAL Framework**. Boulder, CO: Integral Institute. http://www.integralinstitute.org,, 2005.

194

Appendix E
Transformational Inquiry

In Chapter 6, I outlined the program we call Transformational Inquiry (or simply Inquiry). In the years we've been refining this program, individuals have gone through changes ranging from significant to dramatic. The most dramatic was a woman who lost nearly 250 pounds, in part because of the Big Assumptions she uncovered and the creative safe tests she used to shift those Big Assumptions.

I explain this program more fully here in the hope that you will use it in your congregation. Even though I offer an extensive explanation of my adaptation of this process, it is vital that you study the sources because they are filled with compelling and essential insights. The first part of Transformational Inquiry is based on the work of Harvard researchers Robert Kegan and Lisa Laskow Lahey. In their 2001 book, *How the Way We Talk Can Change the Way We Work*, they developed the basic process we use in Inquiry. In their 2009 book, *Immunity to Change*, they deepen the process, particularly the work with Big Assumptions. In Transformational Inquiry I have adapted their work and added *The Work of Byron Katie*[1] as well as a meditation technique.

Immunity to Change

We begin each meeting of Inquiry with a meditation. This may be a few minutes of silence or a body-centered meditation from a process called Breema. The value of the this meditation is that it brings our attention to the body, which is always in the present moment.

Most of our lives are active; we are always moving ahead to the next thing. Spiritual development is about stepping back, about going within or what Zen calls "the backward step." Inquiry is about questioning what you believe you know, entering silence, and learning how to listen to yourself and to others so that creative, context appropriate solutions can emerge. By pausing and *not solving* we learn a new way of knowing in the world, the kind of knowing that can serve you in the increasing complexity of today's world.

As meaning-making creatures we continuously create stories, make judgments, compare and evaluate. The vehicle for meaning-making is language, so Inquiry uses language as the means of approaching the hidden assumptions and commitments that guide our lives. As Kegan/Lahey state, "The forms of speaking we have available to us regulate the forms of thinking, feeling and meaning-making to which we have access, which in turn constrains how we see the world and act in it."[2] In the following pages I will guide you through the process of discovering a Big Assumption that is running your life and making you immune to personal change. I will then present ways in which you can nudge or even change these assumptions.

This kind of work is foundational to spiritual development. Awakening is a developmental process. Whatever tools we can use to loosen ego's hold on us opens us to the Divine. We may have tastes of the awakened state that alter our perception of the world. Once tasted, the work is to bring all dimensions of self into the light of awareness for their transformation. As the spiritual teacher, Jack Kornfield says, "After the ecstasy, the laundry."[3] Inquiry is about the laundry. It is a process that can lead us into awakening or it can help complete the process once awakening has happened.

Inquiry is most effective in groups of eight to 15 individuals. If you have a larger group, great work can be done by breaking into pairs, triads, or even groups of six or so. Even in smaller groups, it works well to have people pair off (or work in triads) then return to the larger group. Here are some basic ground rules:

- As a speaker, how much you share is up to you.
- As a listener, do not point out what your partner is missing, or try to teach, or insert your own agenda.
- Do not partner with a spouse or someone with whom you work.
- Work with the same person throughout a class session.

The Immunity to Change process developed by Kegan and Lahey uses the chart presented in Table E-1. At each step of the process we will fill in a column that sets the stage for the question in the next column. Kegan and Lahey's model uses the columns numbered 1 through 4. I find that adding Column 0 keeps the process clearer as we move through it.

Column 0: Complaint

At each step along the way we ask questions. The first questions are: "What frustrates you?" Or, "What aggravates you?" Or "What is something you would like to change?" All of these signify some sort of complaint. Ask folks to write a complaint or frustration in Column 0 on their worksheet (Table E-1).

Break into pairs or triads and share these complaints. Do not edit your complaints; leave them as raw and simple as you can and share them with your partner(s). This first step generates a lot of energy and laughter and opens folks to the work. Return to the larger group and share your complaints. Write them down on a flip chart for all to see. Get volunteers willing to share their entire process with the larger group.

Table E-2

Column 0 Complaint Aggravation, or Frustration	Column 1 Commitment I am committed to the value or importance of ...	Column 2 Personal Responsibility What am I doing or not doing that prevents my commitment from being fully realized?	Column 3 Competing Commitments: I may also be committed to ...	Column 4 Big Assumptions I assume that if ... then
People should not gossip or talk behind peoples' backs	I am committed to the value or importance of being direct and clear with people.		Worry Box	

Column 1: Commitment

A vital point needs to be made. We don't complain unless we are committed to something we consider important and valuable. According to Kegan/Lahey, "We would not complain about anything if we did not care about something. Beneath the surface torrent of our complaining lies a hidden river of our caring, that which we most prize or to which we are most committed." [4]

In Column 1 of Table E-2, ask folks to complete the following sentence: "I am committed to the value or importance of..." After a few minutes of individual reflection break into pairs or groups and share these underlying commitments. Then return to the large group to share some of these commitments. For example, if someone complains about people gossiping and talking behind peoples' backs (Column 0). The underlying commitment (Column 1) might be, "I am committed to the value or importance of being direct and clear with people." This is a noble commitment an individual could stand up for and be proud of.

There is an important insight in this first move from complaints to commitments. The *language of complaint* essentially tells us (and others) what we don't like, while the language of commitment tells us what we stand for. If time permits, this is a good place to end the first class. The take-home assignment is to observe complaints, frustrations, aggravations, or any time they feel impatient. First, they can just notice how often this happens. Then, whenever possible, ask, "What is the commitment behind this complaint?" This can be revelatory. Individuals discover how much they complain and then discover, when they look behind their complaints, that they aren't just whining and sniveling, but that they have some deeply held, noble commitments. Individuals in the business school where I teach report that this exercise has transformed some working groups. At your next gathering allow time for individuals to share what they discovered during the week.

Column 2: Personal Responsibility

The next step in the process asks, "What am I doing or not doing that prevents my commitment from being fully realized?" This is about our personal responsibility for not fulfilling our first column commitment. Of course, there may be any number of external, uncontrollable factors preventing fulfillment of that commitment. The point here is to examine the areas in which we have control.

Continuing with our example. The Column 1 commitment is "I am committed to the value or importance of being direct and clear with people." Upon reflection, we may discover that one of the things we do to keep this commitment from being fulfilled is to gossip and talk behind peoples' backs. This can be startling. With this realization, folks will often be inspired to make what Kegan and Lahey refer to as a New Year's Resolution: "I promise to not do this again." In the moment, this is a sincere commitment but we all know how well New Year's Resolutions fare. Soon we are back to the same behavior. This point sets the Kegan/Lahey process apart from other self-improvement programs. The challenge here is *not* to fix the problem but to make use of this realization to go deeper. It is easy to conclude, and our culture supports the idea, that since we can't live up to our commitment we must be flawed, weak, or insincere. Kegan and Lahey work from the opposite premise: humans are complex and the contradictions between our values and our actions reflect that complexity, not some deficiency.

At this point, invite folks to privately reflect on what they may or may not be doing that keeps their Column 1 commitment from being fulfilled. Then send them into pairs or groups to share these reflections. When you all return to the large group write some of these on the flip chart. This public process is generally infused with laughter as we all recognize common perceived foibles. At this juncture, you should be tracking a few individuals and watching a pattern emerge. It is important to emphasize that this is *not* about trying to change these behaviors; in fact you will subvert the process if you try to change them.

Let's look at our work sheet so far (Table E-3).

Table E-3

Column 0 Complaint Aggravation, or Frustration	Column 1 Commitment I am committed to the value or importance of …	Column 2 Personal Responsibility What am I doing or not doing that prevents my commitment from being fully realized?	Column 3 Competing Commitments: I may also be committed to…	Column 4 Big Assumptions I assume that if … then …
People should not gossip or talk behind peoples' backs	I am committed to the value or importance of being direct and clear with people.	I gossip and talk behind peoples' backs.	Worry Box	

Column 3: Competing Commitments

The move to Column 3 begins our dive into complexity. It is a two step process. The first step is to consider what you wrote in Column 2 and ask "What if I did the opposite of this?" Specifically, in our example, "What if I didn't gossip or talk behind backs? What anxiety or fear arises within me?" Perhaps you fear that if you didn't gossip with your friends you would have nothing to talk about and they would abandon you. This concern goes in the "Worry Box": "My friends might abandon me." To get the best from this process, it is important to get to a concern that really raises your anxiety.

Assuming that "my friends might abandon me" is a serious concern for you; the next question is, "What might I also be committed to?" These competing commitments are not noble like the Column 1 commitments; they are self-protective and likely a bit embarrassing. In this example, it may be "I may also be committed to being liked" or "I may also be committed to not being alone."

The power and brilliance of this process begins to reveal itself at this juncture. It discloses what Kegan and Lahey call our *immunity to change*. Look at Table E-3. Notice that columns 1 and 3 are contradictory. They are both true…and we hold them simultaneously. This is not some deficiency in us but a reflection of the complexity of our true nature. Nonetheless, it does reveal a tension that holds us in a *dynamic equilibrium* that prevents change. If you look at the three columns together they expose a pattern of resistance to change, our immunity to change.

Look at the self-protective commitment in Column 3. You will notice that your Column 2 action is a brilliant response to that commitment: "If I am committed to being liked and not being alone, then it makes perfect sense that I will gossip with my friends so I don't run the risk of losing them." But this commitment is in direct conflict with my Column 1 commitment: to not gossip.

Column 1 represents values we are proud to stand up for. They represent the heaven we want. Column 3 represents the hell we want to avoid. Column 3 is self-serving and self-protective; we would not get on our soapbox to tell the world about it. It is not bad to be self-protective. The problem is that our self-protective commitments are often invisible to us. If they are invisible to us, it's likely that they control us. A lot of creative energy is used maintaining our competing commitments…and keeping them invisible to us.

There is a wonderful quote in Paul's letters that captures this immunity to change: "I do not understand my own actions. For I do not do what I want, but I do the very thing I hate."[5] Here Paul suggests the dynamism of our immunity to change. Our immunity is not static, but is constantly readjusting itself in a manner that finds us doing "not what we want, but what we hate," in this case, gossiping.

At this point allow folks some time to reflect individually on the anxiety or fear they will place in their "Worry Box" and connect that to their self-protective Competing Commitment in Column 3. Generally there is a settling and deepening of the energy of the group at this point. When they move into their pairs, you will notice a quieting of voices and often greater gentleness. In the large group you may need to coach folks a bit to help them get clear on their fears and their competing commitments.

If your schedule allows, this is a good time to send folks home to reflect. I ask folks to spend the week between classes observing the tension between their noble, Column 1 commitments and their Competing Commitments (Column 3), without trying to change anything. This is quite a challenge. It is difficult to recognize personal responsibility for not living up to a value without wanting to fix it. But this is precisely the New Year's Resolution strategy that has not worked in the past. By asking that folks just observe their immunity to change in action, new insights emerge and change begins to happen.

Column 4: Big Assumptions

Big Assumptions are those assumptions that we take to be true. Our Big Assumptions create the deep structure of our meaning making; they are the foundation of the story of *who I am*. As long as our Big Assumptions are assumed to be true, without reflection; they have us, they rule us. They might be right or they might be wrong. When we are caught in our Big Assumptions we don't look any further. Why? *We already have the truth.*

Table E–4

Column 0 Complaint Aggravation, or Frustration	Column 1 Commitment I am committed to the value or importance of …	Column 2 Personal Responsibility What am I doing or not doing that prevents my commitment from being fully realized?	Column 3 Competing Commitments: I may also be committed to…	Column 4 Big Assumptions I assume that if … then …
People should not gossip or talk behind peoples' backs	I am committed to the value or importance of being direct and clear with people.	I gossip and talk behind peoples' backs.	**Worry Box** My friends might abandon me I may also be committed to being liked I may also be committed to not being alone	

I think of Big Assumptions as big, heavy boulders upon which we have erected our egos. The difficulty is they are deep seated and invisible. The opportunity is when you shift one, even slightly, results can be profound.

Our last step on what participants have called "the damn grid" is to use our Column 3 Competing Commitments to unearth one or more important Big Assumptions. We do this by creating an *if/then* statement from a Competing Commitment. Again, we flip that statement to its opposite.

I will use the commitment to being liked in our example: "I assume that if I wasn't liked then…" and complete the sentence quickly. Often we have to follow this pattern down several layers. So,

- I assume that if I *wasn't* liked then I would be alone.
- I assume that if I was alone that I would be miserable and that it would be hard to function.
- I assume that if I was miserable and nonfunctional my life would collapse; I would lose my home, my family, and I'd die alone under a bridge.

"Dying alone under a bridge" has become amusing in my groups, as it seems the ultimate destination on our Big Assumption journey. We laugh together about it while it points to something essential about our Big Assumptions: they generally have dire consequences.

In my experience, if you gently lead folks into deeper connection with their Big Assumptions, words begin to fail and they touch a deep sense of dread. Spiritually, this can be a very important. At the core of our ego is a dirty little secret we guard ourselves against at all costs. The secret is there is no substance to the egoic self; it is intrinsically empty. The inherent non-existence of the separate self is at our core; and our fear of egoic non-existence drives us. As we delve into our Big Assumptions, we may taste this fear. You need not go into the fear, but the darkness folks may experience as you lead them deeper into unexamined assumptions is real and not to be brushed away or denied.

Let's return to our example and create a single statement of this hidden Big Assumption: "I assume that if I wasn't liked I would be alone and miserable, I couldn't function, I couldn't work, I'd lose my job, my home, my family and die alone under the bridge." It sounds dramatic, but this is actually the nature of Big Assumptions. They are often created at a very young age when our perspective was very narrow and we were vulnerable. They weren't absurd then, though they may sound that way to us now.

Notice that holding this Big Assumption makes the Column 3 competing commitment, and the Column 2 action, perfectly reasonable. When I assume dire consequences if I am not liked, I become deeply committed to being liked so my friends won't abandon me; hence, I gossip to stay connected with friends, all the while believing that gossiping is bad. (The whole pattern is laid out in Table E-5)

Each step in the Kegan/Lahey process brings its own revelations. I have led this process in a variety of ways. If time permits, participants spend a week between meetings reflecting on each step.

- *Week 1*: Col. 0 to Col. 1. Noticing complaints and frustrations and looking for the noble commitments beneath those complaints.
- *Week 2*: Col. 1 to Col. 2. Noticing, without judging or fixing, how we undercut or do not live up to our Col. 1 values.
- *Week 3*: Col. 2 to Col. 3. Imagining doing something different (say, not gossiping), observing any anxiety that arises and following it into com peting commitment(s). Sitting with those competing commitments without judgment.
- *Week 4*: Col. 3 to Col 4. Observing my Big Assumption in action. How does it shape my everyday interactions? Noticing how often it shows up.

Working with Big Assumptions

Though it may not appear spiritual on the surface, this work is actually of great spiritual import. I work from the premise that the first person orientation to Spirit is pivotal and often missing from churches. The 1st person orientation, you will recall, concerns our identity with the Divine. It asks not "Should I worship Jesus?" Nor "Should I emulate Jesus?" But "How can I discover what Jesus discovered?" Our Big Assumptions generate the possibilities for our lives, while they simultaneously create the walls of our individual prisons. Since our Big Assumptions construct the parameters of our world, modifying those assumptions changes how we perceive and act in the world. By inquiring into the fundamental architecture of the self, we change how we engage the world and begin to free ourselves.

We use various techniques to inquire into our Big Assumptions. One has already been mentioned, observing the Big Assumption in action. Simply noticing when the Big Assumption is shaping our feelings, beliefs or actions helps shift it from something that _has us_ to something _we have._

Closely related to this exercise is the practice of observing _counter evidence._ Our minds are conditioned to receive and remember data that support our Big Assumption (it's the truth after all!) and to discount any data that disconfirm it. Noticing and attending to evidence that contradicts the Big Assumption allows us to stand back and observe it.

Using our example of gossiping, I begin to understand my Big Assumption (that I will be alone and miserable if I don't gossip) as I watch it in action; even as I gossip I notice my Big Assumption at work. Then, I notice when I refrain from gossiping, my friends don't desert me. This is a piece of evidence that is counter to my Big Assumption. The mind will naturally discount this evidence because it doesn't align with the "truth" of the Big Assumption. Attention is required to bring this evidence into our meaning system. Writing it down, reminding ourselves and actively seeking new counter evidence begins to make space for counter evidence in our awareness.

We can also be more intentional in challenging our Big Assumptions. We do this by creating Safe Tests. Safe Tests are just that: small, modest challenges to the Big Assumption. I emphasize small and modest because one strategy of the mind is to take on big, unsafe tests that are doomed to fail; in failing they confirm the truth of the Big Assumption. This is a perfectly natural function of a mind designed to protect us from harm and guide us safely through the world. Our strategy here is to pile up modest safe tests to create leverage to nudge the Big Assumption, remembering that minor shifts in our assumptions can alter the entire superstructure of our lives.

In our classes, we use a variety of strategies to construct and carry out effective safe tests. We begin with individual self reflection. In their latest book, _Immunity to_

Change, Kegan and Lahey have laid out extremely helpful guidelines for reflecting on Big Assumptions (see Boxes E -1, 2 and 3[6]). It is valuable to have participants spend some time reflecting on the construction of their safe tests prior to meeting. Sharing in pairs or triads helps folks look carefully at the tests they are designing. Are they too ambitious? Will they really test the Big Assumption? What data would confirm the Big Assumption?...Disconfirm it? Can the test be conducted soon? Instructing everyone to help their partners create genuinely safe tests helps to counter the inclination to take on tests doomed to fail.

Table E-5

Column 0 Complaint Aggravation, or Frustration	Column 1 Commitment I am committed to the value or importance of ...	Column 2 Personal Responsibility What am I doing or not doing that prevents my commitment from being fully realized?	Column 3 Competing Commitments: I may also be committed to...	Column 4 Big Assumptions I assume that if ... then ...
People should not gossip or talk behind peoples' backs	I am committed to the value or importance of being direct and clear with people.	I gossip and talk behind peoples' backs.	**Worry Box** My friends might abandon me I may also be committed to being liked I may also be committed to not being alone	I assume that if I wasn't liked I would be alone and miserable, I couldn't function, I couldn't work, I'd lose my job, my home, my family and die alone under a bridge

Role playing in a fishbowl setting or in small groups are good practice for conducting safe tests. Given that the mind does not know the difference between role playing and the real thing, role playing can actually serve as a successful safe test.

Properly designed safe tests can be run between sessions. Invite folks to write down what happened as soon as possible after the safe test (see Box E-2) as well as their initial interpretation (see Box E-3). Bring these to the next meeting. Individual experiences can be explored in pairs, small groups or the larger group. One goal of this discussion is to create a scaled up safe test for another round of practice. As participants become more facile with the process, this can become an ongoing support group for significant development.

Box E-1
Guide Sheet for designing a good test of your big assumption (BA)

Write out a testable version of your big assumption. Then ...

1a. *Write down what you are going to do.* (Make sure you are doing something different from what your big assumption would normally have you do).

1b. *Jot down how your think your test (1a.) will get you information about your big. assumption.*

2a. *Next, what data do you want to collect?* In addition to having people react to you, your feelings can be a very rich data source.

2b. *How will that data help you to confirm or disconfirm your big assumption (BA)?* (What results would lead you to believe your BA is correct? What results would lead you to question the validity of your BA?)

2c. *Is there anyone you'd like to give a "heads-up" to or ask to serve as an observer who can give you feedback after the fact?*

3. Finally, review your test on these criteria:
   - *Is it safe?* (If the worst case were to happen, could you live with the results?)
   - *Are the data relevant to your BA?* (See question 2b.)
   - *Is it valid?* (Does the test actually test your big assumption? See 1b.)
   - *Are the data sources valid?* (Choose sources that are not out to get you or protect or save you.)
   - *Might it actually reinforce your big assumption?* (Is it designed so that it surely will lead to bad consequences, just as your BA tells you? Are you setting yourself up to fail? Are there any data you could collect that could disconfirm your BA?)
   - *Can it be done soon?* (Is the personal situation you need in place to enact the test, are you reasonably certain you know how to do what you plan, and can you run the test within the next week or so?)

Box E-2
Guide sheet for running tests of the Big Assumption

1. What did you actually do?

2. What happened? What did people actually say or do when you ran your test? If you asked someone for feedback, what did she or he say? What were your thoughts and feelings at the time? (These are your data points.)

3. Check the quality of your data to make sure it is valid. Is the data about other people's response to you directly observable, or have you snuck in an interpretation? Would someone else in the room agree with your description? Were there any unusual circumstances in your test?

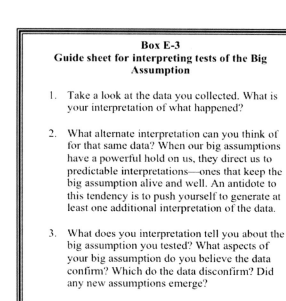

> **Box E-3**
> **Guide sheet for interpreting tests of the Big Assumption**
>
> 1. Take a look at the data you collected. What is your interpretation of what happened?
>
> 2. What alternate interpretation can you think of for that same data? When our big assumptions have a powerful hold on us, they direct us to predictable interpretations—ones that keep the big assumption alive and well. An antidote to this tendency is to push yourself to generate at least one additional interpretation of the data.
>
> 3. What does you interpretation tell you about the big assumption you tested? What aspects of your big assumption do you believe the data confirm? Which do the data disconfirm? Did any new assumptions emerge?
>
> 4. What are your thoughts about a next test of your big assumptions? Pick up on what you've learned about your big assumption. What next test could you design to learn more? If you have additional big assumptions, you might want to test those too.

Big Assumptions and The Work of Byron Katie

We also use a method from Byron Katie. It is a deceptively simple process called The Work. It has broad application and can be very powerful when confronting our Big Assumptions. Katie asks four questions about any thought that brings us stress:

- Is it true?
- Can you be absolutely certain it is true?
- How do you react when you believe the thought is true?
- How would you feel if you couldn't have the stressful thought?

Then turn the thought around and give three good examples of why each turnaround is true (see Box E-4[7]). In our classes we bring this powerful process to bear on the Big Assumptions. We do not confront the Big Assumptions directly, but the *evidence* for the Big Assumptions.

In the example above, we discovered the following Big Assumption: "I assume that if I wasn't liked I would be alone and miserable." It is important to recognize that all of our *evidence* for our Big Assumptions comes from our thoughts and our interpretations of events. Events are simply events; our interpretations make them meaningful. So, I may have a piece of evidence that I believe confirms this Big Assumption: "I was alone last Friday evening and I was miserable." There are two parts to this statement. The first part is empirically verifiable: I was alone. The second part is an interpretation that causes stress, "because I was alone I was miserable."

The Four Questions

- *"Is it true?"* Answering honestly, my first response might be "Yes, I was miserable."
- *"Can you be absolutely certain it is true?"* This question asks us to dive deeper. I might notice that some of the time I felt bad, but I also enjoyed some time alone to read or finish a project. So it may not be entirely true that being alone was a miserable experience. "Can I be absolutely certain that I was miserable when I was alone last Friday?" Perhaps not. Doubt is growing about this piece of evidence for my Big Assumption.
- *"How do you react when you believe the thought?"* How do I react when I believe being alone makes me miserable? I become anxious about being alone. I might become fearful about being alone. How did I react to the prospect of being alone last Friday? I was anxious. Allow that anxiety to re-emerge.
- *"How would you feel if you couldn't have this stressful thought?"* If I couldn't have the thought that I would be miserable if I was alone I simply wouldn't worry about it. I would be alone or with friends and it would be fine.

Some Turn Arounds

- "I was *not* miserable last Friday when I was alone." "I am *not* miserable when I am alone." Think of examples when this was true (like last Friday!).
- "I am happy when I am alone." (Give some examples).
- "I am unhappy when I'm not alone." (Give some examples)

Some Turn Arounds may be as true as the original statement. This can offer important insights but that is not the main point. By inquiring into the evidence for my assumption, "If I am alone I am miserable," the thought loses its power. With Turn Arounds we notice that other thoughts are equally valid. All of this creates doubt about the Big Assumption. We don't need to change the Big Assumption, only create space for it to change on its own.

```
┌─────────────────────────────────────────┐
│                 Box E-4                  │
│             Turn it Around               │
│                                          │
│  After you've investigated your statement with the four │
│  questions, you're ready to turn it around (the │
│  concept you are questioning).           │
│                                          │
│  Each turnaround is an opportunity to experience │
│  the opposite of your original statement and see │
│  what you and the person you've judged have in │
│  common.                                 │
│                                          │
│  A statement can be turned around to the opposite, to │
│  the other, and to the self (and sometimes to "my │
│  thinking," wherever that applies). Find a minimum of │
│  three genuine examples in your life where each │
│  turnaround is true.                     │
│                                          │
│  For example, "Paul doesn't understand me" can be │
│  turned around to "Paul does understand me." │
│  Another turnaround is "I don't understand Paul." A │
│  third is "I don't understand myself."   │
│                                          │
│  Be creative with the turnarounds. They are │
│  revelations, showing you previously unseen aspects of │
│  yourself reflected back through others. Once you've │
│  found a turnaround, go inside and let yourself feel it. │
│  Find a minimum of three genuine examples where the │
│  turnaround is true in your life        │
└─────────────────────────────────────────┘
```

Walking Meditation

Between meetings I ask folks to engage in a simple meditation designed for Westerners who may not want to practice sitting meditation. Every day they walk for an hour or more, listening to an awakened individual. Eckhart Tolle's *The Power of Now* is very powerful and accessible. After listening to the entire volume, they start again from the beginning. Learning the content is not important, the power is in being drawn into a more expanded State of Consciousness through the combination of walking and listening.

Resources

Adyashanti. *Spontaneous Awakening*. Sounds True, Incorporated, Unabridged edition June 1, 2005.

Katie, Byron. *Loving What Is: Four Questions That Can Change Your Life*. Audio Literature, Abridged edition August 9, 2002.

Kegan, Robert and Lisa Laskow Lahey. *How the Way We Talk Can Change the Way We Work: Seven Languages for Transformation*. San Francisco: Jossey-Bass, 2001.

Kegan, Robert and Lisa Laskow Lahey. *Immunity to Change: How to Overcome It and Unlock the Potential in Yourself and Your Organization*. Boston: Harvard Business Press, 2009.

Tolle, Eckhart. *The Power of Now*. New World Library; Unabridged edition, December 10, 2001.

Notes

1 See http://www.thework.com.

2 Kegan, Robert and Lisa Laskow Lahey, *How the Way We Talk Can Change the Way We Work: Seven Languages for Transformation*. San Francisco: Jossey-Bass, 2001, 7.

3 Kornfield, Jack. *After the Ecstasy, the Laundry: How the Heart Grows Wise on the Spiritual Path*. New York: Bantam, 2000.

4 Kegan, Robert and Lisa Laskow Lahey, *How the Way We Talk Can Change the Way We Work: Seven Languages for Transformation*. San Francisco: Jossey-Bass, 2001, 20.

5 Romans 7:15.

6 Kegan, Robert and Lisa Laskow Lahey, *Immunity to Change: How to Overcome It and Unlock the Potential in Yourself and Your Organization*. Boston: Harvard Business Press, 2009, 262-268.

7 The Work of Byron Katie, see Resources, http://www.thework.com/.

About the Author

Tom Thruesher is currently the pastor of a nascent Integral Church in western Washington. Long a student of consciousness and spirituality, Tom's exploration was inspired by eight years of intensive transformational work in a small group setting nearly 40 years ago. Ironically, that experience led him into economics. After completing a Masters in Economics and a Doctorate in Education at Stanford University, Tom taught economics for a decade. Following a personal crisis, he left college teaching and worked for 12 years as an artist/craftsman. A series of extraordinary events led him to seminary in 1998. He is now an ordained minister and spiritual teacher in the emerging field of Evolutionary Christianity. Over the years he studied and worked with a Native American shaman, explored Zen and Yoga, and developed his own Westernized spiritual practices. He has studied and taught Integral Theory for over 15 years. In addition to pastoring, Tom teaches Leadership and Personal Development at Bainbridge Graduate Institute, an MBA program in sustainable business. For the past seven years he has led groups exploring the interface of religion, spirituality and science; he continues to develop and lead workshops in Transformational Inquiry and Integral philosophy. He does his best not to take any of this seriously.

Tom is available for workshops. For more information visit his web site www.ReverentIrreverence.org.

Breinigsville, PA USA
22 December 2010
251990BV00004B/22/P